Products Liability and the Food Consumer

Products Liability
and
the Food Consumer

by

REED DICKERSON

GREENWOOD PRESS, PUBLISHERS
WESTPORT, CONNECTICUT

The Library of Congress has catalogued this publication as follows:

Library of Congress Cataloging in Publication Data

Dickerson, Frederick Reed, 1909-
Products liability and the food consumer.

Bibliography: p.
1. Products liability--Food--U. S. I. Title.
KF1297.F6D5 1972 343'.73'078 77-139130
ISBN 0-8371-5746-3

Originally published in 1951 by Little, Brown and Company, Boston

Reprinted with the permission of Little, Brown and Company, Publishers

Reprinted in 1972 by Greenwood Press,
a division of Congressional Information Service, Inc.
51 Riverside Avenue, Westport, Connecticut 06880

Library of Congress catalog card number 77-139130
ISBN 0-8371-5746-3

Printed in the United States of America

10 9 8 7 6 5 4 3 2

To J. M. D.

Preface

Frederick R. Baird, general counsel of Armour and Company, suggested the need for a book on food products liability to me some years ago when I was doing graduate work in law at Columbia University. Professors Milton Handler, Edwin W. Patterson, and Karl N. Llewellyn of the law school of that university helped me develop the general contours of the work and made valuable specific suggestions. I also received helpful comments from Professors Paul R. Hays and Allison Dunham. I owe a special debt to Professor Llewellyn, because he helped me uncover merit in ideas and approaches that would certainly have suffocated had they been left to my care alone.

Thanks are owed to H. Thomas Austern, counsel for the National Canners Association, and to Stanley C. Morris, of Washington and Charleston, who read the manuscript. Both are thoroughly conversant with food products liability law as seen by the practitioner and by the food industry. Mr. Austern also made available a valuable compilation of cases.

The many persons in food or insurance companies who gave me information on claims and complaints must remain unnamed because otherwise I cannot preserve the anonymity of their companies, as I promised to do in each case. Even so, I owe them deep thanks. Fortunately, I am able to name Howard M. Starling, of the National Bureau of Casualty Underwriters, and the late Wayne Merrick, of the Claims Bureau, without violating any confidence.

I am grateful to the personnel of the law library of the Library of Congress (especially to John P. Earner) for their courteous co-operation in making more readily accessible the rich resources of that library.

Finally, thanks go to the University of Pittsburgh Law Review, for letting me include, in condensed form, an article of mine that appeared in the May, 1942, issue of that review; to the Washington University Law Quarterly, for permission to use parts of a case note which Andrew C. Gunter prepared under my supervision while he was a student at that university; and to The American Law Institute, for permission to include the relevant sections of the proposed final draft of the Uniform Commercial Code.

The cases cited end with those represented by Report Letter No. 71 of the CCH Food Drug Cosmetic Law Reporter, and the April, 1951, advance pamphlet (Vol. 14–2d, No. 3) of the American Digest System (see "Food," §25; "Negligence," §§19, 27; "Sales," §§246, 274, 288½).

REED DICKERSON

Washington, D.C.
May, 1951

Contents

TOPIC C

A Brief Look at Implied Warranties of Quality

TOPIC D

Breach of Warranty Under the Uniform Sales Act

TOPIC E

The Privity Requirement

TOPIC F

Negligence and Other Breaches of Duty Not Based on Warranty

TOPIC G

Fault of the Buyer

TOPIC H

Some Considerations of Public Policy

CHAPTER II

MANUFACTURERS' AND WHOLESALERS' RESPONSIBILITY TO CONSUMERS FOR UNWHOLESOME FOOD

Topic A

Liability of the Manufacturer for Breach of Warranty

Topic B

Liability of the Manufacturer for Negligence

CHAPTER III

RESPONSIBILITY OF THE RESTAURANT KEEPER FOR UNWHOLESOME FOOD

Topic A

Liability for Breach of Warranty

Topic B

Liability for Negligence

CHAPTER IV

WHAT IS "FIT TO EAT"?

Topic A

In General

TOPIC B

The Trichinosis Cases

TOPIC C

Prevention

TOPIC D

Spreading the Risk or Loss

TOPIC E

Focusing Civil Responsibility

Topic F

Conclusions

APPENDICES

Products Liability and the Food Consumer

Introduction[1]

Topic A. *Frame for a Picture*

The growth of agencies that employ modern technology, complex fabrication, and mass production, into "clusters of private collectivisms," has drastically upset any supposed balance of power between the economic entities whose interplay of mutual demands and concessions gave to Adam Smith's self-regulating economy its motive power.

Not only has the resulting disparity in bargaining strength been at the expense of the individual unorganized consumer, but the very technological forces that have given to him in many cases a superior product have made him correspondingly less capable, as compared with those with whom he deals, of telling the better from the worse. Besides the development of elaborate goods with deeply buried technical qualities, the creation of superficially unique "kinds" of products through the exploitation of minor differences, distinctive packaging, and brand names, together with the multiplication of unstandardized grades and sizes, has made consumer confusion the worse confounded.

Of course the vulnerability of the consumer has not gone unrecognized. The protections already available include such extralegal helps as the cooperative, the magazine "institute," the advisory facilities of professional associations

[1] This introduction is a drastically condensed version of the article, "Consumer Protection and the Public Interest," prepared by the writer and published in 8 U. of Pitt. L. Rev. 149 (1942). If the argumentation seems thin, the reader is invited to examine the longer version.

like the American Medical Association and the Better Business Bureaus, and services like Consumer's Research and Consumer's Union. There are also many legal protections. On the directly regulatory side are state and federal food, drug, and cosmetic laws; safety and sanitation regulations for the manufacture of clothing, bedding, and electrical equipment; licensing laws regulating the production of such commodities as spirituous liquor, bakery goods, and milk, and the vending of articles by auctioneers, brokers, and peddlers; statutes regulating advertising and labeling; statutes governing the possession and sale of dangerous commodities like gasoline and firearms; laws protecting trade-marks and guarding against the passing off of the seller's articles as those of another ("unfair competition"); and, in wartime emergency, such measures as rationing. On the money side are antitrust laws, installment sale and usury restrictions, and, with the coming of war, direct price control.

Besides statutes whose purpose is direct protective regulation by the government, the law has furnished weapons to be wielded by the consumer himself. Thus, in private legal controversy, he has the doctrines of negligence, fraud, and deceit; the doctrines of duress and undue influence; the law of warranty; laws protecting in some instances the title of the bona fide purchaser for value; and doctrines of rescission and avoidance for incapacity because of infancy, insanity, and sometimes marriage.

Some of these laws are intended primarily for the protection of the consumer; others benefit him only incidentally. Legal protection of the consumer has developed to the point where we may ask whether a more articulate and unified philosophy of consumer protection is not now needed.

With the increasing superiority of the producer's ability to know the ingredients and capacities of elaborately fabricated commodities, the consumer's vulnerability has also been increasing. Responding to subtle institutional shifts like this, the consumer turns to the law for new protections. One of the broader questions thus raised is how far the law should go beyond merely prohibiting deliberate and positive deception. How fully should it require the seller or manufacturer to educate the consumer in the character and utility of his product? How fully should it require him to underwrite the consumer's usual expectations?

Nor is the broad problem one merely of extending and unifying a fragmentary movement on the consumer's behalf. While much has been done to bolster his position, much has been done to undercut it. Overprotection of patents, protective tariffs, and resale price maintenance laws reflect legislative attitudes that have been sharpened by attempts not only to prefer business demands but even to identify business with the public interest itself. Likewise, labor pressures have frequently focused on immediate labor objectives in substantial disregard of consumer welfare.

Even the most elementary consumer philosophy should recognize (1) the normal adverse disparity in bargaining power between the individual consumer and the persons he deals with, (2) the diffuse and nonorganic nature of group consumer interests, and (3) the position the individual or group consumer interest occupies in the hierarchy of interests that comprise the "public interest."

The slow development of the cooperative movement suggests that the spending aspect of economic life is organized with greater difficulty than the earning side. The reason is not hard to find.

Topic B. *Who Is the "Consumer"?*

A distinction is often made between "consumer" wants ("economic goods that directly satisfy human wants") and "capital" wants ("economic goods destined for use in production"). And yet, whether a man buys golf clubs, or a lathe for his machine shop, he buys to satisfy a material human want. For this reason the difference is often phrased in terms of "ultimate consumer" and "industrial [or commercial] consumer." But even this terminology misleads. To say that the industrial consumer of a lathe is not in the truest sense the ultimate consumer of the lathe is to confuse the lathe with what the lathe helps to produce.

There is a significant distinction to be made, but it lies in something else: the differing degrees of sophistication and bargaining strength of these buyers when dealing with their respective sellers. We sympathize less with the industrial purchaser of capital goods, not because he doesn't "consume" them as an "ultimate" user, but because generally he is supposed to know what he is about. Special economic consideration belongs to those who need it more.

The first mark of the consumer, therefore, is that as normally viewed he is the unsophisticated, individual, noncommercial user.

The second mark of the consumer is that for most practical purposes he is the *buyer* for consumption, whether his own or that of an immediate beneficiary; and his wants are considered as of the moment of sale. You could hardly name a law that benefits the consumer *as* consumer, except as his consumption is somehow hooked to a contract of purchase and sale in which the consumer is a participant or its immediate beneficiary. Similarly, the science of price economics finds itself confined largely to studying the consumer at the point where he impinges upon the rest of the economic system, a contact that occurs where the seller matches the buyer's wit and a sale is accomplished.

The fact that every responsible person is in some respect a consumer has made it easy to assume that his interests as consumer require no special consideration. The position is sometimes supported by the argument that no one will consciously work against his own interests.

Here it is helpful to remember that the word "consumer" means variously (1) an individual buyer, as related to a particular product [2] he wants, (2) an individual buyer, as related to the total of his purchasable wants, (3) all buyers who want a particular product, as they are related to that product, or (4) all buyers (*i.e.*, everybody), as related to the total of their purchasable wants.

In sense (1) the word "consumer" denotes not a whole man, nor even a constant aspect of a man, but a fleeting relationship. True, the individual buyer may not consciously work in this transaction against his interests in this transaction, but he may unconsciously work in this transaction against his interests in other transactions. And conversely. This is just as true for the less concrete and less significant sense (2), where his interest is, in the abstract, more pervasive, but remains in individual situations an aggregate of separate interests no better or differently coordinated.

In most economic situations of general significance, sense (3) is the most important, because concrete problems normally involve particular products or groups of products and all those who are interested as users in those products. Here the relevant consumer group not only is limited in number but is comprised of constantly changing individuals with

[2] In this discussion the word "product" is intended to refer to a single product or group of closely related products.

only a momentary allegiance. The important fact here is that the common interest in a common product provides no such adhesive, necessary to group self-assertion, as it gives, through intimate and continued personal association, to organic entities such as the "laborer" and the "producer." Add to this fact an increased disparity in sophistication between seller and buyer and you can see why the consumer frequently needs special help.

When we say that "everyone is a consumer" (sense (4)), we mean that everyone wants at least something that is purchasable, though not necessarily the same thing or things. Here, the word "consumer" relates to an undifferentiated group with no peculiarities whatsoever. As this everybody-capable-of-buying-anything, the consumer has even less group self-consciousness than under sense (3). The capacity for group self-protection is correspondingly less.

The consumer interest in this fourth and very amorphous sense is often confused with the public interest. But to identify the consumer with the public at large is to lose the interest in consumption in the larger whole, leaving it inadequately understood and inadequately represented. Conversely, to confuse the public interest with the narrower interest of society in material consumption is to forget other interests of equal validity.[3]

Topic C. *What the Consumer Wants*

Generally speaking, the first concern of the individual consumer is to satisfy by purchase (and within his resources) the material want which at the time prompts him to act. This is his "substantive" stake.

[3] Means makes this clear in "The Consumer and the New Deal," 173 Annals 7, 14 (1934).

But there is more. With an eye on saving something for future purchases, he is also interested in satisfying his present demand at the cheapest price he can gracefully get away with paying. This second primary consumer demand in the transaction that makes him a consumer-buyer may be called his "pure price" interest. The fiercest consumer antagonisms exist here.

It is important to keep in mind the difference between issues touching substantive consumer needs and those that involve only the prices at which those needs are met. The former recall Adam Smith's observation that "consumption is the sole end and purpose of all production." Insofar as it is valid, this means that within the limitations permitted by the public interest, and with due regard for the interests of the laborer in fit working conditions and for comparable substantive interests of the manufacturer, farmer, and distributor, the needs of the consumer should be the principal test. On the other hand, to the extent that only price questions are involved, the consumer's claim to preferment ordinarily disappears and the issue between buyer and seller becomes one of spreading purchasing power and fairly apportioning the revenue burden.

Most commercial enterprise has little ultimate meaning except in terms of material human needs to be satisfied. On this score, the interest of the consumer, if not synonymous with the public interest, is for the most part consistent with it. So far as the substantive needs of the consumer depend upon the respective purchases by which those needs are to be satisfied, buyer and seller stand generally in the relationship, metaphorically speaking, of master and servant. Here the consumer's wants are the central value and conflicting demands should be required to prove their case.

Contrast the economic relationship between the consumer and the seller in matters purely of price. Here their positions are not complementary. Service and subservience disappear. Within the area of price differential that measures their initial disagreement and below the figure at which the consumer would be discouraged from buying, buyer and seller stand in the relationship of active competitors.

They do not compete as potential buyers for the product of the same or even similar sellers (the buyer may want to win the price differential to buy a radio, the seller to buy a water softener or to give to his church). However, they are competitors in that each wants as much of the price as possible to strengthen his position as buyer or donor in future transactions. Thus even in the bargaining struggle there is a strain of competition.

If this analysis is sound, the consumer has no claim to preferment where price alone is in question. Issues between buyer and seller on this plane become those of finding a fair balance between persons who, in the absence of qualifying circumstances, should be treated as equals.

Similar comments apply to the relationship between the consumer-buyer and those who stand behind the seller (distributor, manufacturer, farmer, their employees, and owner). As to the consumer's substantive needs, not only the seller but the manufacturer, laborer, and owner stand generally subservient to the consumer, because relative to the particular goods and their flow to the consumer their primary function is to serve his needs.

Also contrast their relationship in the pure price plane. It has been said that seller, middleman, manufacturer, farmer, worker, and owner compete for the consumer's dollar. This is truer when we say that seller, middleman, manufacturer, farmer, worker, owner, *and consumer* compete for the consumer's dollar.[4] On this level qualitative differences disappear.

Most of the consumer's antagonisms with the manufacturer involve, on the manufacturer's side, the money aspect alone, *i.e.*, his interest as a future buyer or donor (or in economic prestige). On the consumer's side, it may typically be either quality or price of the article which is threatened by the manufacturer's attempts to enhance his own purchasing power. Thus the manufacturer may find a greater profit available in an inferior article than in a better one, or a greater profit in an expensive article available to a few than in the same article available at a lower price to many.

With a twofold interest (substantive and pure price) on the part of the adversary as well, it becomes apparent that any given dispute involving the consumer must fall within one or more of four possible frames of reference, each presenting a different hierarchy of interests:

A. As to the quality of the goods —

(1) The consumer's substantive needs must be balanced against the substantive needs of his adversary (*e.g.*, fit working conditions), equally valid in the abstract.

(2) The consumer's substantive needs presumptively prevail over adversary money demands that go

[4] The difference between the consumer's substantive wants and his pure price demands is not always obvious. If he is already buying the article, his only interest in its price is the interest of one who is thinking of his position in future transactions. If, however, the consumer believes he cannot afford it, that part of the price differential which means the difference between buying and not buying represents his substantive interest, for at least as disappointing as a defective article is no article at all. Again, the suit made of inferior cloth looks at first like a matter involving solely the consumer's substantive need. But if the only result of the inferior quality of the article is the shortening of the useful life of the article and

beyond the minimum price concession necessary to make workable any economic system that depends upon the profit motive.

B. As to the price of the goods —

(1) The consumer's pure price demands presumptively yield to the substantive needs of his adversary.

(2) The consumer's pure price demands are, in the abstract, just as valid as those wage, salary, and profit claims that go beyond the minimum inducement necessary to the functioning of any economic system dependent upon the profit motive. Within this price differential, the parties are true competitors. *Caveat:* Above the price that discourages the consumer's purchase of that kind of article a *substantive* consumer need is involved. To that extent the problem is thrown back to A(2).

Although actual controversies tend to fall into more than one of these overneat compartments, it is helpful to know what interests are at stake and where the burden of persuasion lies within the frames of reference into which the various elements of the composite problem fall.

TOPIC D. *Summary of Basic Considerations*

With an understanding of the disparity in bargaining power between the unsophisticated individual buyer and

the buyer can (and probably will) make a satisfactory replacement in the market, when it wears out, at a price he feels able to afford, the significant loss, it can be argued, will be only a monetary one. Such possibilities as embarrassment or disappointment would seem, however, to be truly "substantive." It is another question as to how much weight they should be given in the particular case.

those he deals with, the diffuse nature of the broader consumer interest, and the fact that the consumer is a human activity taken in abstraction rather than a whole man, it becomes apparent why the consumer interest is insufficiently organized and inadequately protected.

The first step in getting comprehensive consumer protection is to determine the specific areas in which a serious inequality of bargaining power exists. This looks beyond arbitrary distinctions between "commercial" and "noncommercial" use, which fall short of separating the consumer who needs protection from the consumer who can look out for himself.

Won piecemeal at best, bargaining equality is achieved in various ways. The least universally satisfactory method seems to be voluntary consumer cooperation. The negligible growth of the cooperative (in the United States at least) suggests that the buyers of a particular product or group of products usually lack the adhesive necessary to effective group collaboration. At the opposite pole, it is equally doubtful that consumer protection is to be comprehensively assured by any wholesale atomization of Big Business, a process which, even if feasible, would not be desirable, certainly if carried to the point where it meant return to a more primitive standard of living.

Between these extremes, positive protection of the consumer takes two general forms: (1) direct regulation and penalization (*i.e.*, legal disarmament of the adversary), and (2) legal aids designed to help the individual consumer protect himself. Public policy and practical considerations largely determine which is more desirable in particular cases. Although some combination of both is usually inevitable, in a legal order still sworn in large part to free competition the organization and legal and educational arming of the consumer interest are preferable, where workable, to regulation from overhead. Nor is this simply ideology. When it can be concentrated, the cumulative effect of individual civil actions can exert a force as persuasive as that of government-enforced regulations, and it does not depend upon the aggressiveness of officials whose incentives to action grow mainly out of the duties of office.

Consumer protection also takes the form of consumer representation in governmental and administrative proceedings in which the consumer has a substantial stake.

Finally, in limiting the field of risk in the worst areas it is necessary to supplement these approaches with direct regulatory legislation and criminal sanctions, wherever the consumer himself, individually and collectively, cannot adequately protect himself.

TOPIC E. *Civil Protection of the Food Consumer*

The following chapters deal with a small part of the consumer problem: the individual consumer's civil remedy in food cases. An attempt to appraise the legal protections now available properly begins with the civil remedy, because until it is known what the consumer can do for himself there is little guidance to desirable direct regulation.

A word as to the category "food." It is true that food is not a class apart. The broad problem is one of the unsophisticated consumer. Even so, it is useful to examine sales law with eyes focused on particular aspects of its application.

Food is significant because, as the commodity species most litigated and regulated, it represents a comprehensive experience valuable as a testing ground for appraising both the civil and directly regulatory aspects of consumer protection, particularly in relation to each other. Moreover, with food, the principal consumer interest is brought into bold relief: substantive needs are much more important than price or title.

On the substantive needs side, the consumer problem is twofold: compensation for injuries incurred, and prevention of potentially harmful defects. Like drugs, food carries a great inherent threat to personality. It is consumed in the most intimate way and the consumer's risk susceptibility is increased by the fact that he buys his food more casually than he does his less frequently purchased durable goods.

On the price side, the consumer problem is to establish a price that is fair and at the same time high enough to spread among the many individual consumers the financial burden of individual losses and the cost of preventive measures.

Our present preoccupation, then, will be the civil remedy, first as a compensation device, secondly as a preventive force, and finally as a means of spreading the financial burden of compensating for, or preventing, loss. If we remember that food is only a part of the problem, we can do a useful study without letting it wag the whole consumer.[5]

[5] The problem of food as approached in this book does not include problems relating to the containers in which food is marketed. For this reason, cases involving injury from exploding soft-drink bottles, defective hood wires, and broken bottle-tops are not discussed. Readers interested in these special classes will find pertinent materials listed in Appendix D.

CHAPTER I

Responsibility of the Retailer for Unwholesome Food

General References

For general discussions of food products liability, see Llewellyn, Cases and Materials on the Law of Sales 340–343 (1930); Melick, The Sale of Food and Drink (1936); Williston, Sales §§241–242b, 243a (3d ed. 1948); Cotton, "A Note on the Civil Remedies of Injured Consumers," 1 Law & Contemp. Prob. 67 (1933); Guiher and Morris, "Handling Food Products Liability Cases," 1 Food Drug Cosmetic L.Q. 109 (1946); Houtz, "The Insurance Response to a Shifting Caveat," Rep. Proc. of Sec. of Ins. Law, A.B.A. 296 (Chicago Meeting, Sept. 1944); Mintener, "Food Products Liability Law," 1 Food Drug Cosmetic L.Q. 96 (1946), 2 *id.* 62 (1947), "Product Liability," 3 *id.* 76 (1948), "Progress of Product Liability Law in 1948," 4 *id.* 110 (1949), "Product Liability Law," 5 Food Drug Cosmetic L.J. 168 (1950); Perkins, "Unwholesome Food as a Source of Liability," 5 Iowa L. Bull. 6 (1919), 86 (1920); Comment, 7 J.B.A. Kan. 183 (1938); Note, 92 U. of Pa. L. Rev. 306 (1944).

CHAPTER I

Responsibility of the Retailer for Unwholesome Food

Topic A. *Breach of Warranty at Common Law — The English Story*

§1.1. The special retail food warranty. The responsibility of the retail food dealer for the quality of his goods cannot be adequately understood without knowing something of its history in English law before the enactment of the English Sale of Goods Act, 1893.[1]

That the Act signalized the mature development of the implied warranty of fitness and the implied warranty of merchantability is well known. Further mention of these warranties will, therefore, be deferred.[2] What is not so clear is the extent to which an implied warranty of wholesomeness peculiar to food and distinct from the other and better-known warranties also may have developed before 1893.

It is common to state that there was such a warranty,[3] but the matter is not free from doubt. Most articulate of the proponents has been Melick, whose support of the warranty is based largely on the following considerations: [4]

§1.1. [1] 56 & 57 Vict. c. 71, enacted Feb. 20, 1894.

[2] For the source of these warranties at common law, see §§1.4, 1.6.

[3] *E.g.*, Ford v. Waldorf System, Inc., 57 R.I. 131, 188 Atl. 633, 635 (1936). See also Williston, Sales §241 (3d ed. 1948); Lessler, "Implied Warranty of Quality in Sales of Food," 14 Conn. B.J. 47, 49–52 (1940).

[4] Melick, The Sale of Food and Drink (1936). Melick was counsel for the defendant retailer in a leading New York food case (Gimenez v. Great Atlantic & Pacific Tea Co.) and his book developed in large part from the preparation of that case. It is reviewed in 50 Harv. L. Rev. 553 (1937).

The year 1266 marked the first of a series of criminal statutes imposing penalties upon victualers, vintners, brewers, butchers, cooks, and other persons handling "corrupt" food and drink for immediate consumption. Though these statutes said nothing about civil liability, there was a general principle that persons failing to show the degree of skill prevailing in their trade were, by the "common custom of the realm," subject to liability in an action on the case.[5]

In a case appearing in the Year Book, 9 Hen. VI, f. 53B, pl. 37 (1431), it was said: ". . . if I come into a tavern to eat and the taverner gives and sells me beer or food which is corrupt, by which I am put to great suffering, I shall clearly have an action against the taverner on the case even though he makes no warranty [6] to me." [7] In 1472 the Year Book, 11 Edw. IV, f. 6B, pl. 10, reported this statement: "For if I sell a man 20 sheep to kill, if they are corrupt, even if I warrant them, he will not have an action of deceit on the warranty, and there will be no traverse for until they are dead I cannot know that they are corrupt . . . but if I sell mutton *for consumption* that is corrupt, he will have an action of deceit even though I do not warrant it . . . the reason is because it is prohibited by law that a man should sell corrupt victuals." (Italics added.) In a note in Keilway's Report (1507),[8] Frowike said: "No man can justify selling corrupt victual, but an action on the case lies against the seller, whether the victual was warranted to be good or not. But if a man sells me cloth or other thing, knowing the cloth

[5] *Id.* at 1 n.1, and at 7.

[6] *I.e.*, express warranty.

[7] In the report of this case in 1 Rolle's Abridgement 90 (P), pl. 1 and 2 (1668), and in Viner's Abridgement 560, 561 (1746), the *scienter* qualification "knowing it to be corrupt" appears. Melick says, in The Sale of Food and Drink 4 n.2 (1936), that this is Rolle's unjustified interpolation, contradicted by Keilway's Report, *infra* note 8.

[8] Page 91; 72 Eng. Rep. 254.

to be bad . . . though he sold it without warranty, still he shall be punished by writ on the case." (This implied, of course, that for victuals *scienter* was unnecessary.) In *Roswel* v. *Vaughan* (1607),[9] the court said, "But if a man sell victuals which is corrupt, without warranty, an action lies, because it is against the commonwealth."

In addition, Melick relied on several treatises[10] and Blackstone's Commentaries.[11] He attempted to explain away certain apparently inconsistent remarks of Chief Justice Popham, in *Chandelor* v. *Lopus* (1603),[12] classing victuals with other goods, on the ground that Popham was talking generally about sales between dealers and not about sales by dealers to consumers.

In 1847 the Court of Exchequer Chamber decided *Burnby* v. *Bollett*,[13] a case involving the casual sale of a pig between farmers. After considering most of the authorities already cited, Baron Parke said by way of dictum that common dealers in victuals were in the same position as dealers in other articles, in being "presumed to undertake to supply a good and merchantable article; but they are also liable to punishment for selling corrupt victuals, by virtue of an ancient statute, (certainly if they do so knowingly, and probably if they do not), and are therefore responsible civilly to those customers to whom they sell such victuals,

[9] Cro. Jac. 196, 79 Eng. Rep. 171.

[10] 1 Fitzherbert, Natura Brevium 94 (1534); 3 Holdsworth, History of English Law 386 (4th ed. 1936).

[11] Book 3, p. 165 (the correct page appears to be 166). Melick severely criticizes Blackstone's statement. The Sale of Food and Drink 11 n.15 (1936).

[12] Cro. Jac. 4, 79 Eng. Rep. 3. Popham's remark is reported in a note to Andrews v. Boughey, 1 Dy. 75a, 73 Eng. Rep. 160 (1552). The role of Chandelor v. Lopus in the development of *caveat emptor* is discussed in Hamilton, "The Ancient Maxim Caveat Emptor," 40 Yale L.J. 1133, 1166 (1931).

[13] 16 M. & W. 644, 17 L.J. Ex. 190, 153 Eng. Rep. 1348.

for any special or particular injury by the breach of the law which they thereby commit." The parenthetical reference to *scienter*, says Melick,[14] was needless caution because it is plain that *scienter* was immaterial in those circumstances. The ancient food statutes had been repealed in 1844,[15] but the court was apparently unaware of the fact.

Here, then, is Melick's evidence for claiming that a retailer's warranty peculiar to food and not requiring *scienter* developed in English law independently of the principal implied warranties of quality.

After weighing the same authorities and noting that they were apparently dicta, Perkins had concluded, some seventeen years earlier (1919), that although "it cannot be said that there was no tendency to introduce into the English law the rule that the dealer of food stuffs is answerable for their wholesomeness, however ignorant he may be of defects . . . the cases do not justify us in saying that this tendency resulted in the actual adoption of such a rule." [16] As adverse authority he cited *Emmerton* v. *Mathews* [17] and *Smith* v. *Baker*,[18] holding that the innocent dealer was not liable, even when selling food, in the absence of a warranty of fitness or merchantability of the orthodox kind.

Melick distinguishes these cases by the fact that the buyers were dealers and not consumers.[19] His view that the special food warranty applied in sales by dealers to consumers, while ordinary warranty principles applied between deal-

[14] Melick, The Sale of Food and Drink 7 n.2 (1936).

[15] 7 & 8 Vict. c. 24, July 4, 1844. Melick, *id.* at 6 n.2, erroneously gives the date as "1845 or 1846."

[16] Perkins, "Unwholesome Food as a Source of Liability," 5 Iowa L. Bull. 6, 8–9 (1919). Others have called Melick's authorities "shadowy, obscure and flickering." Book Review, 50 Harv. L. Rev. 553, 554 (1937).

[17] 7 H. & N. 586, 31 L.J. Ex. 139, 158 Eng. Rep. 604 (1862).

[18] 40 L.T. 261 (1878).

[19] Melick, The Sale of Food and Drink 11 n.15 (1936).

ers, was based on (1) the distinction indicated in the Year Book, 11 Edw. IV, f. 6B, pl. 10, already discussed, (2) Lord Chief Justice Hale's annotations to the seventh edition of Fitzherbert's Natura Brevium,[20] and (3) Baron Parke's comment in *Burnby* v. *Bollett*, also discussed *supra*.

Perkins had anticipated the attempt to distinguish *Emmerton* v. *Mathews* and *Smith* v. *Baker*. It is true, he said, that "It might be found that the buyer 'relied on the skill and judgment of the seller' if he were a consumer more readily than if he were a dealer, but this involves applying the same rule to different sets of facts, not a different rule to be applied." [21] Baron Parke's dictum on *scienter*, he contended, was offset by Baron Channell's remarks during argument in *Emmerton* v. *Mathews*,[22] and rejected by the decision in that case, in which it was said that a seller "is not liable to any penalty" in the absence of knowledge.[23] But if Melick's basis for distinguishing those cases is correct, the court's language, as applied to sales to consumers, was likewise dictum.[24]

[20] Page 214 (1730). "Note a diversity between selling corrupt wines to merchandise, for there an action on the case does not lie without warranty; otherwise, if it be for a tavern [*sic*] or victualler, if it prejudice any."

[21] Perkins, "Unwholesome Food as a Source of Liability," 5 Iowa L. Bull. 6, 9 n.20 (1919).

[22] "As a matter of public policy, the authorities may seize unwholesome meat, but it does not follow that the person who exposes it for sale is liable to the penalty if he did not know that it was unwholesome." 7 H. & N. 586, 588, 158 Eng. Rep. 604, 606 (1862).

[23] *Id.* at 594, 31 L.J. Ex. at 143, 158 Eng. Rep. at 608.

[24] As Llewellyn has often pointed out, the distinctions between sales by casual sellers to casual buyers, sales by dealers to dealers, and sales by dealers to users, are fundamental. The first is the "horse" situation, where *caveat emptor* is appropriate. The second is the "hop" situation, where mercantile considerations should prevail. The third is the ultimate consumer situation, where unsophisticated buyer meets sophisticated seller and the inequality of bargaining power creates a special economic and social problem. Llewellyn, Cases and Materials on the

The possible argument that the food statutes were police regulations requiring no knowledge by the retailer, said Perkins, loses force when applied to a statute that provided for such punishments as the pillory and the tumbrel.[25] Perkins' belief is supported by a note to *Jones* v. *Edney*,[26] referring to Lord Ellenborough's summing up to the jury in *Cooper* v. *Twibill*,[27] an otherwise unreported case involving a beer covenant in a lease:

> If the plaintiff had gone on selling beer of a bad quality, with notice to him that it was so, and any material injury had been produced to any of his Majesty's subjects by drinking it, he would clearly have been liable to all the consequences of a criminal prosecution for selling beer of so noxious a quality.

On the other hand, Baron Parke's dictum in *Burnby* v. *Bollett* on the dispensability of *scienter* seems to have had at least the support of his associate, Baron Rolfe. The latter's remark during argument,[28] that "The case in Croke James [presumably *Roswel* v. *Vaughan*] explains those in the Year Books, as turning on the scienter in the seller, *or* on the peculiar duty of a taverner" (italics added), implied that if the seller were a taverner, *scienter* would not be required.[29]

Law of Sales 204, 268–269, 340–353 (1930); "On Warranty of Quality, and Society," 36 Col. L. Rev. 699, 712–713, 720–721 (1936); "Across Sales on Horseback," 52 Harv. L. Rev. 725, 743 (1939); and "The First Struggle to Unhorse Sales," 52 Harv. L. Rev. 873, 879, 904 (1939). See also Dickerson, "Consumer Protection and the Public Interest, 8 U. of Pitt. L. Rev. 149 (1942).

[25] Perkins, "Unwholesome Food as a Source of Liability," 5 Iowa L. Bull. 6, 9 n.22 (1919).

[26] 3 Camp. 285, 170 Eng. Rep. 1384 (1812). Lessler, in "Implied Warranty of Quality in Sales of Food," 14 Conn. B.J. 47, 49–52 (1940), seems to find more in this case than is visible to the naked eye. Or perhaps his "Jones v. Every" (*sic*) is another case.

[27] 1808.

[28] 16 M. & W. 644, 648, 153 Eng. Rep. 1348, 1350 (1847).

[29] Note also that Burnby v. Bollett and Emmerton v. Mathews did not deal with the same pure food statutes.

Perkins claimed further vindication in the passage of the English Sale of Goods Act, 1893.[30] This Act is generally conceded to have attempted only a codification of existing sales law.[31] It indicates that at least the draftsman, Chalmers, believed that no warranty peculiar to food was then being enforced. However, the Act is not persuasive, because even if it reflected current law it does not rule out a special liability that (a) had died out earlier, (b) had merged (as Williston suggests) [32] with the new warranties of fitness and merchantability, or (c) rested on other than a sales foundation. The Sale of Goods Act may have made the issue academic in England, but the importation of England's common law into the United States has kept it alive, at least in the states that have not enacted the Uniform Sales Act.

The basic point of disagreement between Melick and Perkins is, of course, *scienter*. However, merely to show that retail food dealers were treated differently and more severely than other retail sellers is not conclusive, because it can be argued that this difference consisted merely of (1) the imposition of civil liability for breach of a criminal pure food statute requiring *scienter*, or (2) the relaxation of the early

[30] 56 & 57 Vict. c. 71, February 20, 1894. Perkins, "Unwholesome Food as a Source of Liability," 5 Iowa L. Bull. 6, 11 (1919).

[31] Chalmers, Sale of Goods viii (12th ed. 1945).

[32] Williston, Sales §242a (3d ed., 1948). "When Blackstone wrote, the obligation imposed upon dealers in food was no doubt more extensive than that imposed on dealers in other goods, but with the increased severity of the English law in regard to all dealers this distinction has disappeared; . . . In jurisdictions, therefore, which follow the English law in imposing an implied warranty in sales of goods of any kind by dealers in that kind of merchandise, the doctrine in regard to sales of provisions probably differs little, if at all, from the doctrine prevailing as to other kinds of goods, though circumstances may indicate the justifiable reliance on the skill and judgment of a seller of food, which would not be so conclusive in sales of other goods." This suggests that whether or not the merger was one of legal doctrines, the practical results in the food cases are the same as those resulting from an unconditional food warranty.

rule, best exemplified by *Chandelor* v. *Lopus*, that without *scienter* no obligation as to quality would be raised in the absence of an express warranty couched in appropriate words of art.

Unfortunately, the English historical materials remain inconclusive. Some kind of special civil responsibility undoubtedly attached to retail food sales long before the modern warranties expressed by the sales statutes were developed, and this responsibility ultimately came to be classed as a "warranty" obligation. But whether it presupposed *scienter*, and whether it was simply absorbed into the warranties of fitness and merchantability, atrophied from disuse, died with the repeal of the ancient food statutes in 1844, or survived in legal potentiality until snuffed out in 1894, we cannot be sure.

It is important to note that arguments based on the codification of existing law by the Sale of Goods Act reach only obligations in "warranty." Although Rolle, Blackstone, Parke, and others have presumed that the retailer's quality obligation was properly so labeled, the question may well be asked whether that is the only plausible alternative.[33] The reader is invited to speculate on the logical implications (a) of classifying the retailer's responsibility simply as one kind of "civil liability for breach of criminal statute," and (b) conversely, of classifying the civil consequences of selling unwholesome food in violation of a modern pure food law

[33] Compare Llewellyn's statement in Comment, 27 Yale L.J. 1068, 1070 (1918): "But Blackstone's exception to *caveat emptor* rested in no wise on warranty, but on ancient criminal statutes; the predication on it of the warranty doctrine, by a multitude of dicta, and then by decided cases, seems a case of growth by mistake." See also Pollock, "The Snail in the Bottle, and Thereafter," 49 L.Q. Rev. 22, 24 (1933) (saying that the earlier concern of the common law with the consumer was only in the "sphere of penal regulation"); Benjamin, Sales §672 (4th Am. ed. 1883); Note, 26 Va. L. Rev. 100, 104 (1939); 22 Am. Jur. 882.

as a "breach of implied warranty." More, later, on the significance of proper classification.[34]

TOPIC B. *Breach of Warranty at Common Law — The American Story*

§1.2. The special retail food warranty. The United States has been a more prolific source of pronouncements on the responsibility of the retail food dealer.

In the early case of *Van Bracklin* v. *Fonda*,[1] the New York Supreme Court of Judicature announced this dictum: "In the sale of provisions for domestic use the vendor is bound to know that they are sound and wholesome, at his peril. This is a principle not only salutary, but necessary to the preservation of health and life." Although no authority was cited (other than Blackstone's exaggerated statement that provisions are always warranted to be wholesome), the principle stated coincided with the special food warranty which Melick contends developed in England, except that it was based upon "public policy" and not the violation of local (*i.e.*, New York) pure food laws. A later New York decision [2] criticized the quotation from Blackstone as going

[34] Section 1.24 *infra*.

§1.2. [1] 12 Johns. 467, 7 Am. Dec. 339 (N.Y. 1815).

[2] Moses v. Mead, 1 Denio 378, 387, 43 Am. Dec. 676, 678, (N.Y. 1845), *aff'd*, 5 Denio 617 (1846). For other New York dicta supporting the special food retailer's warranty, see Waring v. Mason, 18 Wend. 425, 439 (N.Y. 1837); Wright v. Hart, 18 Wend. 449, 456 (N.Y. 1837); Miller v. Scherder, 2 N.Y. 262, 267 (1849); Goldrich v. Ryan, 3 E. D. Smith 324, 326 (N.Y. 1854); Hoe v. Sanborn, 21 N.Y. 552, 560 (1860); Burch v. Spencer, 15 Hun 504, 509 (N.Y. 1878); Fairbank Canning Co. v. Metzger, 118 N.Y. 260, 267, 23 N.E. 372, 374 (1890); Rothmiller v. Stein, 143 N.Y. 581, 592, 38 N.E. 718, 721 (1894); Money v. Fisher, 92 Hun 347, 348, 36 N.Y. Supp. 862 (1895). In Wright v. Hart, Senator Tracy said (p. 464) that Blackstone's statement was an "unsupported *dictum*,

too far, but it supported by its own dictum the dictum of the earlier court. The matter was not concluded by direct holding of New York's highest court until 1918, when the Court of Appeals confirmed the special seller's obligation in a situation arising just before the Uniform Sales Act was enacted in that state (1911).[3] It based its decision on public policy and the fact that the buyer had no chance to determine the condition of the article. The same rule seems to have been accepted in a number of other states as well, and matters such as the buyer's reliance or the seller's knowledge have generally been passed over in favor of a liability founded upon general considerations of public health.[4]

---

borrowed probably from the civil law." The first holding appears to have been Divine v. McCormick, 50 Barb. 116, 118 (N.Y. 1867).

David Dudley Field's ill-fated attempt to codify the New York common law in the latter part of the nineteenth century recognized the warranty. "One who makes a business of selling provisions for domestic use warrants by a sale thereof, to one who buys for actual consumption, that they are sound and wholesome." (Proposed N.Y. Civ. Code §889.) The code was not enacted, after three near-successes, but the warranty provision has since appeared in California (Cal. Civ. Code (1929) §1775 (Mar. 21, 1872; repealed by the Uniform Sales Act, 1931) and Montana (Mont. Rev. Codes Ann. (1947) §74-321).

[3] Race v. Krum, 222 N.Y. 410, 118 N.E. 853 (1918). To the same effect: Zenkel v. Oneida County Creameries Co., 104 Misc. 251, 252, 171 N.Y. Supp. 676 (1918).

[4] Heinemann v. Barfield, 136 Ark. 500, 502, 207 S.W. 62 (1918); Wiedeman v. Keller, 171 Ill. 93, 99 (1898); Chapman v. Roggenkamp, 182 Ill. App. 117, 121 (1913); Hoover v. Peters, 18 Mich. 51, 55 (1869); Bark v. Dixson, 115 Minn. 172, 131 N.W. 1078 (1911); McNaughton v. Joy, 1 W.N.C. 470 (Pa. 1875); Catani v. Swift & Co., 251 Pa. 52, 57, 95 Atl. 931 (1914) (common law rule as codified by Act of May 4, 1889, Pa. P.L. No. 87, §1, an act which was repealed July 14, 1917, by P.L. No. 840, §1500, following enactment of the Uniform Sales Act, 1916); Walker v. Great Atlantic & Pacific Tea Co., 131 Tex. 57, 62, 112 S.W.2d 170, 171 (1938); Flessher v. Carstens Packing Co., 93 Wash. 48, 54, 160 Pac. 14, 17 (1916). In Kroger Grocery & Baking Co. v. Schneider, 249 Ky. 261, 264, 60 S.W.2d 594, 595 (1933), involving a retailer-manufacturer, the court ignored the Uniform Sales Act and based its decision on

It is important to distinguish the rule of implied warranty peculiar to food from the general rules of implied warranty as they have been applied to food, for the former is strictly a consumers' rule.[5] Hence the limitation that the sale must be for "immediate use." [6] Sales between dealers,

---

public safety. Under the civil law of Louisiana there is apparently an implied warranty against defects in every sale. MacLehan v. Loft Candy Stores, 172 So. 367, 369 (La. App. 1937). See Nelson v. Armour Packing Co., 76 Ark. 352, 355, 90 S.W. 288, 289 (1905); Lukens v. Frieund, 27 Kan. 664, 669 (1882); Jones v. Murray, 3 T. B. Mon. 83, 85 (Ky. 1825); Marshall v. Peck, 1 Dana 609, 613 (Ky. 1833); Osgood v. Lewis, 2 Harr. & G. 495, 519 (Md. 1829); Craft v. Parker, Webb & Co., 96 Mich. 245, 248, 55 N.W. 812, 813 (1893); Ryder v. Neitge, 21 Minn. 70, 75 (1874). Bragg v. Morrill, 49 Vt. 45, 47, 24 Am. Rep. 102, 103 (1876); Getty v. Rountree, 2 Pinney 379, 386, 54 Am. Dec. 138, 140 (Wis. 1850); Williams v. Slaughter, 3 Wis. 347, 360 (1854). *Contra:* Green v. Ashland Water Co., 101 Wis. 258, 77 N.W. 722 (1898). See Goad v. Johnson, 6 Heisk. 340, 346 (Tenn. 1871).

Several early Massachusetts cases are sometimes cited as supporting the special food retailer's warranty. *E.g.*, Winsor v. Lombard, 18 Pick. 57, 62 (Mass. 1836); Emerson v. Brigham, 10 Mass. 197, 201, 6 Am. Dec. 109, 111 (1813). Examination shows, however, that although the court was ready to presume a representation-in-fact of wholesomeness (and *scienter*) because of the nature of the product and its normal purpose, such a presumption could be negatived. The warranty peculiar to food retailers was repudiated in Farrell v. Manhattan Market, 198 Mass. 271, 284, 84 N.E. 481, 487 (1908), decided before the Uniform Sales Act was adopted in that state (1909). The court said that to prevail the plaintiff must establish reliance on the seller's skill.

Perkins, who could find no more than a "tendency" in English law, agrees that a warranty peculiar to food developed in this country. "Unwholesome Food as a Source of Liability," 5 Iowa L. Bull. 6, 12–16 (1919). *Contra:* Benjamin, Sales §672 (4th Am. ed. 1883). But Perkins would hardly go along with Melick's assertion that it was imported, as part of our common law, from England.

[5] This difference was first clearly pointed out in Jones v. Murray, 3 T. B. Mon. 83, 85 (Ky. 1825). For holdings to this effect, see cases cited in note 2 *supra*, and cases cited as dicta in note 4 *supra*.

[6] Perkins, "Unwholesome Food as a Source of Liability," 5 Iowa L. Bull. 6, 25–27 (1919); Melick, The Sale of Food and Drink 22–23, 61 (1936); Race v. Krum, 222 N.Y. 410, 414, 118 N.E. 853, 854 (1918). "Immediate use" means for consumption rather than resale. The existence of the warranty does not depend upon when the buyer intends to eat the food. The warranty is only that the food will remain wholesome for a

on the other hand, are governed by rules of warranty applicable generally,[7] although where the goods are known to be intended for resale to consumers they often raise warranties of fitness and merchantability of equal stature to that which on the resale flows from the retailer to the consumer.[8]

Another important limitation on the common law warranty peculiar to food is that it applies only to such sales to buyers for consumption as are made by a dealer or a person selling in the open market.[9] Here "dealer" apparently includes manufacturers and growers selling directly to the consumer.[10] As for the casual food seller, he remains subject to general principles of law. Thus, where he has sold goods known by him to be defective he has been held liable in an action in deceit.[11]

§1.3. The special retail food warranty — Sealed containers. A discordant note was sounded in 1896 by a lower New York court which in *Julian* v. *Laubenberger* [1] ex-

reasonable time. Hertzler v. Manshum, 228 Mich. 416, 424, 200 N.W. 155, 157 (1924) (under Uniform Sales Act).

[7] Perkins, *id.* at 16–22; Melick, *id.* at 59–61.

[8] J. Aron & Co., Inc. v. Sills, 240 N.Y. 588, 148 N.E. 717 (1925); Lexington Grocery Co. v. Vernoy, 167 N.C. 427, 429, 83 S.E. 567, 568 (1914). See also Mazzetti v. Armour & Co., 75 Wash. 622, 630, 135 Pac. 633, 636 (1913).

[9] Giroux v. Stedman, 145 Mass. 439, 441, 14 N.E. 538, 540 (1888) (farmer making casual sale of diseased pork not liable in the absence of *scienter*); Burnby v. Bollett, 16 M. & W. 644, 17 L.J. Ex. 190, 153 Eng. Rep. 1348 (1847). *Contra:* Hoover v. Peters, 18 Mich. 51, 55 (1869) (sale of diseased pork by farmer to consumer), where the court said, "The doctrine seems to be that any purchase for domestic consumption is protected."

[10] Perkins, "Unwholesome Food as a Source of Liability," 5 Iowa L. Bull. 6, 22–25 (1919).

[11] French v. Vining, 102 Mass. 132, 3 Am. St. Rep. 440 (1869); Van Bracklin v. Fonda, 12 Johns. 468, 7 Am. Dec. 339 (N.Y. 1815). See also Burnby v. Bollett, 16 M. & W. 644, 17 L.J. Ex. 190, 153 Eng. Rep. 1348 (1847).

§1.3. [1] 16 Misc. 646, 38 N.Y. Supp. 1052 (N.Y. 1896).

cused the seller of defective canned salmon on the ground that he had no greater knowledge of possible defects than the buyer and the buyer knew it. Arkansas, Georgia, Kentucky, Maine, Mississippi, and West Virginia echoed this result.[2]

Although these cases can be construed as repudiating the special food warranty, such a result seems hardly plausible in New York. And yet this decision cannot be reconciled with the notion of a food warranty that depends upon neither reliance by the buyer nor knowledge of the seller. Despite the earlier New York pronouncements, the court expressly repudiated the notion of a special food warranty that did not require *scienter* and questioned whether *scienter* could be wholly dispensed with even in the case of other implied warranties of quality. On the other hand, the sealed container exception has been repudiated under the common law of Florida, Illinois, Kansas, Missouri, North Carolina, and Texas.[3]

[2] Scruggins v. Jones, 207 Ky. 636, 269 S.W. 743 (1925); Bigelow v. Maine Central R.R., 110 Me. 105, 85 Atl. 396 (1912); Kroger Grocery Co. v. Llewelling, 165 Miss. 71, 85, 145 So. 726, 727 (1933); Pennington v. Cranberry Fuel Co., 117 W. Va. 680, 186 S.E. 610 (1936). See H. J. Heinz v. Duke, 196 Ark. 180, 187, 116 S.W.2d 1039, 1042 (1938); Great Atlantic & Pacific Tea Co. v. Gwilliams, 189 Ark. 1037, 76 S.W.2d 65 (1934); Coca-Cola Bottling Co. v. Swilling, 186 Ark. 1149, 57 S.W.2d 1029 (1933); Walden v. Wheeler, 153 Ky. 181, 154 S.W. 1088 (1913); Trafton v. Davis, 110 Me. 318, 325, 86 Atl. 179, 182 (1913); Cotton v. Reed, 25 Misc. 380, 382, 54 N.Y. Supp. 143, 144 (N.Y. 1898). The possibility of an exception to the exception in Georgia in the case of transparent containers is discussed in Davis v. Williams, 58 Ga. App. 274, 278, 198 S.E. 357, 360 (1938).

The application of the sealed container exception by the Maine court in the Bigelow case is surprising, since the defendant operated a dining car and it is hardly likely that the plaintiff was served an unopened can. See also Green v. Wilson, 194 Ark. 165, 105 S.W.2d 1074 (1937).

[3] Sencer v. Carl's Markets, Inc., — Fla. —, 45 So.2d 671 (1950); Sloan v. F. W. Woolworth Co., 193 Ill. App. 620 (1915); Chapman v. Roggenkamp, 182 Ill. App. 117, 121 (1913); Swengel v. F. & E. Wholesale Grocery Co., 147 Kan. 555, 562, 77 P.2d 930, 935 (1938); De Gouveia v. H. D. Lee Mercantile Co., 231 Mo. App. 447, 451, 100 S.W.2d

§1.4. The warranty of fitness. The implied warranty normally relied on in food cases today is the implied warranty of fitness, which in addition to being a common law obligation [1] appears in Section 14 (1) of the English Sale of Goods Act and in Section 15 (1) of the Uniform Sales Act.[2] This warranty was recognized in general form in 1829 in the English case of *Jones* v. *Bright* [3] and was crystallized in 1868 in *Jones* v. *Just*.[4] In effect it says that if the buyer makes known a particular purpose for which he wants an article and if he relies on the skill of the seller to select an article reasonably fit for that purpose, the seller is liable if the article fails to fulfill that purpose. It applies regardless of the kind of commodity involved. The nature of this warranty is developed more fully in Topic D.

In states that have adopted the sealed container doctrine noted in the last section, no warranty of fitness will of course be implied for those products, because the nature of the container is assumed to preclude the necessary element of reliance.

§1.5. The warranty of fitness — Selection by the buyer. An abortive interpretation of the warranty of fitness appeared at common law in Massachusetts, a state that

---

336, 338 (1937); Rabb v. Covington, 215 N.C. 572, 576, 2 S.E.2d 705, 707 (1939); Griggs Canning Co. v. Josey, 139 Tex. 623, 164 S.W.2d 835 (1942); Walker v. Great Atlantic & Pacific Tea Co., 131 Tex. 57, 61, 112 S.W.2d 170, 172 (1938) (the court was moved in part by the facts that (1) the applicable Texas pure food law does not require knowledge of the seller, and (2) the can did not carry the manufacturer's name).

§1.4. [1] *E.g.*, Burgess v. Sanitary Meat Market, 121 W.Va. 605, 5 S.E.2d 785, 6 S.E.2d 254 (1939); and cases cited in §1.3 *supra*, notes 2 and 3.

[2] See §1.13 *infra*.

[3] 5 Bing. 533, 130 Eng. Rep. 1167.

[4] L.R. 3 Q.B. 197, 37 L.J.Q.B. 89, 18 L.T. 208 (1868).

later avoided the sealed container pitfall. In *Farrell* v. *Manhattan Market Co.*,[1] the seller of a diseased chicken via the Saturday bargain counter was excused because the buyer had selected the goods himself. This conclusion was reached after consideration of the English authorities on sales between dealers, and despite an Illinois decision to the contrary.[2] The "buyer's selection" doctrine has not appeared in other states. It has been repudiated under the common law of Texas.[3]

§1.6. The warranty of merchantability. The implied warranty of merchantability, found in Section 14 (2) of the English Sale of Goods Act and in Section 15 (2) of the Uniform Sales Act, dates mainly from the English case of *Gardiner* v. *Gray* (1815).[1] Its modern form at common law, like the warranty of fitness, was crystallized by *Jones* v. *Just*.[2] In effect, this warranty says that in a sale by description goods are warranted to be good enough under mercantile usage to pass without objection under the designation in the contract, and that they shall be reasonably fit for the ordinary and usual purposes for which such goods are used. The nature of this warranty is developed more fully in Section 1.18 *infra*.

§1.7. Combined effect of warranties. Today the American food retailer's responsibility for breach of implied war-

§1.5. [1] 198 Mass. 271, 84 N.E. 481 (1908). See also Gearing v. Berkson, 223 Mass. 257, 259, 111 N.E. 785, 786 (1916).

[2] Wiedeman v. Keller, 171 Ill. 93, 49 N.E. 211 (1898) (that the buyer made the selection appears from the opinion of the lower court in 58 Ill. App. 382, 384 (1895)).

[3] Walker v. Great Atlantic & Pacific Tea Co., 131 Tex. 57, 61, 112 S.W.2d 170, 172 (1938) (self-service store). The doctrine is discussed more fully in §1.15 *infra*.

§1.6. [1] 4 Camp. 144, 171 Eng. Rep. 46. See also Laing v. Fidgeon, 6 Taunt. 108, 128 Eng. Rep. 974, 4 Camp. 169, 171 Eng. Rep. 55 (1815).

[2] See §1.4 *supra*, note 4.

ranty in the fourteen common law states [1] rests upon the general warranties of fitness and merchantability and the warranty peculiar to food. The current standing of the special retail food warranty in particular states, however, is not always clear, because the courts do not always say which warranty they are invoking.[2] The matter is largely academic because, as currently applied to food retailers, the warranties of fitness and merchantability come to the same practical result as the special retail food warranty. This is more fully explained in Section 1.19 *infra*.

Topic C. *A Brief Look at Implied Warranties of Quality*

§1.8. General nature and sources. In the broadest sense, implied warranties are simply warranties that are not expressed. They may be "implied in fact" or " implied in law." [1] Implied warranties of quality, as distinct from the implied warranties of title, were not recognized and enforced until the early part of the nineteenth century,[2] except as a

§1.7. [1] Florida, Georgia, Kansas, Louisiana, Montana, Mississippi, Missouri, New Mexico, North Carolina, Oklahoma, South Carolina, Texas, Virginia, and West Virginia.

[2] *E.g.*, Housand v. Armour & Co., 173 S.C. 268, 175 S.E. 516 (1934); Walters v. United Grocery Co., 51 Utah 565, 172 Pac. 473 (1918).

§1.8. [1] Compare the concepts of "implied" and "express" warranties in the proposed Uniform Commercial Code — Sales §2-313, where a sale by description or sample involves an express warranty, with those in the Uniform Sales Act, where such a sale involves an implied warranty. Uniform Commercial Code (1951), prepared by The American Law Institute and the National Conference of Commissioners on Uniform State Laws.

[2] Prosser, "The Implied Warranty of Merchantable Quality," 27 Minn. L. Rev. 117, 120 (1943), citing Holcombe v. Hewson, 2 Camp. 391, 170 Eng. Rep. 1194 (1810). Compare the implied warranty of identity in a sale by description. If we look at substance, not form, Chandelor v. Lopus, Cro. Jac. 4, 79 Eng. Rep. 3 (1603), involved such a warranty, not

special warranty may have applied to retail food dealers. Despite their differing bases, these warranties, together with express warranties, developed (though not at the same time) as members of a common family group.

The breach of express warranty was originally a tort in which the wrong was considered to be a misrepresentation of fact and the action was case [3] (for many years appropriate words of warranty were necessary to create the obligation).[4] By 1689,[5] it was clear that, unlike its cousin deceit, the express warranty did not depend upon the seller's knowledge of the defect. Even so, the connotation of fraud persisted.

With the general shift in legal thinking from status to contract,[6] it became more fashionable to think in terms of a promise rather than a representation made supplementary to the contractual arrangement of sale, the promise finding its way into the contract first as a "condition." This switch in legal theory was negotiated in large part through the influence of Lord Mansfield, who, with the assurance of his colleague, Buller, that such had been the practice for the space of his memory, held that a suit for breach of express warranty was properly declared in assumpsit.[7]

---

an express warranty. See Llewellyn, "On Warranty of Quality, and Society," 36 Col. L. Rev. 699, 726 n.89 (1936).

[3] Ames, "The History of Assumpsit," 2 Harv. L. Rev. 1, 8 (1888); Prosser, *id.* at 118; Melick, The Sale of Food and Drink 8 (1936); 1 Street, Foundations of Legal Liability 377–378 (1906).

[4] Chandelor v. Lopus, Cro. Jac. 4, 79 Eng. Rep. 3 (1603) ("bare affirmation without warranting it to be so is no cause of action"). Presumably the magic word "warranty" had to be used.

[5] Cross v. Gardner, 1 Show. 68, 89 Eng. Rep. 453; 3 Mod. 261, 87 Eng. Rep. 172 ("Cross v. Garnet"); Carthew 90, 90 Eng. Rep. 656, Comberbach 142, 90 Eng. Rep. 393, Holt 5, 90 Eng. Rep. 900 ("Crosse v. Gardner").

[6] Maine, Ancient Law 165 (1st Am. ed. 1864).

[7] Stuart v. Wilkins, 1 Dougl. 18, 99 Eng. Rep. 15 (1778). Although assumpsit today smells of contract, it had a tort origin. Williston, Sales §195 (3d ed. 1948).

In the meantime the special liability applicable to retail sales of food was apparently treated as a member of the same family. By the time of Rolle (1668), it had come to be considered a "warranty in law,"[8] still later an "implied warranty."[9] By taking on this guise, however, the original basis for liability was obscured by a name that seemed to denote a warranty implied in fact. Thus what started simply as a statute-grounded liability continued as a liability based ostensibly upon false representation. Hence the action in deceit, but (says Melick) without the requirement of *scienter*.[10]

Lord Mansfield, it has been said, had doubted that the declaration in assumpsit, while appropriate to the breach of express warranty, would be appropriate in the case of an implied warranty (presumably of title).[11] But by the time implied warranties of quality were clearly recognized (about 1810), the assumpsit action was taken for granted.[12]

American common law statements upholding the special retail food warranty appear to have founded liability di-

[8] Melick, The Sale of Food and Drink 4 n.2 (1936).

[9] *Id.* at 8; Burnby v. Bollett, 16 M. & W. 644, 649, 153 Eng. Rep. 1348, 1350 (1847).

[10] Melick, The Sale of Food and Drink 8 (1936). Perkins, though skeptical, concedes, in "Unwholesome Food as a Source of Liability," 5 Iowa L. Bull. 6, 8 (1919), that the dictum in Keilway's Report, already discussed (*supra* p. 20), and the statements of Baron Parke and Blackstone support the position taken by Melick. Melick is accepted as authoritative in Ford v. Waldorf System, Inc., 57 R.I. 131, 135, 188 Atl. 633, 635 (1936).

[11] Prosser, "The Implied Warranty of Merchantable Quality," 27 Minn. L. Rev. 117, 120 (1943). Prosser's authority for this statement is not clearly indicated. It takes deep digging to get it out of Stuart v. Wilkins.

[12] On the other hand, the plaintiff in Burnby v. Bollett, who in 1847 tried to recover on the theory of a special food warranty, brought case instead of assumpsit. Melick notes "a surprising lack of cases in England involving food sold for human consumption during the greater part of the eighteenth and nineteenth centuries." The Sale of Food and Drink 10 n.12 (1936).

rectly upon considerations of public safety, without regard to any supposed representation or promise and without regard to the violation of local pure food laws.[13] In this respect, the special food warranty did not undergo the shift in rationale (from representation to promise) that occurred for express warranties.

What of the implied warranties of fitness and merchantability? Both warranties developed after assumpsit had become the orthodox action for breach of express warranty and, as members of the heterogeneous warranty family, fell into procedural line. Does this mean that, like the express warranty, they too are basically contractual or representational? Or did they, like the retailer's food warranty, spring directly from the law, dressed to look like promises or representations?

§1.9. General nature and sources — The warranty of merchantability. It is often said [1] that implied warranties of quality are "implied in law" (as distinct from "implied in fact"). Not so, says Prosser,[2] for the warranty of merchantability. This warranty, he says, is almost wholly contractual in fact, because it merely requires the seller to carry out an undertaking that is understood but not expressed.

Prosser's contention raises two separate, though related, questions: Is the warranty implied in fact or implied in law? Does it rest, in its factual aspects (or legal rationale), on promise or representation?

[13] Perkins, "Unwholesome Food as a Source of Liability," 5 Iowa L. Bull. 6, 12–16 (1919); Melick, *id.*, c. II.

§1.9. [1] *E.g.*, Llewellyn, "The First Struggle to Unhorse Sales," 52 Harv. L. Rev. 873, 880 (1939); Spruill, "Privity of Contract as a Requisite for Recovery on Warranty," 19 N.C.L. Rev. 550, 555 (1941); Comment, 29 Yale L.J. 782, 786–787 (1920).

[2] Prosser, "The Implied Warranty of Merchantable Quality," 27 Minn. L. Rev. 117, 125 (1943).

Before we try to answer these questions, several general assumptions should be made explicit: [3] A warranty of quality in the *legal* sense is the responsibility the law imposes on a seller for the benefit of a buyer or user that the thing sold will, to the extent the law prescribes, satisfy the buyer's or user's actual or supposed wants. Insofar as this responsibility is contingent upon and measured by a warranty in the *factual* sense (express or factually implied promise or representation), it may be called a "warranty in fact." Insofar as it is not contingent upon or measured by a warranty in the factual sense, it may be called a "warranty in law." Thus warranties in fact include all express warranties and such "implied" warranties (warranties "implied in fact") as are contingent upon and measured by actual promises or representations. Warranties in law include such "implied" warranties (warranties "implied in law") as are not so related to actual promises or representations. The mark of a warranty in law, therefore, is not the fact that the law raises it but the fact that the law raises it even though there may be no actual promise or representation fully to support it.

A warranty in the factual sense may be related to a warranty in the legal sense in three distinct ways. First, it may furnish the basis for a warranty in fact (*e.g.*, any express warranty). Second, it may contribute to the underlying rationale for raising a "warranty in law," without actually helping to define its working boundaries (*e.g.*, the reliance factor in the warranty of merchantability). Third, as a result of the natural tendency of actual understandings to

[3] The conventional breakdown of warranties into "express" and "implied" not only is not helpful here but obscures (1) the important distinction between warranties based on the parties' understandings and warranties created by law without that foundation, and (2) the close similarity between warranties based on the parties' tacit understandings and explicit warranties.

conform to what is known in the market about what the law requires, it may emulate a warranty in law based on an independent rationale (*e.g.*, the special retail food warranty). Although only the first two relationships are in themselves legally significant, the third is worth noticing because it is easily confused with the first two. This is important because the fact that sellers-in-general of an article tend to promise (or represent) a minimum standard of quality does not necessarily mean that a legal warranty assuring that standard is a warranty in fact or that the high incidence of actual promise or representation is the reason the law generated the obligation.

If this analysis is sound, the true test of a warranty in fact is not whether actual understanding generally coincides with legal obligation or enters into underlying rationale, but whether the law enforces the arrangement understood by the particular parties because it is *their* arrangement.

If the warranty of merchantability were truly implied in fact, the courts would weigh the issue of promise or representation case by case, aided perhaps by rebuttable presumptions based on average assumptions and general tendencies. Instead, the law raises the warranty wherever there is a sale by description.[4] The difference between enforcing individual arrangements and fitting them into preconceived (and greatly oversimplified) patterns of what is "normal" or "proper" for the market as a whole becomes more apparent when we shift from dealer-dealer sales to dealer-consumer sales, where a uniform mold is not so likely to fit.

That "merchantability" is intended to include more than the minimum specifications of a description may be inferred

[4] Compare the approach of the proposed Uniform Commercial Code — Sales §2-314(1) (1951). This would raise the warranty "if the seller is a merchant with respect to goods of that kind or though not a merchant states generally that they are guaranteed."

from the fact that the contrary assumption would make this warranty a needless duplication of the warranty of description, which is considered a separate warranty.[5] The difference between what is necessary to meet the description (read in the light of normal market word-usage) and what is necessary to meet the tests of merchantability — whatever the specific difference may be in a particular instance — is measured by the extent to which (1) the particular parties' understanding differs from the "normal" understanding reflected by the warranty and (2) the warranty differs from or has shaped, rather than reflected, normal market understanding.[6] This difference, it seems plain, is one created by law.

At most, therefore, the warranty of merchantability is a warranty in law whose rationale lies in the crystallization of factual tendencies.[7] Thus, while approximating actual understanding in many transactions, the obligation transcends it.

The second question is whether the rationale of the implied warranty of merchantability rests on "promise" or "representation," or both. Prosser argues that it is based almost entirely on the former.[8]

[5] Llewellyn, "On Warranty of Quality, and Society, II," 37 Col. L. Rev. 341, 387 (1937). Under Section 2–313 of the proposed Uniform Commercial Code — Sales (1951), description would be handled as a basis for express warranty.

[6] See Comment by K.N.L. (Llewellyn) in 29 Yale L.J. 782, 786, and n.13 (1920).

[7] "Our fields of law, our patterns of legal thinking, our legal concepts, have grown up each one around some 'type' of occurrence or transaction, *felt* as a typical something, *seen* in due course as a legally significant type, and, as a type-picture, made a standard and a norm for judging. 'Implied warranties,' for example, are aspects of typical transactions, aspects conceived as so typical that they are attached, with legal force, by law." Llewellyn, "The First Struggle to Unhorse Sales," 52 Harv. L. Rev. 873, 880 (1939).

[8] Prosser, "The Implied Warranty of Merchantable Quality," 27 Minn. L. Rev. 117, 125 (1943). There is a surprising tendency to associ-

So long as he supposes the situation where, after the buyer describes the kind of article he wants, the seller contracts to supply such an article, it is not difficult to find at least a strong tendency to make a promise to deliver a "merchantable" article of that description. But if we agree (Williston notwithstanding) [9] that the warranty applies also to the sale of specific goods identified by description,[10] what is the promise here?

A promise ordinarily connotes a voluntary undertaking that something will take place in the future.[11] The only undertaking that fits specific goods is one to provide suitable relief if the goods fall short of the description.[12] But this is hardly what we may attribute to the minds of real sellers and buyers, at least in retail sales of food.[13] "Representation," on the other hand, seems a much more plausible description of actual market tendencies, since we can assume that the parties normally think in terms of the desired quality, not what the seller must do if he defaults.

If this analysis is correct, the merchantability warranty has as its factual core promise in some cases and representation in others. Of course, even with respect to contracts to

---

ate warranties in fact with promises and warranties in law with representations. *E.g.*, Spruill, "Privity of Contract as a Requisite for Recovery on Warranty," 19 N.C.L. Rev. 550, 555 (1941); Comment, 42 Harv. L. Rev. 414, 415 n.11 (1929). The converse is just as logical and just as arbitrary.

[9] Williston, Sales §224 (3d ed. 1948).

[10] Prosser, "The Implied Warranty of Merchantable Quality," 27 Minn. L. Rev. 117, 139–145, especially 143–145 (1943).

[11] Restatement, Contracts §2(1) (1932).

[12] *Id.*, §2(2); Williston, Contracts §1A (rev. ed. 1936) ("Even where the undertaking relates to an existing or past fact, as in case of a warranty that a horse is sound, . . . the existence and validity of the undertaking is dealt with in the same way as if the warrantor could cause the fact to be as he asserted.").

[13] See Patterson, "The Apportionment of Business Risk Through Legal Devices," 24 Col. L. Rev. 335, 342 (1924).

sell goods to be appropriated to the contract, the tendency of sellers to make such promises in fact is not in itself persuasive, since if ex post facto conformity is the test the warranty of merchantability can be said, with good logic, to be based equally on representation.

§1.10. General nature and sources — The warranty of fitness. With appropriate revision, similar remarks can be addressed to the implied warranty of fitness for a particular purpose. Here, in view of the condition that the buyer rely on the seller, the warranty seems to have stemmed from a representation generally implied in fact, rather than a promise. The breach of this warranty, therefore, smacks more of deceit and tort than it does of contract, despite the fact that it developed after assumpsit was accepted as the appropriate form of action for all breaches of warranty. If so, the warranty of fitness may be characterized, for the reasons developed in connection with the warranty of merchantability, as a "warranty in law" based presumably on the crystallization of an observed tendency of sellers to imply a representation in such cases.

§1.11. Significance of contract and tort theories. Although a number of courts still accept an action in tort for breach of warranty,[1] it is more common to consider the

§1.11. [1] Shippen v. Bowen, 122 U.S. 575, 30 S. Ct. 1172 (1887) (tort for breach of express warranty that bonds were genuine); Davis v. Williams, 58 Ga. App. 274, 278, 198 S.E. 357, 360 (1938) ("Whether the action be one on warranty or negligence, it comes to the same thing. It sounds in tort"; but the court seems to base liability on some kind of fault); Greenwood v. John R. Thompson Co., 213 Ill. App. 371 (1919); Schuler v. Union News Co., 295 Mass. 350, 353, 4 N.E.2d 465, 466 (1936); Hertzler v. Manshum, 228 Mich. 416, 423, 200 N.W. 155, 157 (1924) ("The implied warranty, so-called, reaching from the manufacturer of food stuffs to the ultimate purchaser for immediate consumption is in the nature of a representation that the highest degree of care has been exercised and a breach of such duty inflicting personal injury is a wrong in the nature of a tort . . ."); Kennedy v. F. W. Woolworth Co.,

breach of implied warranty as a breach of contract. There are five possible explanations. (1) The usual presence of a promise implied in fact (in addition to any representation), where the seller selects in response to the buyer's request for a described article, makes it easy to claim the former as the basis of the warranty in all cases. (2) Warranty causes of action of all types are normally carried in the assumpsit basket. (3) Even though the warranty itself may be a representation, it is ancillary to the contractual undertaking that is the sale itself.[2] (4) Express warranties are commonly considered to be contractual. (5) Under civil law, it has been said,[3] warranty has always been based on contract.

If the courts, through mistake or otherwise, generally consider the implied warranty as contractual rather than representational in character, it would be fatuous not to take into account the prevalence of that assumption. Even so, it should not be forgotten that the implied warranty is in large part an invention of law, irrespective of what is actually promised or represented by implication in the particular case.

The moral of this analysis is not so much that a court should feel obliged to consider the breach of an implied warranty of fitness or merchantability a tort as that it should not feel obliged by logic and history to consider it an unalloyed

---

205 App. Div. 648, 200 N.Y. Supp. 121 (1st Dept. 1923). See Farrell v. Manhattan Market Co., 198 Mass. 271, 274, 84 N.E. 481, 482 (1908).

[2] The fact that a warranty is a phase of a contractual arrangement does not mean that the warranty must be treated as having only contractual significance. "In its last analysis, the word 'contract' indicates the source from which the obligation to act is derived while the word 'tort' is used to indicate the wrongful act upon which liability is predicated." 1 Street, Foundations of Legal Liability xxix (1906).

[3] Morrow, "Warranty of Quality; A Comparative Survey," 14 Tulane L. Rev. 327, 529, at 551 (1940).

breach of contract,[4] with the normal consequences and limitations of such an approach. Results the court may believe desirable can frequently be founded on the tort theory[5] (whether breach of actual representation or duty raised by law) or on a tort-contract hybrid, and it should not be inhibited in reaching those results by false notions of legal history or by other inappropriate assumptions.

TOPIC D. *Breach of Warranty Under the Uniform Sales Act*

§1.12. General effect of the Uniform Sales Act. The Uniform Sales Act was first effective in Arizona (1907) and has since been adopted by thirty-three other states[1] and by Alaska, Hawaii, and the District of Columbia. The American law is a substantial copy of the English Sale of Goods Act, 1893. The warranties of fitness and merchantability in Sections 15 (1) and 15 (2) of the American law correspond to the warranties in Sections 14 (1) and 14 (2) of the English law, which in turn were lifted substantially from *Jones* v. *Just*. These provisions are in a broad sense codifications of existing law.[2]

[4] Contract in the sense of actual agreement, as distinct from legal obligation.

[5] For example, in Kennedy v. F. W. Woolworth Co., 205 App. Div. 648, 200 N.Y. Supp. 121 (1st Dept. 1923), a lower New York court bridged the privity gap by switching to the tort theory. It is doubtful whether this represents the view prevailing in New York. In Lovich v. Salvation Army, Inc., 81 Ohio App. 317, 75 N.E.2d 459 (1947), the court held that since the action against the defendant was *ex delictu* (even if based on breach of warranty) its liability as a charity was limited accordingly. And see §2.3 *infra*, note 3.

§1.12. [1] See Appendix B.

[2] This is truer of English common law than of the common law in the various states. With some notable exceptions, draftsman Williston used as his model the English Act, paying closer attention to its terms than the common law of individual states. According to Bell v. Bowers

As for the special warranty applicable to food retailers, the Uniform Sales Act appears to have made a vital change. The apparent exclusion of this warranty [3] from the Act has left a gap in consumer food protection in any situation where there is no reliance by the buyer (thereby precluding the fitness warranty) and the sale is not one "by description" (thereby precluding the merchantability warranty). Whatever effect the Sale of Goods Act may have had on pre-existing English law, the Uniform Sales Act represents, at least in theory, legal retrogression for the American food consumer.

The significant question is what the net difference has been in practical result. How frequently does the food retailer sell other than by description to a buyer who does not rely on his skill or judgment? The answer seems to be:

Stores, 3 Tenn. App. 590, 600 (1926), the Uniform Sales Act "is but declaratory of the common law." In Ohio, however, the court in Clark Restaurant Co. v. Simmons, 29 Ohio App. 220, 225, 163 N.E. 210, 211 (1927), found that the Act "makes more stringent the rule governing those who sell food and food supplies . . ." A similar statement appears in Ryan v. Progressive Grocery Stores, 255 N.Y. 388, 392, 175 N.E. 105, 106 (1931). See also Kurriss v. Conrad & Co., Inc., 312 Mass. 670, 675, 46 N.E.2d 12, 15 (1942), a nonfood case. The Act has been undergoing thorough revision at the hands of The American Law Institute and the Commissioners on Uniform State Laws (see Appendix C).

[3] Section 15 reads: ". . . there is no implied warranty or condition as to the quality or fitness for any particular purpose of goods supplied under a contract to sell or a sale, except as follows: . . ." Exception (5) reads: "An implied warranty or condition as to quality or fitness for a particular purpose may be annexed by the usage of the trade." Why has no one argued that that exception may serve as a loophole through which to save the special food warranty? Compare Melick's amazing statement that the Uniform Sales Act codified the special food warranty (The Sale of Food and Drink 69 (1936)) with the court's statement in Rinaldi v. Mohican Co., 225 N.Y. 70, 73, 121 N.E. 471, 472 (1918). If the American version of the retailer's food warranty had rested on breach of local pure food statute rather than public policy, there might have been an additional out in the opening clause of Section 15: "Subject to the provisions of this act and *of any statute in that behalf* . . ." (Italics added.)

rarely, if ever. This is shown more fully in the following sections.

§1.13. The warranty of fitness. Section 15 (1) of the Uniform Sales Act holds the retailer as guarantor of the wholesomeness of his food only if the buyer "makes known" to the seller the "particular purpose" of his purchase and then "relies" on the seller's skill or judgment to provide an article meeting that need.[1] The fact that the buyer wants to eat what he buys is almost universally recognized as implicit in the retail food purchase.[2] Thus the buyer has only to ask for the article he wants. But is eating a "particular purpose"? Here again everyone agrees: "Particular purpose" means any purpose made known by the buyer, including a general purpose such as eating. With food, therefore, the word "particular" is ordinarily surplusage.[3]

§1.13. [1] Under Section 2-315 of the proposed Uniform Commercial Code — Sales (1951), this warranty would be revised as follows: "Where the seller at the time of contracting has reason to know any particular purpose for which the goods are required and that the buyer is relying on the seller's skill or judgment to select or furnish suitable goods, there is unless excluded or modified under the next section an implied warranty that the goods shall be fit for such purpose."

[2] Gindraux v. Maurice Mercantile Co., 4 Cal. 2d 206, 47 P.2d 708 (1935); Nocera v. Great Atlantic & Pacific Tea Co., 15 Conn. Supp. 174 (C.P. 1947); Holt v. Mann, 294 Mass. 21, 200 N.E. 403 (1936); Ward v. Great Atlantic & Pacific Tea Co., 231 Mass. 90, 93, 120 N.E. 225, 226 (1918); Greco v. S. S. Kresge, 277 N.Y. 26, 12 N.E.2d 557 (1938); Temple v. Keeler, 238 N.Y. 344, 144 N.E. 635 (1924); Rinaldi v. Mohican Co., 225 N.Y. 70, 73, 121 N.E. 471, 472 (1918); Lieberman v. Sheffield Farms-Slawson-Decker Co., Inc., 117 Misc. 531, 191 N.Y. Supp. 593 (1921); Bonenberger v. Pittsburgh Mercantile Co., 345 Pa. 559, 28 A.2d 913 (1942); Frost v. Aylesbury Dairy Co., [1905] 1 K.B. 608, 74 L.J.K.B. 386, 92 L.T. 527. The same result has been reached at common law. Farrell v. Manhattan Market Co., 198 Mass. 271, 279, 84 N.E. 481, 484 (1908); Colonna v. Rosedale Dairy Co., Inc., 166 Va. 314, 320, 186 S.E. 94, 97 (1936).

[3] See Holmes, J., in Wallis v. Russell, [1902] 2 Ir. R. 585, 633. (Most cases take the point for granted.)

Not so, if the buyer's purpose is to eat the food without taking the pre-

§1.14. The warranty of fitness — Determination of reliance. A more difficult question arises in ascertaining the buyer's reliance. Presumably Section 15 (1) forecloses all warranties of fitness for a particular purpose not founded upon reliance in fact. Yet, how is the presence or absence of reliance to be determined in a particular case? Who can remember what, precisely, was said and done? The situation is usually too ephemeral to be recalled in its entirety (even for such relatively stereotyped operations as the self-service store), and actual reliance depends upon states of mind to which a court has no access. The courts have no alternative to establishing a few crude fact categories and, in each general type of case, presuming that the parties in fact reflect what the courts believe to be the general tendency of parties in that kind of situation. The Uniform Sales Act itself takes such a step, in Section 15 (4), in excluding the implied warranty of fitness for a particular purpose when the article is sold under its trade name.[1]

It is not surprising, therefore, to find the New York Court of Appeals saying that the mere purchase from a food dealer, "where the buyer may assume that the seller has the opportunity to examine the article sold, unexplained, is also con-

---

cautions normally taken to guard against possible injury (*e.g.*, Cheli v. Cudahy Bros. Co., 267 Mich. 690, 255 N.W. 414 (1934), involving pork to be eaten raw). Since the warranty made by the seller does not go beyond the bounds of the purpose made known by the buyer, cases marking out the limitations of the warranty obligation frequently help to define the scope of the legally disclosed purpose. See discussion of what food is legally "fit to eat" in Chapter IV.

§1.14. [1] The notion is that when a buyer asks for a product by its trade name he is relying on his own judgment, not that of the seller, to provide him with an article fulfilling his wants. Ryan v. Progressive Grocery Stores, 255 N.Y. 388, 175 N.E. 105 (1931); Moreno v. France Milling Co., 261 App. Div. 991, 26 N.Y.S.2d 400 (2d Dept. 1941). See §1.17 *infra*.

clusive evidence of reliance on the seller's skill or judgment." [2] The general rule appears to go even further: Except where the sealed container doctrine is recognized and except for apparent defects in the inspection cases it presumes buyer's reliance in *all* retail food sales.[3] That the defect is latent does not excuse the seller.[4]

§1.15. The warranty of fitness — The sealed container and buyer's selection doctrines. How have the sealed container and buyer's selection doctrines fared under the Uniform Sales Act? [1] For the former, New York furnishes

[2] Rinaldi v. Mohican Co., 225 N.Y. 70, 74, 121 N.E. 471, 472 (1918).

[3] Sapiente v. Waltuch, 127 Conn. 224, 15 A.2d 417 (1940); Nocera v. Great Atlantic & Pacific Tea Co., 15 Conn. Supp. 174 (C.P. 1947); Martin v. Great Atlantic & Pacific Tea Co., 301 Ky. 429, 192 S.W.2d 201 (1946); Ward v. Great Atlantic & Pacific Tea Co., 231 Mass. 90, 93, 120 N.E. 225, 226 (1918); Rinaldi v. Mohican Co., 225 N.Y. 70, 121 N.E. 471 (1918); Race v. Krum, 222 N.Y. 410, 118 N.E. 853 (1918); Bonenberger v. Pittsburgh Mercantile Co., 345 Pa. 559, 28 A.2d 913 (1942).

[4] In addition to the sealed container cases, see Gindraux v. Maurice Mercantile Co., 4 Cal. 2d 206, 47 P.2d 708 (1935); Vaccarezza v. Sanguinetti, 71 Cal. App. 2d 687, 163 P.2d 470 (1945); Botti v. Venice Grocery Co., 309 Mass. 450, 35 N.E.2d 491 (1941); Holt v. Mann, 294 Mass. 21, 200 N.E. 403 (1936); Hertzler v. Manshum, 228 Mich. 416, 200 N.W. 155 (1924); Wadleigh v. Howson, 88 N.H. 365, 189 Atl. 865 (1937); Greco v. S. S. Kresge Co., 277 N.Y. 26, 12 N.E.2d 557 (1938); McSpedon v. Kunz, 271 N.Y. 131, 2 N.E.2d 513 (1936); Rinaldi v. Mohican Co., 225 N.Y. 70, 121 N.E. 471 (1918); Race v. Krum, 222 N.Y. 410, 118 N.E. 853 (1918); Weiner v. Mager & Throne, 167 Misc. 338, 3 N.Y.S.2d 918 (1938); Baum v. Murray, 23 Wash. 2d 890, 162 P.2d 801 (1945); Nelson v. West Coast Dairy Co., 5 Wash. 2d 284, 105 P.2d 76 (1940); Flessher v. Carstens Packing Co., 93 Wash. 48, 160 Pac. 14 (1916); Frost v. Aylesbury Dairy Co., [1905] 1 K.B. 608, 74 L.J.K.B. 386, 92 L.T. 527. And see Great Atlantic & Pacific Tea Co. v. Eiseman, 259 Ky. 103, 108, 81 S.W.2d 900, 902 (1935).

§1.15. [1] See §§1.3 and 1.5 *supra.* The sealed container exception is here discussed as if it were only an exception to the warranty of fitness. Although no known case applies it to a retail sale which the court characterizes as a sale by description, the exception is usually phrased as if it applied to all implied warranties of quality by the retailer. How it could be applied under the Uniform Sales Act to a sale by description would be hard to explain.

the most interesting case-study. The sealed container exception to the food retailer's responsibility had been recognized, in 1896, by a lower New York appellate court in *Julian* v. *Laubenberger*.[2] The Uniform Sales Act was adopted in New York in 1911. In 1929 the issue again came before the lower appellate courts. In *Aronowitz* v. *F. W. Woolworth Co.*,[3] the court held that while the seller's opportunity to inspect "will constitute conclusive evidence of reliance," the mere purchase of food, where it is in the original can and the buyer cannot take for granted that the seller could examine it, does not conclusively establish reliance. Reliance was not necessarily ruled out by the decision, but it would need further establishing. What that might entail, the court did not say.

The Court of Appeals first dealt with the question in *Gimenez* v. *Great Atlantic & Pacific Tea Co.*[4] Here the defendant retailer was held liable for breach of the implied warranty of fitness with respect to defective canned crabmeat, and there is no indication from the opinion that the plaintiff, in establishing reliance, did more than prove the purchase. Since that time the sealed container doctrine does not appear to have been applied in New York.[5]

[2] 16 Misc. 646, 38 N.Y. Supp. 1052.

[3] 134 Misc. 272, 236 N.Y. Supp. 133. But *cf.* Lieberman v. Sheffield Farms-Slawson-Decker Co., Inc., 117 Misc. 531, 191 N.Y. Supp. 593 (1921), where the court held for the plaintiff in a sealed container case in which the defendant gave the impression that it was the producer.

[4] 264 N.Y. 390, 191 N.E. 27 (1934). A sealed container was involved in Ryan v. Progressive Grocery Stores, 255 N.Y. 388, 175 N.E. 105 (1931), but the sale was one by description with its warranty of merchantability, which does not depend upon showing reliance in the particular case.

[5] In Hopkins v. Amtorg Trading Corp., 265 App. Div. 278, 38 N.Y.S. 2d 788 (1st Dept. 1942), the purchase took place in New Jersey. Since there was no evidence on the question whether the New Jersey pure food law created a civil action, the court held that New York common law rules with respect to negligence and warranty applied. It then pro-

The change of view in New York seems attributable more to the fact that the Court of Appeals differed from the lower court than to the enactment of the Uniform Sales Act. As for Arkansas and Maine, the Uniform Sales Act has made no apparent difference. This is to be expected, because there is nothing in the Act that would necessarily alter any sealed container exception to retailer responsibility.[6] If the basis for the rule is an alleged lack of buyer's reliance, no greater or less reliance is to be expected under the Uniform Sales Act. If its basis is simply the ignorance of the seller, there is no more legal justification for the rule after the Act than there was before. The Kentucky court, on the other hand, has found in the Act sufficient reason to repudiate its earlier position upholding the sealed container rule.[7] Georgia, Mississippi, and West Virginia have not enacted the Act.

Apart from its adoption under the Uniform Sales Act in Alabama and Tennessee,[8] the sealed container doctrine does

---

ceeded to apply the rule of Julian v. Laubenberger, 16 Misc. 646, 38 N.Y. Supp. 1052 (1896).

[6] With this exception: Some of the common law cases adopting the sealed container exception used general warranty language that did not distinguish between the warranty of fitness, which is conditioned upon a showing of reliance, and the warranty of merchantability, which is not. The Uniform Sales Act should dispell any notion that the sealed container exception could properly apply (even assuming that a sealed container precludes actual reliance) to a retail food sale by description. No case has been found in which the sealed container exception has been so applied.

[7] Martin v. Great Atlantic & Pacific Tea Co., 301 Ky. 429, 432–433, 192 S.W.2d 201, 202 (1946).

[8] Kirkland v. Great Atlantic & Pacific Tea Co., 233 Ala. 404, 406, 171 So. 735, 737, 738 (1937); Wilkes v. Memphis Grocery Co., 23 Tenn. App. 550, 555, 134 S.W.2d 929, 932 (1939) (the court, in relying on the seller's innocence rather than on the lack of the buyer's reliance, seems clearly out of tune with the Uniform Sales Act); Bell v. Bowers Stores, 310 Tenn. App. 590 (1926). Under Article 1527 of the Quebec Code, providing that the seller must pay damages suffered by the buyer "in all

not appear to be gaining headway. These instances have been more than offset by its repudiation under the Act in California, Connecticut, the District of Columbia, Illinois, Massachusetts, New Jersey, New York, North Dakota, Pennsylvania, and Rhode Island.[9]

As for the buyer's selection doctrine developed at common law by the Massachusetts court, it has been discredited by that court under the Uniform Sales Act in a recent nonfood

---

cases in which he is legally presumed to know the defects," it has been held that a retailer is not presumed to know hidden defects. Bouvier v. Thrift Stores, Ltd., 74 Que. S.C. 93 (1936) (defective canned sardines).

[9] Burkhardt v. Armour & Co., 115 Conn. 249, 259–263, 161 Atl. 385, 389–390 (1932) (tin in canned corned beef); Nocera v. Great Atlantic & Pacific Tea Co., 15 Conn. Supp. 174 (C.P. 1947) (glass in jar of baked beans); Cleary v. First National Stores, 291 Mass. 172, 196 N.E. 868 (1935) (moldy canned cocoa); Groce v. First National Stores, Inc., 268 Mass. 210, 167 N.E. 308 (1929) (metal in canned cocoanut); Ward v. Great Atlantic & Pacific Tea Co., 231 Mass. 90, 120 N.E. 225 (1918) (pebble in canned pork and beans); Stave v. Giant Food Arcade, 125 N.J.L. 512, 16 A.2d 460 (1940) (deleterious canned pineapple juice); Griffin v. James Butler Grocery Co., 108 N.J.L. 92, 96, 156 Atl. 636, 638 (1931) (contaminated canned peaches); Bonenberger v. Pittsburgh Mercantile Co., 345 Pa. 559, 562, 28 A.2d 913, 915 (1942) (oyster shell in canned oysters). See Goetten v. Owl Drug Co., 6 Cal. 2d 683, 688, 59 P.2d 142, 144 (1936); Gindraux v. Maurice Mercantile Co., 4 Cal. 2d 206, 208, 47 P.2d 708, 709 (1935).

The sealed container doctrine is apparently not accepted in England. Jackson v. Watson & Sons, [1909] 2 K.B. 193, 100 L.T. (N.S.) 799, 3 B.R.C. 182 (defective canned salmon; the court discussed only the question of damages). Likewise in Ontario. Shandloff v. City Dairy, [1936] 4 D.L.R. 712, O.R. 579, O.W.N. 531 (glass in bottle of chocolate milk).

The following cases involved sales by description and are therefore not necessarily authority for rejecting the exception in the case of the fitness warranty. Ryan v. Progressive Grocery Stores, 255 N.Y. 388, 175 N.E. 105 (1931) (pin in bread); Brussels v. Grand Union Co., 14 N.J. Misc. 751, 187 Atl. 582 (1936) (unwholesome canned peas); Goljatowska v. Fred W. Albrecht Co., Inc., 17 Ohio L. Abs. 294 (1934) (pin in bread); D'Onofrio v. First National Stores, Inc., 68 R.I. 144, 26 A.2d 758 (1942) (wire in canned corn); Young v. Great Atlantic & Pacific Tea Co., 15 F. Supp. 1018 (W.D. Pa. 1936) (mouse in preserves).

case.[10] Although this case emphasized the enactment of the Act, it is difficult to see how the Act can have altered the force of what is essentially a question of fact. Elsewhere the buyer's selection exception has shown few signs of sprouting.[11] Nor has the courts' readiness to presume reliance been lessened by the rapid growth of the self-service store.

The buyer's selection doctrine makes sense only to the extent that it overlaps the buyer's *inspection* doctrine. But the latter needs no help from the former. As usually applied, it simply refuses to extend the concept of legal defect to those particular qualities of the goods which it is generally fair to assume the buyer has accepted as satisfactory.[12]

§1.16. The warranty of fitness — Nature of buyer's reliance. The real issue in both the sealed container and buyer's selection situations seems to be this: Granting that it is almost always impossible to capture the essence of a single past retail food sale, what is the tendency which it will be most normal to expect in the given type of situation?

[10] Kurriss v. Conrad & Co., Inc., 312 Mass. 670, 683, 46 N.E.2d 12, 19 (1942). According to the earlier dictum in Ward v. Great Atlantic & Pacific Tea Co., 231 Mass. 90, 93, 120 N.E. 225, 226 (1918), the buyer's selection doctrine applied to goods open to inspection (this excluded most sealed containers) "where there is opportunity for the exercise of an independent judgment by both the buyer and the seller, and where, therefore, the fact as to the one who makes the selection is of no significance . . ." How "open to inspection" might apply to unpackaged goods with latent defects, the court did not say.

[11] It was repudiated in Nocera v. Great Atlantic & Pacific Tea Co., 15 Conn. Supp. 174 (C.P. 1947); Walker v. Great Atlantic & Pacific Tea Co., 131 Tex. 57, 112 S.W.2d 170 (1938).

In Wallis v. Russell, [1902] 2 Ir. R. 585, there is a clear implication that selection of the defective crabs by the purchaser instead of by the retailer would have prevented recovery. But the phrase "*necessarily* relies" (italics added) in Section 14(1) of the Sale of Goods Act, which influenced the court, does not appear in the American statute.

[12] But *cf.* Williston, Sales §234 (3d ed. 1948), where the reason is said to be want of reliance. See §1.17 *infra*, note 4. What is a reasonably apparent defect is a jury question. Friend v. Childs Dining Hall Co., 231 Mass. 65, 75, 120 N.E. 407, 411 (1918).

That question cannot be answered without first ascertaining the respects in which it can reasonably be said the buyer might rely on the seller's skill or judgment. The decisions themselves are obscure. In *Ward* v. *Great Atlantic & Pacific Tea Co.*,[1] the court said that the plaintiff buyer was bound to rely on the seller's skill in selecting the can which was offered him because it was almost an irresistible inference that the seller had selected the can. This seems to say that the crucial fact was whether the seller or the buyer selected the particular can, as against other cans on the same shelf. But for packaged goods such a choice hardly relates to the question of reliance. Once the cans are on the shelf the seller has almost no further means of distinguishing between them, except for size or brand, and the buyer knows it. This suggests that whatever it is that the buyer may be relying on (1) normally occurs before the goods get on the shelf, and (2) consists of the exclusion of goods known or suspected to be unwholesome, rather than the affirmative selection of goods known to be wholesome.

The buyer knows or should know that the retail seller cannot guard against all latent defects, whether they come in cans or otherwise. Yet, the buyer can, and usually does, rely on the seller to take appropriate steps to exclude unwholesome foods from the retail counter. The seller can (1) select reputable wholesale suppliers, (2) select reputable manufacturers and brands, (3) exclude goods found or reasonably believed to be unwholesome while in the seller's hands, (4) make complaints and take other appropriate action, where the discovered defect existed while the goods were in the hands of the supplier or manufacturer, and (5) take adequate precautions to keep goods from becoming unwholesome after they reach the seller.

This kind of reliance relates to an exercise of skill and

§1.16. [1] 231 Mass. 90, 121 N.E. 225 (1918).

judgment that cannot reasonably be expected to intercept every possible source of injury.[2] At the same time, it seems plain that the kind of reliance that is made a condition precedent to the operation of the implied warranty of fitness is not reliance upon a degree of skill that is aimed at eliminating every possible defect, however subtle. If the buyer relies on the seller's skill in any material regard with respect to the wholesomeness of the food bought, the Act generates an obligation that extends to all factors that threaten wholesomeness, except those which upon actual inspection by the buyer are reasonably apparent. In other words, it is no objection under Section 15 (1) of the Act that the area of reliance is not coextensive with the area of protection claimed under the warranty.[3] If this is not true for reasons of abstract principle, it is certainly true for reasons of practicability. Who can measure in meaningful terms the *degree* of reliance in particular cases, and who, failing to measure it in particular cases, can take and measure a market average?

Waite talks about "reasonable" reliance.[4] Is "reasonableness" to be tested by the knowledge of sophisticated buyers? Probably not. If normal buyer-expectation is the test, is it reasonable to expect that such a buyer knows the inherent limitations of his seller? The average retail food

[2] In Nocera v. Great Atlantic & Pacific Tea Company, 15 Conn. Supp. 174 (C.P. 1947), the court apparently distinguishes between reliance upon the seller's general skill and judgment in selecting his goods and reliance upon his skill and judgment in selecting the particular article bought by the plaintiff (the former is sufficient under the Uniform Sales Act).

[3] Cases holding that inspection by the buyer negatives implied warranties even against latent defects are not inconsistent with this view, since they presume (however unjustifiably) that there is *no* reliance in those cases. Section 15(3), in distinguishing between latent and reasonably observable defects, is also consistent with the text, and it is more realistic in its assumptions as to the degree of reliance.

[4] Waite, "Retail Responsibility and Judicial Law Making," 34 Mich. L. Rev. 494, 506 (1936).

buyer has only the cloudiest notions of what the retail food operation involves. Or should we expect the courts to measure differing degrees of reliance by a sophisticated patron in a small independent grocery and an uninformed buyer in a supermarket? In any event, there is no indication from the cases that the courts are attempting to measure reliance either in individual instances or for buyers generally. Even the sealed container cases, the buyer's selection cases, and Section 15 (4) seem to rest on the assumption (however false) that there is *no* reliance, rather than *insufficient* reliance, in those cases.

Since practicality requires the use of presumptions of fact, the courts will be closer to reality if they presume a reliance in all cases that exists in most. To require more of the plaintiff is to foster perjury.

That reliance may well be present in a sealed container case was forcefully stated in a North Carolina decision [5] involving the purchase of defective sausage, the casing of which the court treated as a "sealed container."

> One who purchases an article of food for consumption is usually not equal in opportunity with the person who sells it, since the latter has the first opportunity of being assured that the goods he sells are merchantable and fit for human consumption, because of his experience in buying, his acquaintance with the manufacturer, and his knowledge of the brands, and of the responsibility of the concerns with which he deals.

Even where the buyer selects, there is good reason in the retail food cases to find that the buyer is relying on the seller

[5] Rabb v. Covington, 215 N.C. 572, 574, 2 S.E.2d 705, 707 (1939) (the Uniform Sales Act is not in force in North Carolina, but the case loses no force thereby). The product involved in this case illustrates the absurdity of making legal results turn on the presence or absence of a "sealed container." Why is latency any more latent because it comes in cans? The significant issue is whether the seller is to be made liable for undiscoverable defects, and the situation is the same whether it involves canned

at least to exclude unwholesome goods from the total stock from which the buyer makes his selection, very likely on the basis of considerations other than minimum wholesomeness. The plausibility of this supposition was accepted and well considered in a New York case arising under the Uniform Sales Act.[6]

§1.17. **Purchase by trade name.** When the buyer asks for a food product by trade name, warranties of fitness "for any particular purpose" are excluded by Section 15 (4).[1] The reason for the provision is presumably that, to fulfill a special rather than the general purpose served by the goods, the buyer is relying on his own skill and not the skill of the seller. This assumption is as anomalous as that underlying the sealed container exception.[2]

With respect to reliance, it is interesting to compare Section 15 (3), dealing generally with inspection by the buyer, with Section 15 (4), dealing with one kind of selection by the buyer. Inspection by the buyer excludes from the protections of implied warranty only reasonably apparent defects,[3] whereas purchase by trade name excludes latent defects as well. The former provision, therefore, insofar as it rests on lack of reliance, takes account of a fact which

---

peas, trichinous pork, or Malta fever germs in milk. Actually, a bolt in a glass jar of beans may be easier to see than ground glass in a loaf of bread.

[6] Rinaldi v. Mohican Co., 225 N.Y. 70, 74, 121 N.E. 471, 472 (1918).

§1.17. [1] Botti v. Venice Grocery Co., 309 Mass. 450, 35 N.E.2d 491 (1941); Ryan v. Progressive Grocery Stores, 255 N.Y. 388, 175 N.E. 105 (1931); Moreno v. France Milling Co., 261 App. Div. 991, 26 N.Y.S.2d 400 (2d Dept. 1941); Goljatowska v. Fred W. Albrecht Co., Inc., 17 Ohio L. Abs. 294 (1934); D'Onofrio v. First National Stores, 68 R.I. 144, 26 A.2d 758 (1942).

[2] See §§1.3, 1.15, and 1.16, *supra*.

[3] Selection and inspection are, of course, two distinct concepts. In Wallis v. Russell, [1902] 2 Ir. R. 585, for example, there was full inspection by the buyer, but the seller did the selecting. Such inspection did

exposes the fallacy underlying Section 15 (4) and the sealed container and buyer's selection exceptions: That the buyer is relying partly on his own judgment does not mean that he is not also relying on the seller's. What also sets Section 15 (3) apart is the fact that it is based at least in part on a principle, distinct from reliance, with more far-reaching consequences: Features which it is reasonable to assume have been examined and found acceptable by a buyer are not to be considered defects from his viewpoint. Taken in this light, Section 15 (3) is not out of line with the conclusion, noted above, that the courts are not limiting the degree of protection according to the degree of reliance.[4]

That the underlying assumption of Section 15 (4) (that there is no reliance by the buyer) may be unfounded, at least in the retail food cases, does not remove the provision from the Act.[5] The practical question remains: What is the net effect on the rights of the buyer? An answer is suggested in the next section.

§1.18. The warranty of merchantability. It is generally agreed that a purchase by trade name is a purchase by

---

not bar recovery with respect to latent defects; there is a strong implication from the opinions that selection would have. See also Ryan v. Progressive Grocery Stores, 255 N.Y. 388, 175 N.E. 105 (1931).

[4] Williston says that the rationale in the inspection cases is want of reliance. Sales §234 (3d ed. 1948). If so, how does it happen that, unlike the sealed container doctrine, the inspection doctrine applies also to the merchantability warranty under Section 15(2), where reliance in the particular case is irrelevant? Rather, says Prosser, in "The Implied Warranty of Merchantable Quality," 27 Minn. L. Rev. 117, 153–154 (1943), "The reason is that he [the buyer] must understand that the seller is offering for sale what is before him, as it appears to be . . . and when the buyer accepts that offer, he agrees to buy the goods according to the appearance they present." Prosser's statement seems to support the analysis made in the text.

[5] Sections 2–314 and 2–315 of the proposed Uniform Commercial Code — Sales (1951) make no room for the rule of Section 15(4).

description within the meaning of Section 15 (2),[1] which gives the buyer the protection of the implied warranty of merchantability. But Section 15 (2) does not fully compensate the retail food buyer for the inroads of Section 15 (4) unless "merchantability" as applied to retail food sales is equivalent to "fit for eating purposes."

As well explained by Prosser,[2] merchantability seems to require several things. First, where the seller is a dealer, the description calls "for the kind of goods usually sold by that name by such dealer, and the usages of the trade become part of the understanding of the parties." Second, the goods must be of the kind or quality commonly sold in the market (that is, such that the buyer can resell, if he is a dealer; or get what dealers usually sell, if he is a user, assuming that the true character of the goods were known). Third, the goods must be reasonably fit for the ordinary uses to which goods of that kind are put, and free from defects interfering with sale or ordinary use.[3] For food, this adds up to one thing: It must be fit to eat.[4]

§1.18. [1] Botti v. Venice Grocery Co., 309 Mass. 450, 35 N.E.2d 491 (1941); Ryan v. Progressive Grocery Stores, 255 N.Y. 388, 175 N.E. 105 (1931); Goljatowska v. Fred W. Albrecht Co., Inc., 17 Ohio L. Abs. 294 (1934); D'Onofrio v. First National Stores, Inc., 68 R.I. 144, 26 A.2d 758 (1942); Wren v. Holt, [1903] 1 K.B. 610, 72 L.J.K.B. 340, 88 L.T. 282.

The court seemed unmindful of this fact in Moreno v. France Milling Co., 261 App. Div. 991, 26 N.Y.S.2d 400 (2d Dept. 1941). See also Alphonso v. Stavnitsky, discussed in §1.19 *infra*, note 4.

When a sale is "by trade name" is sometimes hard to determine. The mere fact that the article sold has a trade name and the trade name is used to refer to the article does not bring the sale under Section 15(4). J. A. Campbell Co. v. Corley, 140 Ore. 462, 475, 13 P.2d 610, 613 (1932).

[2] Prosser, "The Implied Warranty of Merchantable Quality," 27 Minn. L. Rev. 117, 125–139 (1943). Llewellyn, Cases and Materials on the Law of Sales 324 (1930): "There is no more puzzling question than what this word 'merchantable' means under the Sales Act."

[3] Section 2–314(2) of the proposed Uniform Commercial Code — Sales (1951) spells out this concept in detail.

[4] Botti v. Venice Grocery Co., 309 Mass. 450, 455, 35 N.E.2d 491, 494

There is one respect in which Section 15 (2) may not compensate for the operation of Section 15 (4). There is some doubt whether merchantability calls for a standard of excellence typical only of the brand asked for or whether it also requires food that is good to eat where the entire brand is deficient. Several writers have suggested that where the buyer asks for a deficient brand, that is all he is entitled to get. But why merchantability should not mean fit to eat in the case of food is not explained by saying that it may be more than the buyer expressly requested.

Section 14 provides that in a sale by description the buyer is entitled to what he asked for. Granting that a sale of food under a trade name is a sale by description, equivalent to asking for a typical member of the classification, why should it be assumed that Section 15 (2) is a needless repetition of Section 14? Unlike Section 14, the former does not provide that the article sold must merely fulfill the description. It must be "merchantable." Is it reading too much into the Act to suggest that merchantable food is food that is good to eat?

Where the deficient brand claims membership in the broad category of food, together with other brands which are not deficient, there would seem to be inherent in the normal transaction an overriding characterization of the product as food, especially where the product has no other use. If the buyer asks for Holden's beer, which (let us suppose) uniformly contains too much arsenic and which is intended only for drinking, is he not normally asking (how-

---

(1941); Ryan v. Progressive Grocery Stores, 255 N.Y. 388, 394, 175 N.E. 105, 107 (1931); Galjatowska v. Fred W. Albrecht Co., Inc., 17 Ohio L. Abs. 294 (1934). The problem of when food is fit to eat (the measure of the seller's obligation) is discussed in Chapter IV. For present purposes, it is sufficient to say that "fit to eat" means "fit to eat after the buyer takes the normal precautions."

ever inconsistently) for (a) Holden's beer and (b) something that serves the general purpose of drinking beer?

The problem, at any rate, is largely academic because the kind of defect that is subtle enough to pass as typical of the brand is not likely to be the subject of a civil suit. Cases invoking Section 15 (4) in such a situation are rare. The few cases dealing with the question are divided as to whether the warranty reaches this kind of defect.[5]

§1.19. Combined effect of Sales Act warranties. In practice, there is a strong tendency to assume that Sections 15 (1) and 15 (2), taken together, raise a warranty of wholesomeness in all retail food sales. Whatever may be true of other commodities, the jigsaw puzzle of the Uniform Sales Act, as pieced together in many states, spells out in consumer food cases a liability in warranty as strict as that existing under the special common law warranty peculiar to food. In the remaining states the questionable spots are the sealed container group and products that are uniformly defective.

Prosser's able analysis of the warranty of merchantability[1] suggests that a preoccupation with the mysteries of reliance under the warranty of fitness has frequently led court and counsel to neglect the more important warranty of merchantability, particularly with regard to the possibility of finding sales "by description" where some orthodox investi-

[5] Compare Wren v. Holt, [1903] 1 K.B. 610, 72 L.J.K.B. 340, 88 L.T. 282 (warranty of wholesomeness), with Outhwaite v. A. B. Knowlson Co., 259 Mich. 224, 242 N.W. 895 (1932) (nonfood case; no warranty that stucco sold was better than the brand). If the defect was common to the brand, Kelvinator Sales Corp. v. Quabbin Improvement Co., 234 App. Div. 96, 254 N.Y. Supp. 123 (1st Dept. 1931), which did not discuss the point, agrees in effect with Wren v. Holt.

§1.19. [1] Prosser, "The Implied Warranty of Merchantable Quality," 27 Minn. L. Rev. 117, 120 (1943).

gators (such as Williston) have not, that is, in sales of specific goods identified by description. So far as the retail food cases are concerned, there is at least the justification of practicality in treating the warranty of merchantability as part of a larger theoretical pattern which, when fitted together, largely removes the need to determine the precise pattern of sale in particular cases.[2] Of course, where the individual pattern does emerge, the court should hesitate to direct a verdict for the defendant for want of the buyer's reliance, until it makes certain that the buyer is not entitled to the protection of another warranty not contingent on a showing of reliance.

The Uniform Sales Act fails in literal performance in the retail food cases because its terms presume a degree of formality and deliberation that does not exist.[3] Most courts, being willing to presume reliance and to plug the trade-name gap with the warranty of merchantability, continue to apply Section 15 shotgunwise in the direction of absolute liability. This has the support of practical logic and it avoids the fatuous trying of elusive issues. Nevertheless, the Uniform Sales Act is a continuing invitation to unsophisticated courts to apply the intricacies of the law of sales to

[2] This is not wholly true. In a state accepting the sealed container exception, it is to the plaintiff's advantage to establish a sale by description, because the resulting warranty of merchantability does not depend upon a showing of reliance.

[3] The proposed Uniform Commercial Code — Sales (1951) would largely avoid this difficulty. For example, the merchantability warranty (Section 2–314) would be raised wherever the seller was a merchant with respect to the goods, making it unnecessary to determine whether the particular sale was "by description" or even to use the warranty of fitness (except in unusual cases). The implied warranty of fitness (Section 2–315) would depend upon the seller's having "reason to know any particular purpose . . . and that the buyer is relying on the seller's skill or judgment . . ." Here the warranty could be founded on the general relationship of the parties, if necessary, without resorting to any pretense of determining particular words and mental attitudes.

informal situations where nice distinctions are either impracticable or absurd.[4] Reliance is a sound underlying basis for raising a warranty of fitness because it measures inequalities in bargaining power. But, where the plaintiff is a consumer, practicality forces the courts to relegate reliance to being part of the basic rationale of including the provision, but no part of the mechanics of determination.

§1.20. Special warranties in sales by description or sample. Sections 14 and 16 of the Uniform Sales Act, covering sales by description and by sample, are probably of little help to the food consumer. If not simply duplicated by Section 15 (2), Section 14 [1] gives even less protection, since it assumes only the standard of the brand or description requested (unless "food" can be read into the description). As for Section 16, retailers rarely sell food by sample. Where they do, Subsection (3), covering sample sales by a dealer, assures the buyer of the "merchantability" of his purchase. The latter section, then, may someday be useful to a few

[4] A good example is Alphonso v. Stavnitsky, 8 Conn. Supp. 34 (C.P. 1940). Here the buyer among other things broke his tooth on a sliver of wood in chocolate-covered peanuts which he bought from the defendant's vending machine. The court, in finding reliance under Section 15(1) of the Sales Act, made much of the fact that there was only one brand of peanuts in the machine. It implied that had there been several brands of peanuts to choose from the case might have gone the other way. Actually, the plaintiff might well rely on the defendant even in such a situation; conversely, the fact that there was only one brand did not mean that the plaintiff had not already decided to buy that brand. The court seemed haunted by Section 15(4), which it did not cite but treated as inherent in Section 15(1). It needlessly assumed that, had there been several brands of peanuts, putting a nickel in the "Goober" slot would have been equivalent to asking for peanuts by that brand name. The court then forgot that such a sale would be one "by description" with its warranty of merchantability. Hence its relief that only one brand had appeared in the machine.

§1.20. [1] See Botti v. Venice Grocery Co., 309 Mass. 450, 457, 35 N.E.2d 491, 495 (1941).

retail food purchasers, in case the courts reverse their apparent tendency to ignore the precise manner of purchase.

§1.21. Express warranties. Express warranties of quality are given by the retail food dealer in only an infinitesimal proportion of cases. Even then they are hard to establish. Where such a warranty can be proved, it offers valuable protection.[1] The legal problems involved in those cases require no additional discussion here.

Topic E. *The Privity Requirement*

§1.22. Want of privity as a bar to recovery. Suppose a housewife buys a can of tomatoes from a local grocery. There are glass fragments in the can and the housewife, her husband, her daughter, and a guest suffer throat lacerations. Can they recover against the retailer for breach of warranty?

Consider the little girl and the guest first. If the suits are brought in Alabama, Arkansas, Connecticut, the District of Columbia, Maine, Maryland, Massachusetts, Montana, New Hampshire, New Jersey, New York, North Carolina, South Dakota, Tennessee, Virginia, West Virginia, Wisconsin, Nova Scotia, or England, the answer is almost certainly no.[1] The reason is that there is no "privity of contract"

§1.21. [1] This is purely hypothetical. No case appears in which a consumer recovered against a food retailer for breach of an express warranty of quality. In Scruggins v. Jones, 207 Ky. 636, 296 S.W. 743 (1925), the court found that the retailer did not expressly warrant the goods when he said the canner was "reliable." In Albrecht v. Rubinstein, 135 Conn. 243, 63 A.2d 158 (1948), the restaurateur's statement that the sandwich was "good" was held too indefinite to constitute an express warranty.

§1.22. [1] The following cases involved suits against retailers or restaurant keepers. Borucki v. MacKenzie Bros. Co., 125 Conn. 92, 3 A.2d 224 (1938) (child of purchaser injured by glass in liverwurst); Cleary v. First National Stores, 291 Mass. 172, 196 N.E. 868 (1935) (wife injured by defective canned cocoa); Bolitho v. Safeway Stores, 109 Mont. 213, 95 P.2d

between the plaintiff and the defendant. The states named are both common law and Sales Act states.

The privity requirement in warranty cases rests on the notion that the warranty, or the sale to which it attaches, is

---

443 (1939) (daughter made ill by defective food); Hazelton v. First National Stores, 88 N.H. 409, 190 Atl. 280 (1937) (wife and two children infected with trichinosis); Stave v. Giant Food Arcade, 125 N.J.L. 512, 16 A.2d 460 (1940) (child made ill by deleterious canned pineapple juice); Brussels v. Grand Union Co., 14 N.J. Misc. 751, 187 Atl. 582 (1936) (son and maid injured by defective canned peas); Bourcheix v. Willow Brook Dairy, 268 N.Y. 1, 196 N.E. 617 (1935) (chauffeur injured by glass in milk); Redmond v. Borden Farm Products Co., 245 N.Y. 512, 157 N.E. 838 (1927) (baby injured by broken glass in milk); Massey v. Borden Co., 265 App. Div. 839, 37 N.Y.S.2d 571 (2d Dept. 1942) (child killed by defective milk); Block v. Empire State Doughnut Corp., 233 App. Div. 774, 250 N.Y. Supp. 440 (2d Dept. 1931) (son injured by defective doughnut); Smith v. Hanson, 228 App. Div. 634, 238 N.Y. Supp. 86 (2d Dept. 1929) (child injured by glass in milk); Dickinson v. Sperling, 158 Misc. 905, 286 N.Y. Supp. 934 (1936) (child injured by foreign substance in roll); Shepard v. Beck Bros., Inc., 131 Misc. 164, 166, 225 N.Y. Supp. 438, 440 (1927) (grandson injured by nail in coffee cake); Colonna v. Rosedale Dairy Co., Inc., 166 Va. 314, 186 S.E. 94 (1936) (son infected with Malta fever from milk); Prinsen v. Russos, 194 Wis. 142, 215 N.W. 905 (1927) (guest infected by trichinae in ham sandwich); Hanback v. Dutch Baker Boy, Inc., 107 F.2d 203 (App. D.C. 1939) (child injured by defective éclair); Conner v. Great Atlantic & Pacific Tea Co., 25 F. Supp. 855 (W.D. Mo. 1939) (wife and sister-in-law made sick by unfit meat); Square v. Model Farm Dairies (Bournemouth), Ltd., [1939] 2 K.B. 365, [1939] 1 All E.R. 259, 55 T.L.R. 384, 83 Sol. J. 152. See Heinemann v. Barfield, 136 Ark. 456, 465, 207 S.W. 58, 61 (1918); John B. Thompson Co. v. Smith, 8 Higgins 95 (Tenn. Civ. App. 1916); Burgess v. Sanitary Meat Market, 121 W. Va. 605, 5 S.E.2d 785, 6 S.E.2d 254 (1939). *Cf.* Singer v. Zabelin, 24 N.Y.S.2d 962 (N.Y. City Ct. 1941) (third party beneficiary rule invoked in favor of purchaser's daughter, who had been injured by defective canned salmon); Lieberman v. Sheffield Farms-Slawson-Decker Co., Inc., 117 Misc. 531, 191 N.Y. Supp. 593 (1921) (baby infected by worms in milk). In Kennedy v. F. W. Woolworth Co., 205 App. Div. 648, 200 N.Y. Supp. 121 (1st Dept. 1923), an intermediate New York court hurdled the privity obstacle by putting liability in tort.

The Kentucky rule requiring privity in suits against the manufacturer (Nehi Bottling Co. v. Thomas, 236 Ky. 684, 33 S.W.2d 701 (1930)) may be more lenient where the defendant is a retailer. In Snead v. Waite, 306 Ky. 587, 208 S.W.2d 749 (1948), at least one of the plaintiffs who were not in privity with the defendant recovered. Unfortunately, the privity problem was not discussed.

In Missouri, privity has been requirea as against a wholesaler (De

primarily contractual.[2] Since neither the daughter nor the guest is a party to the contract, neither is entitled to complain of its breach.

That there is some dissatisfaction with the majority rule has been shown in several ways. States such as California, Florida, Illinois, Iowa, Kansas, Louisiana, Mississippi, Oklahoma, Pennsylvania, Texas, and Washington [3] have rejected the privity requirement altogether (here, again, the list includes common law and Sales Act states). In at least one state, the matter has been the subject of special legislation.[4] Even the states that claim to follow the majority rule have been liberal in discovering privity of contract, in some instances where less imaginative courts might not.

So far as the husband is concerned, the jury is usually sympathetic enough to find that the wife has purchased as

---

Gouveia v. H. D. Lee Mercantile Co., 231 Mo. App. 447, 100 S.W.2d 336 (1937)) but dispensed with as against a manufacturer (Madouros v. Kansas City Coca-Cola Bottling Co., 230 Mo. App. 275, 90 S.W.2d 445 (Kan. City Ct. of App. 1936)). Presumably it would be required as against a retailer.

The situation in Ohio is uncertain. Compare Canton Provision Co. v. Gauder, 130 Ohio St. 43, 196 N.E. 634 (1935), with Ward Baking Co. v. Trizzino, 27 Ohio App. 475, 161 N.E. 557 (1920), and Kneiss v. Armour & Co., 134 Ohio St. 432, 17 N.E.2d 734 (1938).

The statement in the text with respect to the other states named is based upon cases involving sellers other than retailers. See Chapter II, Topics A and D.

[2] See Williston, Sales §244 (3d ed., 1948).

[3] The following cases involved suits against retailers. Vaccarezza v. Sanguinetti, 71 Cal. App. 2d 687, 163 P.2d 470 (1945) (two children); Welter v. Bowman Dairy Co., 318 Ill. App. 305, 47 N.E.2d 739 (1943) (*rev'd* on other grounds) (infant daughter); Griggs Canning Co. v. Josey, 139 Tex. 623, 164 S.W.2d 835 (1942) (stepson). See Blarjeske v. Thompson's Restaurant Co., 325 Ill. App. 189, 196, 59 N.E.2d 320, 323 (1945) (guest). Under the civil law, Louisiana does not require privity. Arndt v. D. H. Holmes Co., 9 La. App. 36, 119 So. 91 (1928) (husband and two daughters).

That privity has been rejected in the other states named in the text is established in cases involving sellers other than retailers. See Chapter II, Topics A and D.

[4] Conn. Gen. Stat. (Supp. 1939) §1276e.

his agent, which establishes privity between the husband and the retailer.[5] The injured husband, therefore, rarely loses for want of privity. When the wife alone is involved (as both purchaser and victim), the courts are frequently willing to stack the cards in her favor by presuming that she is purchasing in her own behalf unless her agency affirmatively appears.[6] Recovery by her is then assured by allowing the question of agency to go to the jury. Where the husband buys, on the other hand, the injured wife usually, though not always, fails.[7] Where the wife buys and both

[5] Holt v. Mann, 294 Mass. 21, 200 N.E. 403 (1936); Gearing v. Berkson, 223 Mass. 257, 111 N.E. 785 (1916); Wadleigh v. Howson, 88 N.H. 365, 367, 189 Atl. 865, 867 (1937); Stave v. Giant Food Arcade, 125 N.J.L. 512, 16 A.2d 460 (1940); Ryan v. Progressive Grocery Stores, 255 N.Y. 388, 175 N.E. 105 (1931); Visusil v. W. T. Grant Co., 253 App. Div. 736, 300 N.Y. Supp. 652 (2d Dept. 1937); Singer v. Zabelin, 24 N.Y.S.2d 962 (N.Y. City Ct. 1941); Jackson v. Watson & Sons, [1909] 2 K.B. 193, 100 L.T. (N.S.) 799, 3 B.R.C. 182. See Vaccarino v. Cozzubo, 181 Md. 614, 617, 31 A.2d 316, 318 (1943); Young v. Great Atlantic & Pacific Tea Co., 15 F. Supp. 1018 (W.D. Pa. 1936).

If the wife is normally the agent of the husband, why shouldn't the husband also be able to recover where the wife buys through a child as subagent? Hopkins v. Amtorg Trading Corp., 265 App. Div. 278, 284–285, 38 N.Y.S.2d 788, 794–795 (1st. Dept. 1942), seems to say that the child must buy as direct agent of the husband.

[6] Colby v. First National Stores, Inc., 307 Mass. 252, 254, 29 N.E.2d 920, 921 (1940); Timmins v. F. N. Joslin Co., 303 Mass. 540, 22 N.E.2d 76 (1939); Groce v. First National Stores, Inc., 268 Mass. 210, 167 N.E. 308 (1929); Gimenez v. Great Atlantic & Pacific Tea Co., 264 N.Y. 390, 393, 191 N.E. 27, 28 (1934); Rinaldi v. Mohican Co., 225 N.Y. 70, 121 N.E. 471 (1918) (the record shows that the husband was not supporting his wife at the time of purchase); Meyer v. Kerschbaum, 133 Misc. 330, 232 N.Y. Supp. 300 (1928). *Contra:* Vaccaro v. Prudential Condensed Milk Co., 133 Misc. 556, 232 N.Y. Supp. 299 (1927). If the agency is established but it was undisclosed to the retailer, the wife is treated as contracting in her own behalf. Colby v. First National Stores, Inc., *supra*, at 254, 29 N.E.2d at 921; Timmins v. F. N. Joslin Co., *supra*, at 542, 22 N.E.2d at 77; Groce v. First National Stores, Inc., *supra*, at 213, 167 N.E. at 310. *Cf.* Hunt v. Rhodes Bros. Co., 207 Mass. 30, 92 N.E. 1001 (1910), where the question of the husband's agency was held to be one for the jury.

[7] Binion v. Sasaki, 5 Cal. App. 2d 15, 41 P.2d 585 (1935); Zotto v. Merkel Bros., 229 App. Div. 793, 242 N.Y. Supp. 749 (2d Dept. 1930);

are injured, recovery has been allowed to the husband but denied to the wife on the ground that she acted only as agent.[8] The converse result has been reached where the fact of agency did not affirmatively appear.[9]

In some of these cases an assault on the privity rule is hidden in the fact that the court passes the agency buck to a sympathetic jury, which can usually be counted on to make a factual finding sufficient to justify relief. The straining to bridge the privity gap without legally filling it appears more clearly in cases like *Jensen* v. *Berris.*[10] Here the poisoning accident occurred at a luncheon meeting of a women's pinochle club, where the members took turns paying the check. With respect to the particular meeting the California court found a separate contract between the defendant and each member, even though a single member footed the bill. Thus the plaintiff recovered even though another member had paid.

In *Lockett* v. *A. & M. Charles, Ltd.*,[11] an English case, husband and wife were injured by defective whitebait served in the defendant's restaurant. It was agreed that the husband paid the check. The court performed some deft hairsplitting.

Conner v. Great Atlantic & Pacific Tea Co., 25 F. Supp. 855 (W.D. Mo. 1939). But see Dryden v. Continental Baking Co., 11 Cal. 2d 33, 37, 77 P.2d 833, 835 (1938) (dictum that wife might be "third party beneficiary").

[8] Gearing v. Berkson, 223 Mass. 257, 111 N.E. 785 (1916). *Cf.* Lockett v. A. & M. Charles, Ltd., 159 L.T.R. 547, 55 T.L.R. 22, [1938] 4 All E.R. 170, 82 Sol. J. 951 (1938).

[9] Schlosser v. Goldberg, 123 N.J.L. 470, 9 A.2d 699 (1939); Gimenez v. Great Atlantic & Pacific Tea Co., 264 N.Y. 390, 191 N.E. 27 (1934) (the husband's only injuries were loss of consortium and medical expenses). The Gimenez case was followed in McSpedon v. Kunz, 245 App. Div. 824, 281 N.Y. Supp. 147 (2d Dept. 1935).

[10] 31 Cal. App. 2d 537, 88 P.2d 220 (1939).

[11] 159 L.T.R. 547, 55 T.L.R. 22, [1938] 4 All E.R. 170, 82 Sol. J. 951 (1938).

It was simply a case where a man and a woman sat down at a table and ordered their food . . . where there is no evidence to indicate to the proprietor of the hotel what the relationship between the parties is, and there is no evidence that one or the other is in charge of the proceeding and yet one or the other takes on himself the position of a host entertaining his guests, the proper inference of law is that the person who orders and consumes the food is liable to pay for it as between himself and the proprietor of the restaurant.

On this theory, both husband and wife recovered.

In *Singer* v. *Zabelin*,[12] a lower New York court protected the buyer's daughter as a "third party beneficiary" in a fictional application of that doctrine. The case seems out of step with New York law.[13]

Cases such as these indicate an uneasiness as to the soundness of the privity rule itself. It may explain what some have observed to be a trend toward emasculating it, and perhaps doing away with the rule altogether.[14]

One result of the privity requirement has been to encourage the privity-blocked wife, child, relative, or guest to try the alternative remedy of a suit for negligence or a suit based upon the violation of a pure food statute. How effective these alternatives are will be considered in the following Topic.

[12] 24 N.Y.S.2d 962 (N.Y. City Ct. 1941).

[13] Gimenez v. Great Atlantic & Pacific Tea Co., 264 N.Y. 390, 395, 191 N.E. 27, 29 (1934); Salzano v. First National Stores, 268 App. Div. 993, 994, 51 N.Y.S.2d 645, 646 (2d Dept. 1944). The third party beneficiary approach was also repudiated in Borucki v. MacKenzie Bros. Co., 125 Conn. 92, 98, 3 A.2d 224, 226 (1938).

[14] Llewellyn has shrewdly noted the "tremendous extent to which any shift in *tendency to classify facts* is likely to be accompanied by a parallel (though delayed) tendency to change the words, or scope, or nature of the 'Rules' concerned." Llewellyn, "On Warranty of Quality, and Society," 36 Col. L. Rev. 699, 723 (1936). The privity requirement would be expressly abolished as against the retailer under Section 2–318 of the proposed Uniform Commercial Code — Sales (1951).

Because the problem of privity is even more serious where the seller is the manufacturer, a full discussion of the substantive merits of the requirement will be deferred until the positions of the manufacturer and processor can be fully considered.[15]

Topic F. *Negligence and Other Breaches of Duty Not Based on Warranty*

§1.23. Common law negligence. Although "Negligence as a basis of civil liability was unknown to mediaeval law . . . ," [1] persons following a common calling were held to the standard of skill prevailing in that calling.[2] Those who fell below were liable to those injured in an action on the case "by the common custom of the realm." This notion not only added force to the allegedly absolute responsibility of retail food dealers but it persisted, in diluted form, as part of the later doctrine of negligence as applied to the sale and use of articles generally.

Most suits against the food retailer claim breach of warranty, because the plaintiff does not have to show that the

[15] See Chapter II, Topic A.

The possibility of holding the retailer liable to beneficiaries of the purchaser on the basis of express warranties in advertising done by the retailer is one which has not been explored. On several occasions manufacturers have been held on the strength of literature intended to influence the retail trade. But it is very doubtful that such a principle would be useful in retailer suits, in view of the different type of advertising which the food retailer does. See §1.21 *supra*, note 1.

§1.23. [1] Cardozo, J., in Palsgraf v. Long Island R.R., 248 N.Y. 339, 345, 162 N.E. 99, 101 (1928).

[2] See Melick, The Sale of Food and Drink 1 n.1, and 7 (1936); Ames, "The History of Assumpsit," 2 Harv. L. Rev. 1, 8 (1888); Burdick, "The Origin of Duties Peculiar to Public Service Corporations," 11 Col. L. Rev. 514 (1911) (the concept of "common" calling was originally much broader than it is today).

defendant was at fault. This has made the negligence action only a gap-filler. The main gap is that created by the privity requirement. Another arises where the transaction between the consumer and his supplier is held not to be a "sale," as where the food is received as a perquisite incidental to employment, or where, in some states, the food is served by a restaurant.[3] Other gaps in the warranty action include the sealed container doctrine and possibly the seller's disclaimer.

For the injured consumer, the negligence action against the retailer is small consolation. The successful plaintiff is comparatively rare.[4] Many defects are such as to indicate

[3] The special problem of restaurants is treated in Chapter III.

[4] The few cases in which the plaintiff has recovered have almost always involved food sold in other than the package in which the producer packed the goods. Great Atlantic & Pacific Tea Co. v. Meeks, 38 So.2d 891 (Ala. App. 1949), *cert. denied*, 251 Ala. 576, 38 So.2d 895 (maggots in red snapper); Kraft-Phenix Cheese Corp. v. Spelce, 195 Ark. 407, 113 S.W.2d 476 (1938) (glass in sandwich spread, indicated by crack in container); Kroger Grocery & Baking Co. v. Turner, 191 Ark. 650, 100 S.W.2d 82 (1936) (unwholesome sausage); Great Atlantic & Pacific Tea Co. v. Gwilliams, 191 Ark. 650, 87 S.W.2d 581 (1935) (knife used to cut cheese unclean); Heinemann v. Barfield, 136 Ark. 456, 207 S.W. 58 (1918) (flour kept in bin near rat poison); Astor v. Safeway Stores, Inc., 26 Cal. App. 2d 163, 79 P.2d 146 (1938) (glass in bottle of buttermilk); Great Atlantic & Pacific Tea Co. v. Eiseman, 259 Ky. 103, 81 S.W.2d 900 (1935) (tainted chicken); Hunt v. Rhodes Bros. Co., 207 Mass. 30, 92 N.E. 1001 (1910) (leg of lamb containing tack); Scott v. Swift & Co., 214 N.C. 580, 200 S.E. 21 (1938) (unwholesome sausage); Madden v. Great Atlantic & Pacific Tea Co., 106 Pa. Super. 474, 162 Atl. 687 (1932) (mouse in tea purchased in bulk).

The plaintiff's right to have the issue of the retailer's negligence tried despite a demurrer, directed verdict, nonsuit, or improper charge to the jury in the trial court was upheld in the following cases (whether the plaintiff ultimately succeeded in proving negligence does not appear): Great Atlantic & Pacific Tea Co. v. Crabtree, 230 Ala. 443, 161 So. 508 (1935) (tainted meat; error in charge); Davis v. Williams, 58 Ga. App. 274, 198 S.E. 357 (1938) (glass in Coca-Cola bottle; demurrer); Crowley v. Lane Drug Stores, 54 Ga. App. 859, 189 S.E. 380 (1936) (glass in ice cream; nonsuit); Maddox Coffee Co. v. Collins, 46 Ga. App. 220, 167 S.E. 306 (1932) (glass in coffee; demurrer); Copeland v. Curtis, 36 Ga. App. 255, 136 S.E. 324 (1926) (tainted pork sandwiches; directed verthe fault of a handler preceding the retailer. Thus, in states that recognize the sealed container exception, the same reasons for raising the exception usually exonerate the retailer of negligence.[5] Even where the sole barrier to war-

---

dict); Craft v. Parker, Webb & Co., 96 Mich. 245, 55 N.W. 812 (1893) (tainted bacon; directed verdict).

But even in this type of case (goods not in original container), plaintiffs' casualties run high. Green v. Wilson, 194 Ark. 165, 105 S.W.2d 1074 (1937) (unwholesome lemon meringue pie); Kroger Grocery & Baking Co. v. Melton, 193 Ark. 494, 102 S.W.2d 859 (1937) (unwholesome pork chops); Flaccomio v. Eysink, 129 Md. 367, 100 Atl. 510 (1916) (wood alcohol in whiskey); Gearing v. Berkson, 223 Mass. 257, 111 N.E. 785 (1916) (unwholesome pork chops); Farrell v. Manhattan Market Co., 198 Mass. 271, 285, 84 N.E. 481, 487 (1908) (diseased chicken); Cheli v. Cudahy Bros. Co., 267 Mich. 690, 255 N.W. 414 (1934) (trichinae in pork); Lucey v. Harstedt, 270 App. Div. 900, 61 N.Y.S.2d 157 (2d Dept. 1946) (trichinae in fresh pork); Witham v. Kroger Grocery & Baking Co., 51 Ohio App. 499, 1 N.E.2d 949 (1935) (glass and mouse in flour); Galda v. Maurer's Dairy Co., 15 Northumb. L.J. 54 (Pa. 1941) (foreign substance in ice cream); Connelly v. Kroger Grocery & Baking Co., CCH Food Drug Cosmetic Law Serv. ¶18,060 (W.D. Pa. 1938) (Dethol spray on vegetables).

Several nonfood cases imposing a duty of inspection on the retailer are analyzed and criticized in Eldredge, "Vendor's Tort Liability," 89 U. of Pa. L. Rev. 306, 330–333 (1941).

[5] Kirkland v. Great Atlantic & Pacific Tea Co., 233 Ala. 404, 171 So. 735 (1937) (flour in original bag); Coca-Cola Bottling Co. v. Swilling, 186 Ark. 1149, 57 S.W.2d 1029 (1933) (centipede in Coca-Cola); Davis v. Waycross Coca Cola Bottling Co., 60 Ga. App. 390, 3 S.E.2d 863 (1939) (glass in bottle of Coca-Cola); Blount v. Houston Coca Cola Bottling Co., 184 Miss. 69, 185 So. 241 (1939) (mouse in Coca-Cola); Sullivan v. Henry, CCH Food Drug Cosmetic Law Serv. ¶18,195 (Tenn. App. 1940) (glass in bottle of Coca-Cola); Wilkes v. Memphis Grocery Co., 23 Tenn. App. 550, 555, 134 S.W.2d 929, 931 (1939) (dead flies in bottle of Coca-Cola); Bell v. Bowers Stores, 3 Tenn. App. 590 (1926) (unwholesome canned sardines); Pennington v. Cranberry Fuel Co., 117 W. Va. 680, 186 S.E. 610 (1936) (mouse in can of cocoa).

The same is true, of course, in states not adopting the sealed container exception. H. J. Heinz v. Duke, 196 Ark. 180, 116 S.W.2d 1039 (1938) (defective canned chili); Cleary v. First National Stores, 291 Mass. 172, 196 N.E. 869 (1935) (unwholesome canned cocoa); Lipari v. National Grocery Co., 120 N.J.L. 97, 100, 198 Atl. 393, 395 (1938) (defective canned tuna); Greenway v. Great Atlantic & Pacific Tea Co., 114 S.W.2d 435 (Tex. Civ. App. 1938) (defective canned corn); Linker v. Quaker Oats Co., 11 F. Supp. 794 (N.D. Okla. 1935) (glass in packaged cereal).

ranty action is want of privity, the negligence action is usually unsuccessful, either because the defendant was not negligent or because there is inadequate evidence of his fault.[6] On the other hand, where the retailer is also the manufacturer, or where as brander he represents himself to be the manufacturer, the courts tend to impose the liability of a manufacturer.[7]

[6] Gearing v. Berkson, 223 Mass. 257, 111 N.E. 785 (1916); Lipari v. National Grocery Co., 120 N.J.L. 97, 198 Atl. 393 (1938); Hopkins v. Amtorg Trading Corp., 265 App. Div. 278, 284, 38 N.Y.S.2d 788, 794 (1st Dept. 1942); Dickinson v. Sperling, 158 Misc. 905, 286 N.Y. Supp. 934 (1936). In Greenway v. Great Atlantic & Pacific Tea Co., 114 S.W.2d 435 (Tex. Civ. App. 1938), and Safeway Stores, Inc. v. Fuller, 189 Okla. 556, 557, 118 P.2d 649, 651 (1941), the plaintiff lost because he failed to prove causation. The latter court suggested, however, that a dealer in food products might be liable "regardless of due care."

[7] The plaintiff was successful in Dalton Coca-Cola Bottling Co. v. Watkins, 70 Ga. App. 790, 29 S.E.2d 281 (1944) (safety pin in Coca-Cola); Rost v. Kee & Chapell Dairy Co., 216 Ill. App. 497 (1920) (glass in milk); Flynn v. First National Stores, 296 Mass. 521, 6 N.E.2d 814 (1937) (wire in hamburg steak ground by defendant); Shindelus v. Sevcik, 211 Minn. 432, 1 N.W.2d 399 (1941) (unwholesome éclairs; breach of statute also involved); Amabile v. Kramps, 121 N.J.L. 219, 2 A.2d 178 (1938) (unwholesome creamcakes); McKittrick v. Dugan Bros., 119 N.J.L. 605, 197 Atl. 905 (1938), *aff'd*, 121 N.J.L. 49, 1 A.2d 331 (1938) (glass in muffin); Danker v. Fischer Baking Co., 5 N.J. Super. 248, 68 A.2d 774 (1949) (wood in cruller); McAteer v. Sheffield Farms Co., Inc., 9 N.J. Misc. 33, 152 Atl. 469 (1930) (unfit milk); Stein v. Woodlawn Farm Dairy Co., 50 Lack. Jur. 1 (Pa. C.P. 1949) (glass in milk); Irick v. Peoples Baking Co., 187 S.C. 238, 196 S.E. 887 (1938) (glass in cake); Chevy Chase Dairy, Inc. v. Mullineaux, 71 F.2d 982, 984, 985 (App. D.C. 1934) (glass in milk); Arendale v. Canada Bread Co., Ltd., [1941] 2 D.L.R. 41, O.W.N. 69 (glass in bread); Chaproniere v. Mason, [1905] 21 T.L.R. 633 (stone in bun). See Welter v. Bowman Dairy Co., 318 Ill. App. 305, 47 N.E.2d 739 (1943) (lead in milk).

A leading labeling case is Walker v. Great Atlantic & Pacific Tea Co., 131 Tex. 57, 112 S.W.2d 170 (1938).

The words "tend to" are used in the text because not every retailer who does some processing incidental to his retailing (*e.g.*, cutting or grinding meat) is considered a "manufacturer" of the product. Suppose, for example, that the retailer rebottles whiskey (see Flaccomio v. Eysink, 129 Md. 367, 100 Atl. 510 (1916)).

When a person is a "producer" or "manufacturer" is discussed in

§1.24. Violation of pure food law. In most jurisdictions a sale in violation of local pure food laws is "negligence per se." [1] Knowledge of the defect is usually not an element

Topic E of Chapter II. The restaurant cases appear to be *sui generis* (see Chapter III).

Even where the retailer is a manufacturer, it is difficult to show negligence. The plaintiff was unsuccessful, for example, in Swenson v. Purity Baking Co., 183 Minn. 289, 236 N.W. 310 (1931) (retailer-baker); Shepard v. Beck Bros., Inc., 131 Misc. 164, 225 N.Y. Supp. 438 (1927); Rosonsky v. Union Bakery, 83 Pitt. Leg. J. 378 (1934). And see Chapter II, Topic B.

§1.24. [1] Donaldson v. Great Atlantic & Pacific Tea Co., 186 Ga. 870, 872 *et seq.*, 199 S.E. 213, 215 *et seq.* (1938), later appeal in 59 Ga. App. 79, 200 S.E. 498 (1938); Great Atlantic & Pacific Tea Co. v. DuPee, 71 Ga. App. 148, 30 S.E.2d 365 (1944); Southern Grocery Stores, Inc. v. Donehoo, 59 Ga. App. 212, 200 S.E. 335 (1938); Kelley v. John R. Daily Co., 56 Mont. 63, 181 Pac. 326 (1919); Salzano v. First National Stores, 268 App. Div. 993, 51 N.Y.S.2d 645 (2d Dept. 1944); Catalanello v. Cudahy Packing Co., 264 App. Div. 723, 34 N.Y.S.2d 37 (2d Dept. 1942); Wolfe v. Great Atlantic & Pacific Tea Co., 143 Ohio St. 643, 56 N.E.2d 230 (1944); Kurth v. Krumme, 143 Ohio St. 638, 56 N.E.2d 227 (1944), *aff'g* 73 Ohio App. 524, 57 N.E.2d 177 (1943); Rubbo v. Hughes Provision Co., 138 Ohio St. 178, 34 N.E.2d 202 (1941); Great Atlantic & Pacific Tea Co. v. Hughes, 131 Ohio St. 501, 3 N.E.2d 415 (1936), *aff'g* 53 Ohio App. 255, 4 N.E.2d 700 (1935); Portage Markets Co. v. George, 111 Ohio St. 775, 146 N.E. 283 (1924); Drock v. Great Atlantic & Pacific Tea Co., 61 Ohio App. 291, 22 N.E.2d 547 (1939); Doherty v. S. S. Kresge Co., 227 Wis. 661, 278 N.W. 437 (1938) (restaurant case); Troietto v. G. H. Hammond Co., 110 F.2d 135 (C.C.A. 6th, 1940); White v. East Tennessee Packing Co., CCH Food Drug Cosmetic Law Rep. ¶85, 107 (Tenn. 1947). See Sloan v. F. W. Woolworth Co., 193 Ill. App. 620, 625 (1915); Leonardi v. A. Habermann Provision Co., 143 Ohio St. 623, 56 N.E.2d 232 (1944), *aff'g* 52 N.E.2d 85 (Ohio App., Cuyahoga Co. 1943); Pierce v. City Baking Co., 28 Ohio L. Abs. 503 (Ohio App., 9th Jud. Dist. 1938).

From the opinion of the lower court it appears that the DuPee case, *supra*, involved a Georgia ordinance requiring fault or knowledge of the retailer. DuPee v. Great Atlantic & Pacific Tea Co., 69 Ga. App. 144, 24 S.E.2d 858 (1943) ("knowingly or carelessly"). Failure to make a mandatory inspection that would have disclosed the defect was held to be carelessness. New Mexico allows "reasonable diligence" as a defense. N.M. Stat. Ann. §71-605 (1941).

Pure food laws, strictly construed, are often found not to apply to the type of defect causing the injury. Norris v. Pig'n Whistle Sandwich

of the crime [2] and the resulting liability approximates liability for breach of warranty.[3] Most courts are squeamish about calling this "absolute statutory liability" because the statute is couched in criminal terms only. But to speak of

---

Shop, Inc., 53 S.E.2d 718 (Ga. App. 1949) (bone in meat sandwich); Zorger v. Hillman's, 287 Ill. App. 357, 4 N.E.2d 900 (1936) (trichinae in pork); Bourcheix v. Willow Brook Dairy, Inc., 268 N.Y. 1, 196 N.E. 617 (1935), *rev'g* 243 App. Div. 721, 277 N.Y. Supp. 292 (2d Dept. 1935) (glass in cream); Gimenez v. Great Atlantic & Pacific Tea Co., 264 N.Y. 390, 191 N.E. 27 (1934) (crystals in canned crabmeat); Feinstein v. Daniel Reeves, Inc., 14 F. Supp. 167 (S.D.N.Y. 1936) (trichinae in pork). See Flynn v. First National Stores, 296 Mass. 521, 524, 6 N.E.2d 814, 815 (1937) (wire in hamburg steak). The doctrine of negligence per se was repudiated with respect to the New Hampshire pure food law in Wadleigh v. Howson, 88 N.H. 365, 366, 189 Atl. 865, 867 (1937). To the same effect: Cheli v. Cudahy Bros. Co., 267 Mich. 690, 255 N.W. 414 (1934) (involving liability of manufacturer).

The foregoing cases involved retailers. See Chapter II for sales by manufacturers and wholesalers.

[2] See §1.1 *supra*, note 33.

[3] Holt v. Mann, 294 Mass. 21, 200 N.E. 403 (1936); Wolfe v. Great Atlantic & Pacific Tea Co., 143 Ohio St. 643, 56 N.E.2d 230 (1944) ("neither is it any excuse that the seller chose to offer the food in a sealed container whereby he could not examine the contents"); Kurth v. Krumme, 143 Ohio St. 638, 56 N.E.2d 227 (1944), *aff'g* 73 Ohio App. 524, 57 N.E.2d 177 (1943) ("Under the quoted statutes, a violation may occur even though the seller has no knowledge that the food he is selling is contaminated. . . ." (trichinae in pork)); Portage Markets Co. v. George, 111 Ohio St. 775, 146 N.E. 283 (1924); Nelson v. West Coast Dairy Co., 5 Wash. 2d 284, 105 P.2d 76 (1940). See Leonardi v. A. Habermann Provision Co., 143 Ohio St. 623, 56 N.E.2d 232 (1944), *aff'g* 52 N.E.2d 85 (Ohio App., Cuyahoga Co. 1943) (trichinae in pork butt); Walker v. Great Atlantic & Pacific Tea Co., 131 Tex. 57, 61, 112 S.W.2d 170, 172 (1938) (unwholesome canned corn).

In Square v. Model Farm Dairies (Bournemouth), Ltd., [1939] 2 K.B. 365, [1939] 1 All E.R. 259, 55 T.L.R. 384, 83 Sol. J. 152, the court held that the applicable pure food law was intended to impose a criminal penalty in cases that might otherwise give rise to a civil action and that therefore "If there is any civil duty under the Act, it is owed only to the purchaser." Many pure food laws, however, excuse the defendant if he has a guarantee from the supplier. See The Proprietary Association of America, Compilation of Laws (1945); Walker v. Great Atlantic & Pacific Tea Co., *supra*, at 61, 112 S.W.2d at 172.

That *negligence* per se is not necessarily *liability* per se is pointed out by

"negligence" in a case where knowledge is irrelevant is to pay only lip service to principles of culpability. A few courts have been more forthright.[4]

An intermediate position is taken in Illinois, Massachusetts, and a few other states, where breach of a criminal food statute not requiring *mens rea* is only "evidence" of negligence.[5] In cases where the breach of such a statute is the only straw in the wind to indicate actual culpability[6] (a fictional one at best), this doctrine is only an invitation to the consumer-minded jury to follow its sympathies under cover of a spurious finding of "fact." It is more forthright to stick to orthodox theories of negligence or to find absolute liability.

Despite the frequent tag of "negligence," civil liability for violating a pure food statute is a truer counterpart of the action for violating the early English food statutes than the special American food warranty, which, though it adopted

---

Prosser in "Contributory Negligence as Defense to Violation of Statute," 32 Minn. L. Rev. 105, 111 (1948). Thus assumption of risk and contributory negligence may still be defenses in appropriate cases. *E.g.*, see Kelley v. John R. Daily Co., 56 Mont. 63, 75, 181 Pac. 326, 330 (1919).

[4] Bolitho v. Safeway Stores, Inc., 109 Mont. 213, 95 P.2d 443 (1939). In Martin v. Herzog, 228 N.Y. 164, 168, 126 N.E. 814, 815 (1920), Judge Cardozo said, "There may be times, when, if jural niceties are to be preserved, the two wrongs, negligence and breach of statutory duty, must be kept distinct in speech and thought. . . . In the conditions here present they come together and coalesce." And see Melick, The Sale of Food and Drink 288 (1936).

That the tort aspect of a breach of statute is not married to "negligence" has been pointed out by Prosser, *id.* at 108–110.

[5] Welter v. Bowman Dairy Co., 318 Ill. App. 305, 366, 47 N.E.2d 739, 764 (1943); Flynn v. Growers Outlet, Inc., 307 Mass. 373, 378, 30 N.E.2d 250, 253 (1940); Schuler v. Union News Co., 295 Mass. 350, 4 N.E.2d 465 (1936). See Gearing v. Berkson, 223 Mass. 257, 111 N.E. 785 (1916); Irick v. Peoples Baking Co., 187 S.C. 238, 196 S.E. 887 (1938). For several other states sharing this view, see Prosser, Torts 275 (1941).

[6] Flynn v. Growers Outlet, Inc., 307 Mass. 373, 30 N.E.2d 250 (1940).

the tag of "warranty," sprang from a different source. It is ironical that two doctrines with different (and equally fictitious) names should be more alike than two doctrines with the same name. It is suspected that many authorities [7] have paid more attention to labels than to substance.

What's in a name? Perkins and others have found a retailer obligation peculiar to food, as "implied warranty," incompatible with the English Sale of Goods Act; the doctrine of *Van Bracklin* v. *Fonda*, as "implied warranty," incompatible with the Uniform Sales Act. But no one has suggested that the doctrine of negligence per se, as applied to a retail sale made in violation of a pure food law, is barred by the Uniform Sales Act.[8]

When the fiction of "negligence" is stripped away from negligence per se, it is clear that the American food consumer has four possible strings to his bow as against the retailer: (1) breach of implied warranty of fitness or merchantability (all states); (2) breach of special food warranty (where recognized at common law and not killed by enactment of the Uniform Sales Act); (3) negligence (all states); and (4) breach of pure food statute not requiring knowledge of the defect (some states only).

TOPIC G. *Fault of the Buyer* *

§1.25. The problem. If the plaintiff leaves a bottle of milk open on the kitchen table she can hardly expect to collect from the dairy if her infant son happens to drop a lead

[7] But not including the writers represented in §1.1 *supra*, note 33.

[8] In its civil aspects, why isn't the statutory obligation not to sell unwholesome food properly a "warranty" obligation?

* Because the problem of buyer's fault does not depend upon who the defendant is, this Topic will also include cases against manufacturers, intermediate distributors, and restaurateurs.

soldier in it; the defendant is in no wise implicated.[1] Compare with this the more significant legal situation where the defective condition is traceable to the defendant but the plaintiff has not been vigilant in intercepting it. Will the plaintiff be barred by her own lapse?

§1.26. Negligence cases. In food actions for negligence, the affirmative defense of contributory negligence is as doctrinally alive as it is elsewhere. Thus cases appear in which a judgment for the plaintiff has been reversed because the trial judge failed adequately to cover the defense in his charge.[1]

At the same time, a thorough search has failed to disclose more than a few reported instances in which the plaintiff has failed in a food action because his own fault canceled that of the defendant. Out of many hundreds of food cases this is hardly a substantial body of authority, and in spite of the frequent reiteration of the doctrine and the proper instruction of juries, unsuccessful plaintiffs continue to lose almost entirely on other grounds. Whether the unappealed cases parallel the reported cases is another question.

As eater, the consumer has no legal incentive to examine what he is eating, and a failure to take this precaution is

§1.25. [1] In Amabile v. Kramps, 121 N.J.L. 219, 2 A.2d 178 (1938), the question arose whether the plaintiff had kept creamcakes too long before eating them. The court found that she had not. To consider the question as one of plaintiff's fault would be to use a back-door approach to the fundamental issue: Had the defendant breached any duty relating to the plaintiff's injury? Food is not legally defective if it remains edible for a reasonable length of time, and injuries from spoilage caused by the plaintiff rather than the defendant are written off more appropriately on the basis of want of causation or want of defendant's fault, not the cancellation of a nullity. Cases of this type, therefore, have no significant bearing on the question under discussion.

§1.26. [1] Buffalo Rock Bottling Co. v. Stephenson, 22 Ala. App. 605, 118 So. 498 (1928); Albany Coca Cola Bottling Co. v. Shiver, 63 Ga. App. 755, 12 S.E.2d 114 (1940); Moree v. Shiver, 63 Ga. App. 761, 12 S.E.2d 118 (1940).

uniformly held not to bar recovery.[2] At the table, or otherwise in the act of eating, most guards are down and the law imposes a standard of care commensurate with the consumer's normal inclination to protect himself in that situation. To require him to verify all suspicions might produce, in the words of an Illinois appellate court, "hunger in the midst of plenty." [3]

Accordingly, the courts have been liberal in letting the consumer continue to eat even after he discovers distasteful characteristics.[4] One court has distinguished between the standards of care applicable to the seller and the buyer by saying that the latter's arises only after he has actual knowledge of the defect.[5] Another has said that the consumer has a right to presume that the seller has complied with pure food laws.[6] Whether these courts accurately

[2] Armour & Co. v. Roberts, 63 Ga. App. 846, 12 S.E.2d 376 (1940); Coleman v. Dublin Coca-Cola Bottling Co., 47 Ga. App. 369, 170 S.E. 549 (1933); Atlanta Coca-Cola Bottling Co. v. Sinyard, 45 Ga. App. 272, 164 S.E. 231 (1932); Coca Cola Bottling Works v. Curtis, 302 Ky. 199, 194 S.W.2d 375 (1946); Nehi Beverage Co. v. Hall, 295 Ky. 353, 174 S.W.2d 509 (1943); Kenney v. Wong Len, 81 N.H. 427, 128 Atl. 343 (1925); Boyd v. Coca-Cola Bottling Works, 132 Tenn. 23, 177 S.W. 80 (1914); Texas Coca-Cola Bottling Co. v. Wimberley, 108 S.W.2d 860 (Tex. Civ. App. 1937); Tennessee Dairies v. Seibenhausen, 99 S.W.2d 323 (Tex. Civ. App. 1936).

[3] Sloan v. F. W. Woolworth Co., 193 Ill. App. 620, 626 (1915).

[4] Dryden v. Continental Baking Co., 11 Cal. 2d 33, 77 P.2d 833 (1938); Criswell Baking Co. v. Milligan, 77 Ga. App. 861, 50 S.E.2d 136 (1948); Patargias v. Coca-Cola Bottling Co. of Chicago, 332 Ill. App. 117, 74 N.E. 2d 162 (1947); Duval v. Coca-Cola Bottling Co. of Chicago, 329 Ill. App. 290, 68 N.E.2d 479 (1946); Bark v. Dixson, 115 Minn. 172, 131 N.W. 1078 (1911); Wilson v. Coca Cola Bottling Company of New York, Inc., 65 A.2d 630 (N.J. Super. 1948); McAteer v. Sheffield Farms Co., 9 N.J. Misc. 33, 152 Atl. 469 (1930); Madden v. Great Atlantic & Pacific Tea Co., 106 Pa. Super. 474, 162 Atl. 687 (1932). See Dunn v. Texas Coca-Cola Bottling Co., 84 S.W.2d 545 (Tex. Civ. App. 1935).

[5] Albany Coca Cola Bottling Co. v. Shiver, 67 Ga. App. 359, 20 S.E.2d 181 (1942); Davis v. Williams, 58 Ga. App. 274, 198 S.E. 357 (1938).

[6] Caines v. Marion Coca-Cola Bottling Co., 198 S.C. 204, 17 S.E.2d 315 (1941).

reflect the views of most courts, we can be sure that the courts are holding the consumer, as eater, to a very low standard of vigilance. Unless there is a flagrant disregard of obvious indications of unwholesomeness, the plaintiff will not lose on this ground. Plaintiffs' disappointments from this source have been negligible.

In *Friedmann* v. *Beck*,[7] the plaintiff appears to have disregarded an eloquent warning from the product itself. The court said, "We think that this repeated tasting of the alleged contaminated lobster with forewarning [awareness of unwholesome taste and smell], and knowledge of possible consequences, justified the finding that plaintiff herself had been guilty of such negligence as would preclude a recovery in the action as based on ordinary negligence." In *Saddlemire* v. *Coca Cola Co. of Canada*,[8] a Canadian court held that by continuing to drink after he had noticed a bad odor and taste the plaintiff had made a voluntary choice to incur the risk. In *Jones* v. *Armour & Co.*,[9] the plaintiff was barred after tasting pigs' feet that had a phenomenal odor and were covered with yellow scum. In *Walker* v. *Hickory Packing Co.*,[10] the North Carolina Supreme Court held that evidence that the lard in question had an inescapable odor "like carrion" defeated recovery for negligence.

Most of the contributory negligence cases deal with the plaintiff as eater, where the danger is not disclosed beforehand. On the other hand, as selector of the food or as cook (or as one vicariously accountable for its preparation) [11] the

[7] 250 App. Div. 87, 88, 293 N.Y. Supp. 649, 651 (1st Dept. 1937). See Dunn v. Texas Coca-Cola Bottling Co., 84 S.W.2d 545 (Tex. Civ. App. 1935).

[8] [1941] 4 D.L.R. 614, O.W.N. 392.

[9] Ohio App., Summit Co., Feb. 19, 1937. CCH Food & Drug Serv. ¶21,017 (1937).

[10] 220 N.C. 158, 16 S.E.2d 668 (1941).

[11] *Cf.* Troietto v. G. H. Hammond Co., 110 F.2d 135 (C.C.A. 6th,

plaintiff may find himself held, and properly so, to a higher standard of care. But there is no discernible pattern.

In *Green* v. *Ashland Water Co.*,[12] a suit by the administratrix of a typhoid victim who had been infected by the defendant's water came to grief because the court found that it was common knowledge in the decedent's community that the water source was contaminated. The holding is a little surprising in that the court overturned a specific finding by the jury that the plaintiff had not been negligent.

Several trichinosis cases have raised the question whether the plaintiff was barred by failing to come up to accepted standards of cookery. In *Arena* v. *John P. Squire Co.*,[13] the court held that the plaintiff had surmounted this hurdle; in *Leonardi* v. *A. Habermann Provision Co.*,[14] the court held that the plaintiff probably had not. Trichinosis cases raise special problems which are more adequately discussed in a later chapter.[15]

§1.27. Warranty cases. Where the suit is for breach of warranty, the plaintiff likewise risks losing at least his right to consequential damages if his own fault contributed to the result. Here the doctrinal basis for barring him is not always made explicit. At least the doctrine of contributory negligence as such does not apply.[1]

1940), where the court refused to impute to the plaintiff the negligence of the plaintiff's landlady in cooking the food.

[12] 101 Wis. 258, 77 N.W. 722 (1898).

[13] 321 Mass. 423, 73 N.E.2d 836 (1947).

[14] 143 Ohio St. 623, 56 N.E.2d 232 (1944), *aff'g* 52 N.E.2d 85 (Ohio App. 1943).

[15] See Chapter IV, Topic B.

§1.27. [1] Challis v. Hartloff, 136 Kan. 823, 828, 18 P.2d 199, 202 (1933); Friend v. Childs Dining Hall Co., 231 Mass. 65, 75, 120 N.E. 407, 411 (1918). But *cf.* Eisenbach v. Gimbel Bros., Inc., 281 N.Y. 474, 24 N.E.2d 131 (1939), discussed in note 5 *infra*, and in Chapter IV, §4.6.

Section 15 (3) of the Uniform Sales Act provides, "If the buyer has examined the goods, there is no implied warranty as regards defects which such examination ought to have revealed."[2] No case has been found in which a food consumer has been barred under this section. No common law case has been found in which a comparable principle has been applied. If the plaintiff knew or clearly should have known of the defect when he bought the goods, action should be barred, possibly on the theory that conditions which are ostensibly acceptable to the buyer are not to be considered defective from his viewpoint.[3] Where the plaintiff's laxity occurs after purchase, however, Section 15 (3) does not apply. Willful or careless disregard of facts made obvious after purchase would presumably reduce the plaintiff's recovery under the doctrine of "avoidable consequences." Accordingly, several cases have indicated that the plaintiff's recovery will be limited by his own fault, even in warranty suits, where the lapse occurred after purchase.[4] The precise rationale of these cases is, unfortunately, left to surmise.[5]

[2] See Friend v. Childs Dining Hall Co., 231 Mass. 65, 75, 120 N.E. 407, 411 (1918).

[3] See §1.17 *supra*, note 4.

[4] Eisenbach v. Gimbel Bros., Inc., 281 N.Y. 474, 24 N.E.2d 131 (1939) (suit by restaurant keeper); Walker v. Hickory Packing Co., 220 N.C. 158, 16 S.E.2d 668 (1941).

[5] The Eisenbach case, cited in the preceding footnote, although talking the language of avoidable consequences, smells of contributory negligence, since instead of granting nominal relief the court dismissed the action altogether. It should also be noted that the avoidable consequences doctrine in its orthodox form can be made to do for the warranty action what contributory negligence has been doing for the negligence action only if the defendant's actionable wrong takes place at the time of the sale in the former case and at the time of the injury in the latter. Otherwise, either the avoidable consequences doctrine has been playing a broader role in contract than it has in tort or the courts have been applying contributory negligence in the tort cases when they should have been applying the doctrine of avoidable consequences.

Practically, the legal problems here have little significance. Whatever the underlying basis, anything less than inexcusable disregard of the obvious during eating has little chance of legally barring the plaintiff, whether the suit lies in negligence or for breach of warranty.[6] A higher standard of care is expected of the consumer when selecting, handling, or preparing his food. Here, again, the plaintiff's lapse will probably have the same substantive result whatever his theory of suit.[7]

From a policy standpoint, the courts seem to be reaching a realistic and just result.

[6] Additional cases in which the plaintiff was found not to have been contributorily negligent *as eater*: Coca-Cola Bottling Co. v. Barksdale, 17 Ala. App. 606, 88 So. 36 (1920); Kraft-Phenix Cheese Corp. v. Spelce, 195 Ark. 407, 113 S.W.2d 476 (1938); Great Atlantic & Pacific Tea Co. v. Eiseman, 259 Ky. 103, 81 S.W.2d 900 (1935); Kelley v. John R. Daily Co., 56 Mont. 63, 181 Pac. 326 (1919); Rudolph v. Coca-Cola Bottling Co., 4 N.J. Misc. 318, 132 Atl. 508 (1926); DeGroat v. Ward Baking Co., 102 N.J.L. 188, 130 Atl. 540 (1925). *As cook:* Coca-Cola Bottling Works v. Kennedy, 13 Tenn. App. 199 (1931); Catalanello v. Cudahy Packing Co., 264 App. Div. 723, 34 N.Y.S.2d 37 (2d Dept. 1942); Kurthe v. Krumme, 143 Ohio St. 638, 56 N.E.2d 227 (1944); Great Atlantic & Pacific Tea Co. v. Hughes, 131 Ohio St. 501, 3 N.E.2d 415 (1936), *aff'g* 53 Ohio App. 255, 4 N.E.2d 700 (1935). In the following cases the court upset a nonsuit or directed verdict for the defendant and held that the question of contributory negligence was for the jury. Cordell v. Macon Coca-Cola Bottling Co., 56 Ga. App. 117, 192 S.E. 228 (1937); Craft v. Parker, Webb & Co., 96 Mich. 245, 55 N.W. 812 (1893); Ternay v. Ward Baking Co., 167 N.Y. Supp. 562 (S. Ct. 1st Dept. 1917).

[7] The fact that the transaction by which the plaintiff acquired the food was illegal has been held not to bar recovery by the plaintiff. Bagre v. Daggett Chocolate Co., 126 Conn. 659, 13 A.2d 757 (1940) (fact that candy was won in illegal bingo game no bar to recovery in negligence); Anderson v. Tyler, 223 Iowa 1033, 274 N.W. 48 (1937) (Sunday purchase no bar to recovery in negligence or for breach of warranty; rationale unclear); Jacob E. Decker & Sons v. Capps, 144 S.W.2d 404 (Tex. Civ. App. 1940) (fact that sausage was bought illegally on Sunday no bar to recovery for breach of warranty). *Contra:* Johnson v. Swift & Co., Inc., 186 Miss. 803, 191 So. 423 (1939) (warranty barred because retail purchase was on Sunday); Boliver v. Monnat, 130 Misc. 660, 665, 227 N.Y. Supp. 535, 542 (1927) (warranty barred because retail purchase violated liquor laws).

Topic H. *Some Considerations of Public Policy*

§1.28. Arguments for and against holding the retailer absolutely liable. Waite [1] has argued that a retailer should not be liable for defective food, even to his immediate buyer, unless (1) he is negligent, or (2) he has "undertaken to *assume* the burden" (expressly or by factual implication). Waite would in effect carry the sealed container exception to its logical conclusion by doing away with any retailer warranty undertaking insofar as it may be "implied in law." It is apparent from his initial example that, in determining the "facts" of particular situations, he would not find implied promises of wholesomeness in many of the cases where Prosser [2] and others find sales by description with resulting warranties of merchantability. There is no hidden reservation, therefore, in Waite's championship of the retailer.

Waite, like Holmes,[3] sees no point in raising legal obligations that exceed the voluntary and conscious undertakings of the parties unless there are compelling reasons of public policy to transfer the burdens of litigation and liability from innocent buyers to innocent sellers. He challenges the necessity or desirability of using the retailer as a conduit to reach the manufacturer, because he believes the consumer already has adequate recourse to the manufacturer. As for the inaccessibility of foreign manufacturers, Waite feels that the convenience to the consumer of being able to sue a local defendant is more than offset by the corresponding incon-

§1.28. [1] Waite, "Retail Responsibility and Judicial Law Making," 34 Mich. L. Rev. 494 (1936); "Retail Responsibility—A Reply," 23 Minn. L. Rev. 612 (1939).

[2] Prosser, "The Implied Warranty of Merchantable Quality," 27 Minn. L. Rev. 117, 143 (1943).

[3] ". . . sound policy lets losses lie where they fall, except where a special reason can be shown for interference." Holmes, The Common Law 50 (1881).

venience to an equally innocent retailer, who, in addition, is subjected to the risk of fraudulent claims (to which he is more vulnerable than the manufacturer since he lacks the manufacturer's means to refute them).

The opposition to the position represented by Waite is impressive. Brown, in a strong attack on Waite's thesis, makes these arguments in support of retailer liability: [4]

(1) The consumer's power to reach the manufacturer is inadequate from a legal standpoint.[5] A negligence action against the manufacturer may be ruled out either because the manufacturer was not negligent, or because it is too difficult to show negligence, at least in those states where the doctrine of *res ipsa loquitur* is not recognized. If the plaintiff sues for breach of warranty, he will be barred in many states because of the lack of privity.

(2) The consumer's power to reach the manufacturer is inadequate from a practical standpoint.[6] The distance between consumer and manufacturer makes it impractical to sue in many cases and the expense of suit may well exceed the amount sued for.[7]

(3) The retailer's superior bargaining position gives him the better chance of settling with the manufacturer out of court.[8]

(4) If the retailer has the same practical difficulty in suing the producer as the consumer, the retailer cannot complain since it was he who selected the producer.[9]

[4] Brown, "The Liability of Retail Dealers for Defective Food Products," 23 Minn. L. Rev. 585 (1939).

[5] *Id.* at 596.

[6] *Id.* at 600.

[7] See, for example, Griffin v. James Butler Grocery Co., 108 N.J.L. 92, 156 Atl. 636 (1931), where the cannery was in California, the consumer in New Jersey.

[8] Brown, "The Liability of Retail Dealers for Defective Food Products," 23 Minn. L. Rev. 585, 606 (1939).

[9] *Ibid.*

(5) If the retailer is unable, as a practical matter, to pass on a loss that is rightfully the manufacturer's, it is (quoting Cardozo) "one of the hazards of the business." Anyway, the retailer has a better chance of avoiding this hazard.[10]

Although Brown has proved the better prophet, and although some of his points are supported by strong authority,[11] his arguments taken on merit alone are not entirely persuasive. Argument (1) was dealt with by Waite in his original argument: A public policy strong enough to hold the retailer ought to be strong enough to remove the privity requirement as against the manufacturer.[12] Likewise, argument (2): Inconvenience to the consumer is no warrant in itself for shifting the inconvenience to someone who is equally innocent, even though the inconvenience to the latter may be less.[13] Argument (3), which was not considered by Waite, is valid, but for more basic reasons (see Llewellyn, *infra* pp. 88–89) than those given by Brown. Argument (4) seems pointless, since distance has nothing to do with quality. To the extent that it means anything it would actually boomerang, because in borderline cases it would tempt the retailer to put proximity above quality. Its premise is also false in any case where the retailer buys (as most small independents do) from a wholesaler. If the retailer "selects the manufacturer" in such a case, so does the consumer. Argument (5), in talking about business hazard, begs the ques-

[10] *Id.* at 607.

[11] "Public safety" was the keynote in Wiedeman v. Keller, 171 Ill. 93, 49 N.E. 210 (1898); Chapman v. Roggenkamp, 182 Ill. App. 117 (1913); Race v. Krum, 222 N.Y. 410, 415, 118 N.E. 853, 854 (1918). Relative inconvenience to the consumer was emphasized in Sencer v. Carl's Markets, Inc., — Fla. —, 45 So.2d 671, 673 (1950); Ward v. Great Atlantic & Pacific Tea Co., 231 Mass. 90, 94, 120 N.E. 225, 226 (1918).

[12] Waite, "Retail Responsibility and Judicial Law Making," 34 Mich. L. Rev. 494, 511 n.43 (1936).

[13] *Id.* at 514.

tion. As for comparative ability to pass on the loss, this only repeats the earlier argument. Brown does not answer Waite's argument about the greater vulnerability of the retailer to fraudulent claims.[14]

Although Waite seems generally justified in suggesting that Brown, like the authorities he cites, does little more than assert that "public policy" supports his position,[15] others have come to Brown's support.

Melick, for example, says that retailer liability in warranty is justified on grounds of general fairness. A person who receives a sound price for a sound article ought to assume the risk.[16] If this argument is valid, it nevertheless has a strange ring because, outside of the law merchant, notions of a "sound" or "fair" price have had little effect in Anglo-American law or in the public policy that shaped it.

Perkins, writing in 1919, seems to have something more substantial in mind:

> While there may be less opportunity for the dealer to know of defects in canned goods, than in goods open to inspection, the purchase, handling and selling of such articles does not present a field in which "care" is unimportant. . . . This being true no sound reason exists why the law should withdraw the stimulus from such situations . . . it is not at all true . . . that insurer's liability does not tend to correct the evil at its source." [17]

The point touched on by Perkins, which Waite, Brown, and Melick apparently ignored, has been adequately devel-

[14] The North Carolina court dealt with the point in Rabb v. Covington, 215 N.C. 572, 575, 2 S.E.2d 705, 707 (1939): "The fact, if it is a fact, . . . that a ruling of this sort would open the gate to a fertile field of spurious litigation does not appeal to us. That some might abuse the processes of the court affords no reason for denying them to others who have meritorious causes of action."

[15] Waite, "Retail Responsibility — A Reply," 23 Minn. L. Rev. 612, 614 (1939).

[16] Melick, The Sale of Food and Drink 69 (1936).

[17] Perkins, "Unwholesome Food as a Source of Liability," 5 Iowa L. Bull. 6, 33 (1919), 86, 110 (1920).

oped only in recent years. For example, a fuller statement of the public policy whose existence Waite has challenged is found in *Rabb* v. *Covington*,[18] a North Carolina case decided in 1939. Here the court said:

> . . . we not only recognize the superior opportunity of the retailer over that of the consumer to be assured of the quality of the products sold by him through his opportunity of selection of brands and purchase from reliable manufacturers, but also recognize the fact that the internal pressure of commerce in this field, as well as in others, will, through the necessity of meeting competition, of improving methods, and of rigid attention to matters relating to the quality and fitness of the product, strongly tend to minimize untoward happenings of the kind complained of in this suit . . .

Similar notions are found in the opinion of the Texas Supreme Court in *Griggs Canning Co.* v. *Josey*.[19]

The "public policy" here expressed goes beyond the concern of the prior statements with merely balancing the interests of the immediate parties. It directs attention also to broader social and economic considerations where individual civil actions help to bring about results often left to direct governmental control.

[18] 215 N.C. 572, 575, 2 S.E.2d 705, 707 (1939).

[19] 139 Tex. 623, 633–634, 164 S.W.2d 835, 840 (1942). ". . . if the retailer is held responsible he will exercise greater precaution in determining the reliability and responsibility of the distributor or manufacturer. In the second place, it would amount to a practical denial, in some instances, of the right of the consumer to redress to hold that he must look exclusively to the manufacturer. . . . An action against the retailer would afford him a remedy close at hand, which could be practically realized on; whereas, a right to sue a manufacturer in a foreign country might be of no avail. In the third place, the local dealer can protect himself against financial loss by demanding a guarantee of protection from his vendor. . . . He, the retailer, is in much better position to put pressure on the one with whom he has dealt, and thus bring about an equitable adjustment of the loss. And in the fourth place, by making everybody responsible who handles food products intended for human consumption a greater stimulus is provided to insure that none but wholesome food is sold . . ."

Here Llewellyn's oft-repeated[20] distinctions between sales by (1) commercial sellers to commercial buyers, (2) casual sellers to casual buyers, and (3) commercial sellers to casual buyers are fundamental. Different situations call for different treatment, and what is sound public policy in situation (1) or (2) may be unsound public policy in situation (3). Therein, he suggests, lie the limitations of Waite's approach.

> What is wanted is to protect the [dependent] consumer. . . . That needed protection is twofold: to shift the immediate incidence of the hazard of life in an industrial society away from the individual over to a group which can distribute the loss; and to place the loss where the most pressure will be exerted to keep down future losses.[21]

There are several key ideas here. Situation (3), the one at issue, involves a disparate bargaining struggle between unequals, with "public policy," acting through law, seeking to add its counterbalance. As part of the counterbalance, threat of civil liability, like direct regulation, has economic use as a preventive measure where a higher degree of care is possible and a higher degree of care makes a difference in result. In addition, actual liability, appropriately channeled, spreads unavoidable losses and thus serves as a kind of publicly shared insurance policy.[22] (The latter idea belongs more to the commentators than to the courts.)

In this picture the retailer occupies two positions. As one whose care, skill, and vigilance are important in their own right (even as to sealed containers), he is in a position where

[20] See §1.1 *supra*, note 24.

[21] Llewellyn, Cases and Materials on the Law of Sales 341 (1930).

[22] Cushing v. Rodman, 82 F.2d 864, 869 (App. D.C. 1936); Llewellyn, Cases and Materials on the Law of Sales 311 (1930); Douglas, "Vicarious Liability and the Administration of Risk," 38 Yale L.J. 584, 720 (1929); Patterson, "The Apportionment of Business Risk Through Legal Devices," 24 Col. L. Rev. 335, 358 (1924); Comment, 37 Col. L. Rev. 97 (1937).

the threat of liability offers a substantial inducement. Secondly, even with privity requirements abolished, the retailer is a useful conduit for transmitting a similar inducement to earlier handlers and finally to the person on whom the ultimate burden of correcting the evil or of administering and distributing the risk or loss ought to lie. Here is "public policy" in a dimension untouched by Waite and Brown. Whether it is sound public policy is another question. For present purposes, the important thing is that it is getting increasing consideration and acceptance by the courts.

Some of the advocates of civil liability as a preventive, including Llewellyn,[23] admit that the principle has practical limitations, and there is a small body of authority, with Judge Augustus Hand's much admired opinion[24] as its core, that has repudiated the use of civil absolute liability for this purpose in favor of direct regulation by pure food laws. But the current trend is increasingly to hold the retailer to the liability of an insurer, even for latent defects, and to make this responsibility an instrument of social control.

[23] Llewellyn, "On Warranty of Quality, and Society," 36 Col. L. Rev. 699, 712 (1936).

[24] Valeri v. Pullman Co., 218 Fed. 519 (S.D.N.Y. 1914). Disagreement has been expressed in Cushing v. Rodman, 82 F.2d 864, 870 (App. D.C. 1936); Perkins, "Unwholesome Food as a Source of Liability," 5 Iowa L. Bull. 86, 110 (1920); Wasserman, "Commentary on Diners' Protection," 6 N.J.L.J. 57, 59 (1938).

C H A P T E R I I

Manufacturers' and Wholesalers' Responsibility to Consumers for Unwholesome Food

General References

On the general subject of the liability of the manufacturer to the consumer, see Melick, The Sale of Food and Drink, c. IV (1936); Clark, "Let the Maker Beware," 19 St. John's L. Rev. 85 (1945); Jeanblanc, "Manufacturers' Liability to Persons Other than Their Immediate Vendees," 24 Va. L. Rev. 134 (1937); Russell, "Manufacturers' Liability to the Ultimate Consumer," 21 Ky. L.J. 388 (1933); Underhay, "Manufacturers' Liability, Recent Developments," 14 Can. B. Rev. 283 (1936); Note, 96 U. of Pa. L. Rev. 863 (1948); Note, 33 Calif. L. Rev. 637 (1945); Note, 14 St. John's L. Rev. 110 (1939) (food only); Note, 46 W. Va. L.Q. 82 (1939).

CHAPTER II

Manufacturers' and Wholesalers' Responsibility to Consumers for Unwholesome Food *

TOPIC A. *Liability of the Manufacturer for Breach of Warranty*

§2.1. The privity gap as a barrier to recovery. There are two main reasons why the manufacturer appears as defendant in food products liability suits: The defect is frequently traceable to his doorstep, and his financial position, more often than not, is strong enough to keep a judgment from being a hollow victory. Even so, the way to a judgment is not simple and direct.

The position of the injured consumer is strongest where the manufacturer is also the retailer. The most typical examples are the local dairy, the local bakery selling "homemade" breads and pastries, and the bottling company that operates its own vending machines. Much less common are the several large retail chains that pack their own preserves, jams, and jellies, or other canned products.

Here the plaintiff may sue the manufacturer in warranty, as he might sue any retailer.[1] In states such as Arkansas and

* Problems of contributory fault are considered in Chapter I, Topic G.

§2.1. [1] See Chapter I. See also Nemela v. Coca-Cola Bottling Co. of St. Louis, 104 S.W.2d 773 (Mo. 1937), and Beyer v. Coca-Cola Bottling Co. of St. Louis, 75 S.W.2d 642 (Mo. App. 1934), where the retailer was also the consumer.

Maine he is actually in a better position than he would be against one who was simply a retailer, because the fact that the defendant is also the manufacturer removes any occasion for applying the sealed container exception.

Although an action for breach of warranty might seem, at first glance, the most attractive alternative to an injured consumer, only a small volume of food is sold directly by the manufacturer to consumers. This means that in most cases there is no privity of contract [2] between the plaintiff and the defendant. In most states, want of privity is fatal.[3]

[2] On privity in warranty generally, see Spruill, "Privity of Contract as a Requisite for Recovery on Warranty," 19 N.C.L. Rev. 551 (1941); Comment, 23 Calif. L. Rev. 621 (1935); Comment, 7 J.B.A. Kan. 183 (1938); Note, 25 Minn. L. Rev. 83 (1940); Note, 21 Minn. L. Rev. 315 (1937). See also General References, page 91.

[3] Birmingham Chero-Cola Bottling Co. v. Clark, 205 Ala. 678, 89 So. 64 (1921); Nelson v. Armour Packing Co., 76 Ark. 352, 90 S.W. 288 (1905); Nehi Bottling Co. v. Thomas, 236 Ky. 684, 33 S.W.2d 701 (1930); Pelletier v. Dupont, 124 Me. 269, 128 Atl. 186 (1925); Carlson v. Turner Centre System, 263 Mass. 339, 161 N.E. 245 (1928); Duley v. Coca-Cola Bottling Co. of St. Louis, CCH Food Drug Cosmetic Law Rep. ¶22,223 (St. Louis Ct. of App. 1950); Smith v. Salem Coca-Cola Bottling Co., Inc., 92 N.H. 97, 25 A.2d 125 (1942); Bourcheix v. Willow Brook Dairy, 268 N.Y. 1, 196 N.E. 617 (1935); Chysky v. Drake Bros. Co., 235 N.Y. 468, 139 N.E. 576 (1923); Thomason v. Ballard & Ballard Co., 208 N.C. 1, 179 S.E. 30 (1935); Whitehorn v. Nash-Finch Co., 67 S.D. 465, 293 N.W. 859 (1940); Coca-Cola Bottling Works v. Sullivan, 178 Tenn. 405, 158 S.W.2d 721 (1942); Hoback v. Coca-Cola Bottling Works of Nashville, 20 Tenn. App. 280, 98 S.W.2d 113 (1936); Hanback v. Dutch Baker Boy, Inc., 107 F.2d 203 (App. D.C. 1939); Karger v. Armour & Co., 17 F. Supp. 484 (D.C. Munic. Ct. 1936); Ferstenfeld v. Kik Co., 77 Que. S.C. 165 (1939). See Cassini v. Curtis Candy Co., 113 N.J.L. 91, 172 Atl. 519 (1934); Burgess v. Sanitary Meat Market, 121 W. Va. 605, 611, 5 S.E.2d 785, 787, 6 S.E.2d 254 (1939); Buckley v. Mott, 50 D.L.R. 408 (Nova Scotia, 1919). But *cf.* Snead v. Waite, 306 Ky. 587, 208 S.W.2d 749 (1948), where privity with defendant retailer was apparently lacking for at least one plaintiff and the problem was apparently ignored.

That privity is required in Connecticut, Maryland, Montana, New Jersey, Virginia, Wisconsin, and England is to be inferred from the application of that doctrine in suits against retailers. See Chapter I, Topic E.

In Alabama and Michigan, there is talk of a warranty directly to the

This deprives the consumer of the remedy which in the case of a suit against the retailer is his most useful weapon.

§2.2. Bridging the privity gap — The fictional approach. In a growing minority of states (about twelve), the requirement of privity has been discarded, or emasculated by legal fictions. Some of the cases have spelled out a warranty that "runs with the goods" [1] or "inures" to the consumer's benefit.[2] At least two have paid it lip service by speaking of a third party beneficiary contract between the manufacturer and his vendee for the benefit of the consumer.[3] Several have said that food [4] (or food in sealed

---

consumer, but inspection shows this to be illusory since the warranty is only that the defendant has not been negligent. Alabama Coca-Cola Bottling Co. v. Ezzell, 22 Ala. App. 210, 114 So. 278 (1927); C. C. Hooper Cafe Co. v. Henderson, 223 Ala. 579, 137 So. 419 (1931); Hertzler v. Manshum, 228 Mich. 416, 200 N.W. 155 (1924). This leaves the tentative score: Privity states (including D.C.), 18; non-privity states, 12; uncertain, 19.

§2.2. [1] Patargias v. Coca-Cola Bottling Co. of Chicago, 332 Ill. App. 117, 74 N.E.2d 162 (1947); Anderson v. Tyler, 223 Iowa 1033, 274 N.W. 48 (1937); Biedenharn Candy Co. v. Moore, 184 Miss. 721, 186 So. 628 (1939); Coca-Cola Bottling Works v. Lyons, 145 Miss. 876, 111 So. 305 (1927); Jacob E. Decker & Sons, Inc. v. Capps, 144 S.W.2d 404 (Tex. Civ. App. 1940). See Coca-Cola Bottling Co. of Fort Worth v. Smith, 97 S.W.2d 761 (Tex. Civ. App. 1936). Even a donee may sue. Coca-Cola Bottling Works v. Lyons, 145 Miss. 876, 883, 111 So. 305, 307 (1927). The "assignment" theory was criticized in Note, 22 Wash. U.L.Q. 406, 418 (1937).

[2] Klein v. Duchess Sandwich Co., 14 Cal. 2d 272, 283, 93 P.2d 799, 804 (1939); Biedenharn Candy Co. v. Moore, 184 Miss. 721, 725, 186 So. 628, 629 (1939); Jacob E. Decker & Sons, Inc. v. Capps, 144 S.W.2d 404 (Tex. Civ. App. 1940). See Coca-Cola Bottling Co. of Fort Worth v. Smith, 97 S.W.2d 761, 767 (Tex. Civ. App. 1936).

[3] Ward Baking Co. v. Trizzino, 27 Ohio App. 475, 161 N.E. 557 (1920). See Dryden v. Continental Baking Co., 11 Cal. 2d 33, 37, 77 P.2d 833, 835 (1938). See also cases cited in preceding note. In Singer v. Zabelin, 24 N.Y.S.2d 962 (N.Y. City Ct. 1941), the third party beneficiary rule was invoked against a retailer in favor of the purchaser's daughter. The case is out of line with New York law. Gimenez v. Great Atlantic & Pacific Tea Co., 264 N.Y. 390, 395, 191 N.E. 27, 29 (1934);

containers)[5] is a special exception to the privity rule. A larger number have repudiated privity on the ground of public policy.[6] Some have simply brushed it aside or ignored it.[7]

Salzano v. First National Stores, 268 App. Div. 993, 51 N.Y.S.2d 645 (2d Dept. 1944).

The third party theory was criticized in Note, 22 Wash. U.L.Q. 406, 417 n.71 (1937); Comment, 23 Calif. L. Rev. 621, 625 (1935).

[4] See Hertzler v. Manshum, 228 Mich. 416, 421, 200 N.W. 155, 156 (1924).

[5] Davis v. Van Camp Packing Co., 189 Iowa 775, 800, 176 N.W. 382, 392 (1920); McNicholas v. Continental Baking Co., 112 S.W.2d 849, 854 (St. Louis Ct. of App. 1938); Nock v. Coca-Cola Bottling Works of Pittsburgh, 102 Pa. Super. 515, 521, 156 Atl. 537, 538 (1931); Mazetti v. Armour & Co., 75 Wash. 622, 630, 135 Pac. 633, 636 (1913). "These, however, are not decisions which limit the rule to such situations [sealed container], but are cases in which the article having been in fact transferred in that form the court uses language which will dispose of the issue without necessarily including other situations which may come before it later." Perkins, "Unwholesome Food as a Source of Liability," 5 Iowa L. Bull. 86, 92 (1920).

[6] Klein v. Duchess Sandwich Co., 14 Cal. 2d 272, 282–283, 93 P.2d 799, 804 (1939); Blanton v. Cudahy Packing Co., 154 Fla. 872, 19 So.2d 313 (1944); Davis v. Van Camp Packing Co., 189 Iowa 775, 176 N.W. 382 (1920); Madouros v. Kansas City Coca-Cola Bottling Co., 230 Mo. App. 275, 90 S.W.2d 445 (Kan. City Ct. of App. 1936); Helms v. General Baking Co., 164 S.W.2d 150 (St. Louis Ct. of App. 1942); Catani v. Swift & Co., 251 Pa. 52, 95 Atl. 931 (1914); Sincavage v. Armour & Co., 41 Luz. Leg. Reg. 183 (Pa. C.P. 1950); Jacob E. Decker & Sons, Inc. v. Capps, 139 Tex. 609, 164 S.W.2d 828 (1940); Coca Cola Bottling Co. v. Enas, 164 S.W. 2d 855 (Tex. Civ. App. 1942); Mazetti v. Armour & Co., 75 Wash. 622, 135 Pac. 633 (1913) (suit by restaurateur); Williams v. Campbell Soup Co., 80 F. Supp. 865 (W.D. Mo. 1948). See Eisenbeiss v. Payne, 42 Ariz. 262, 25 P.2d 162 (1933).

The position of the Kansas court respecting manufacturers is to be inferred from its decisions respecting wholesalers. Swengel v. F. & E. Wholesale Grocery Co., 147 Kan. 555, 77 P.2d 930 (1938).

[7] Rainwater v. Hattiesburg Coca Cola Bottling Co., 131 Miss. 315, 95 So. 444 (1922); Jackson Coca-Cola Bottling Co. v. Chapman, 106 Miss. 864, 64 So. 791 (1914); Holyfield v. Joplin Coca Cola Bottling Co., 170 S.W.2d 451 (Mo. App. 1943); Griffin and Ada Coca-Cola Bottling Co. v. Asbury, 196 Okla. 484, 165 P.2d 822 (1945); Amarillo Coca-Cola Bottling Co., Inc. v. Loudder, 207 S.W.2d 632 (Tex. Civ. App. 1947); Coca-Cola Bottling Co. of Fort Worth v. Burgess, 195 S.W.2d 379 (Tex. Civ.

Dissatisfaction with the privity rule is also shown in cases that strain to find agency arrangements with intermediate parties in order to develop a deal directly between the plaintiff and the defendant.[8] Another approach technically satisfying the privity requirement is the development of a unilateral contract between the manufacturer and the anonymous purchaser who completes the arrangement by buying and using the product in response to the manufacturer's general offer.[9]

Concepts of "third party beneficiaries," "warranties running with the goods," and "purchasing agents" suggest that, where successful, the consumer is being protected by a warranty existing in the first instance between the manufacturer and his immediate buyer, the distributor. But if the consumer's rights rest on such a warranty, they are dependent on its existence and subject to its defects. Thus a disclaimer [10] by the manufacturer, or want of reliance by

---

App. 1946); Nelson v. West Coast Dairy Co., 5 Wash. 2d 284, 105 P.2d 76 (1940). See Foley v. Coca-Cola Bottling Co. of St. Louis, 215 S.W.2d 314 (St. Louis Ct. of App. 1948); Geisness v. Scow Bay Packing Co., Inc., 16 Wash. 2d 1, 132 P.2d 740 (1942).

[8] Hall Manufacturing Co. v. Purcell, 199 Ky. 375, 251 S.W. 177 (1923); Wisdom v. Morris Hardware Co., 151 Wash. 86, 91, 274 Pac. 1050, 1053 (1929); Timberland Lumber Co. v. Climax Mfg. Co., 61 F.2d 391 (C.C.A. 3d, 1932) (nonfood).

[9] Carlill v. Carbonic Smoke Ball Co., [1893] 1 Q.B. 256. Waite, Sales 199 (2d ed. 1938).

[10] The potential position of the disclaimer in food products liability law is uncertain. Theoretically, the seller can contract out of any warranty, express or implied, except insofar as the minimum description necessary to identify the goods actually ordered is considered an "implied warranty." Practically, it must be kept in mind that, so far as warranties implied by law are concerned, the courts construe disclaimers very narrowly. This unfriendliness can be expected to increase in proportion to the buyer's lack of economic sophistication or bargaining power. In Linn v. Radio Center Delicatessen, 169 Misc. 879, 9 N.Y.S.2d 110 (1939), a lower New York court went so far as to hold that "it is against natural justice and good morals to permit an individual or corporation to manu-

his immediate buyer in a sale not by description,[11] might well undercut any claim for recovery if this approach were followed to its logical extreme. Gaps such as these might be considerable.[12]

---

facture food containing dangerous foreign substances and to escape the consequences of his acts by a disclaimer." The doctrinal validity of this conclusion is open to question in Sales Act states in view of the Act's careful dichotomy between "description" and "quality" in the sections dealing with warranty. A more appealing approach might, by interpretation, reach the same result in many instances: No straight disclaimer, regardless of its terms, should be construed as attempting to negative responsibility for minimum wholesomeness where (1) the article is sold as food, and (2) the sale of the unwholesome article as food is forbidden by statute. Whether the same result would be justified in the absence of condition (2) is open to question, since the identification of "food" with "wholesome food" might well run counter to a sound interpretation of the Uniform Sales Act.

Fortunately, the matter may well be academic. The almost complete absence of reported food cases dealing with the disclaimer problem suggests that, outside of an occasional salvage sale ("as is") between dealers, disclaimers relating to minimum standards of wholesomeness simply are not made in the food industry. Casual inquiry confirms this impression.

For disclaimers-in-general, see Llewellyn, "On Warranty of Quality, and Society, II," 37 Col. L. Rev. 341, 384–388 (1937); Prosser, "The Implied Warranty of Merchantable Quality," 27 Minn. L. Rev. 117, 157–167 (1943); Comment, 31 Col. L. Rev. 1325 (1931); Comment, 7 Ford. L. Rev. 238, 250 (1938); Note, 7 Fort. L.J. 280 (1938); Note, 32 Iowa L. Rev. 784 (1947); Note, 23 Minn. L. Rev. 784 (1939); Note, 22 Wash. U.L.Q. 536 (1937); Note, 1939 Wis. L. Rev. 459.

Disclaimers would be expressly dealt with under the proposed Uniform Commercial Code — Sales (1951). Subsection (1) of Section 2–316 would preclude the disclaimer of express warranties. Subsection (2) would permit the disclaimer of implied warranties in certain cases. It is important to remember in this connection that the dichotomy between "express" and "implied" under the proposed Code would be different from that under the Uniform Sales Act. For instance, a sale by description or sample involves an implied warranty under the Sales Act, but an express warranty under the Code. Uniform Commercial Code — Sales §2–313 (1951). For the status of the disclaimer under civil law, see Morrow, "Warranty of Quality; A Comparative Survey," 14 Tulane L. Rev. 529, 570 (1940).

[11] See Note, 22 Wash. U.L.Q. 406, 416 n.64 (1937).

[12] The difference between a warranty made to the wholesaler which benefits the consumer and a warranty made directly to the consumer is

The question whether in a particular case a warranty actually arose between the manufacturer and his immediate buyer is usually ignored by courts adopting these fictions, although its existence is implicit in this approach. Thus it is held that a warranty does exist and that it protects the consumer. To make such an assumption in all cases is in effect to set up a warranty by the manufacturer directly to the consumer, distinct from any obligation which the manufacturer may have assumed to his immediate buyer and independent of any obligation which the retailer may have assumed to the consumer.

If this is the desired result, courts wanting to dispose of the privity requirement for reasons of policy will sound technically more convincing if they eschew such feeble fictions as third party beneficiaries and warranties running with the goods. They would better direct their energies toward examining the historical, legal, and social justifications for imposing such a requirement and, if fictions are helpful, adopt assumptions better suited to their purpose.

§2.3. Bridging the privity gap — The tort approach. Can a warranty directly to the consumer be supported in terms of traditional legal concepts?

It has already been shown that the implied warranties of fitness and merchantability are as fully representation-in-fact as promise-in-fact and in either event are impositions of law over the armature of factual tendencies.[1] Accordingly, the contractual strain (in the sense of promise-in-fact) is highly attenuated.

If this is so, and if it is true that the privity requirement

---

rarely noted. Exceptions: Note, 42 Harv. L. Rev. 414, 418 n.39 (1929); Note, 25 Wash. U.L.Q. 293, 295 (1940). Andrew Gunter will observe that in the text I have borrowed liberally from his excellent case note.

§2.3. [1] See Chapter I, Topic C.

rests on the questionable assumption that causes of action for breach of the implied warranty of fitness or merchantability are necessarily circumscribed by contractual considerations, would not going back to the original tort theory of warranty overcome the difficulty? [2]

A number of states have, for collateral purposes, recognized the tortlike qualities of a breach of warranty.[3] In the two following cases recovery for breach of warranty was allowed to the consumer in actions brought directly in tort. Although neither case involved the privity problem, both made significant comments on the legal character of the defendant's breach. In *Flessher* v. *Carstens Packing Co.*,[4] the plaintiff sued a retailer in tort for negligence based on injuries caused by unfit beef purchased from the defendant. The Supreme Court of Washington held that despite his failure to show actual negligence the plaintiff was entitled to recover in tort for breach of implied warranty, the obligation being "created by implication of law independent of the contract." Liability was said to rest on "the demands of

[2] It has been suggested that privity became a requirement only because the early cases happened to satisfy it. Note, 21 Minn. L. Rev. 315, 323 (1937). Another explanation is that assumpsit was more convenient because it permitted the addition of common counts for money "had and received." Note, 18 Corn. L.Q. 445, 446 (1933).

[3] Death statutes: See §5.4 *infra*, note 4. Statutes of limitations: *E.g.*, Schlick v. New York Dugan Bros., 175 Misc. 182, 22 N.Y.S.2d 238 (1940). In Jones v. Boggs & Buhl, 355 Pa. 242, 49 A.2d 379 (1946), the court held that the plaintiff, who had gotten a skin disease from a coat purchased from the defendant, was barred in recovering for personal injury by a two-year statute of limitations applicable to suits for "injury wrongfully done to the person." In Finck v. Albers Super Markets, Inc., 135 F.2d 191 (C.C.A. 6th, 1943), the court held that the plaintiff, who had been injured by bugs in a soft drink, was barred by a one-year statute of limitations applicable to actions for injuries to persons and was not subject to the statute applicable to liabilities created by statute (even though the Sales Act is in effect in Kentucky) and actions on unwritten contracts. But *cf.* Challis v. Hartloff, 136 Kan. 823, 18 P.2d 199 (1933).

[4] 93 Wash. 48, 52, 55, 160 Pac. 14, 15, 17 (1916).

social justice." In *Greenwood* v. *John R. Thompson Co.*,[5] an Illinois appellate court granted recovery in an action on the case brought by the administrator of a restaurant patron mortally injured by defective food served by the defendant. The court said:

> Where an action on the case is brought for breach of warranty, the gravamen of the action is not fraud and deceit but merely lies in the wrongful act of the defendant in making a false warranty . . .

Similar cases appear in several other states.[6]

The possibility of bridging the privity gap by an action in tort for breach of warranty was apparently realized in *Mazetti* v. *Armour & Co.*[7] Here, in an action in tort for negligence, a packer was held liable for breach of implied warranty of canned tongue purchased by the plaintiff for service in his restaurant. The goods had been obtained through a grocery house. As the same court later explained in the Flessher case,[8] "Whether the action be called one on warranty or of negligence it comes to the same thing. It sounds in tort." The court limited its holding to goods in sealed containers.

This approach was also used by a lower New York court.[9] Its opinion does not represent the prevailing view in that state.

[5] 213 Ill. App. 371, 374 (1919). See Rost v. Kee & Chapell Dairy Co., 216 Ill. App. 497, 501 (1920).

[6] Schuler v. Union News Co., 295 Mass. 350, 353, 4 N.E.2d 465, 466 (1936); Burgess v. Sanitary Meat Market, 121 W. Va. 605, 611, 5 S.E.2d 785, 787, 6 S.E.2d 254 (1939). See Farrell v. Manhattan Market Co., 198 Mass. 271, 84 N.E. 481 (1908); Lovich v. Salvation Army, Inc., 81 Ohio App. 317, 75 N.E.2d 459 (1947). *Contra:* Howson v. Foster Beef Co., 87 N.H. 200, 206, 177 Atl. 656, 660 (1935).

[7] 75 Wash. 622, 625, 135 Pac. 633, 634 (1913).

[8] 93 Wash. 48, 56, 160 Pac. 14, 17 (1916).

[9] Kennedy v. F. W. Woolworth Co., 205 App. Div. 648, 200 N.Y. Supp. 121 (1st Dept. 1923) (retailer case).

Several commentators have found in the tort approach of these cases an attractive legal rationale for bridging or closing the privity gap.[10] Another has found it the least promising approach.[11] Either way, few courts have been persuaded by tort theories of warranty to hold the manufacturer in the face of privity objections.

The controlling factor seems to be "public policy." Most courts are unwilling to dispense with privity requirements unless they are persuaded that absolute liability of the manufacturer is a good thing substantively. Privity, whether or not historically and doctrinally sound, offers legal sanction for maintaining the *status quo* where, on policy, the *status quo* appears to be the safer bet. The most the tort theory can claim is that it offers a legal vehicle for courts that are persuaded that liability without fault is desirable. The question is how good a vehicle it is for this purpose.

It is not clear whether the privity requirement is based on the contractual character of the sale or the contractual character of the warranty. Analysis of the development of the law respecting negligence in the manufacturer and sale of goods suggests that, in part at least, it may be the latter. In the leading negligence case dealing with manufacturers, *MacPherson* v. *Buick Motor Co.*,[12] Judge Cardozo said that the duty not to injure third parties arises out of the law inde-

[10] Spruill, "Privity of Contract as a Requisite for Recovery on Warranty," 19 N.C.L. Rev. 551, 565 (1941); Note, 29 B.U.L. Rev. 107 (1949); Note, 18 Corn. L.Q. 445, 446 (1933); Note, 25 Minn. L. Rev. 83, 91 (1940).

[11] Comment, 33 Col. L. Rev. 868, 870 (1933). But the main argument advanced is only that the courts have so far not accepted this approach as a bridge. Thus in Roberts v. Anheuser-Busch Brewing Association, 211 Mass. 449, 98 N.E. 95 (1912), the court said, "While there may be no inherent difficulty in maintaining an action of tort upon a false warranty . . . it yet remains true that there cannot be a warranty where there is no privity of contract."

[12] 217 N.Y. 382, 390, 111 N.E. 1050, 1053 (1916).

pendently of the sales contract. There are two aspects of this decision: (1) emancipation of the obligation from the contractual limitations of the sale, and (2) affirmative generation of the duty directly to the consumer. The latter aspect stands on its own feet. It is not an inevitable consequence of the former.

Similarly for implied warranties. To emancipate the implied warranty obligation from the contractual boundaries of the sale may well allow the warranty to operate according to its inherent capacities. Here the legal parallel with *MacPherson* v. *Buick Motor Co.* ends. Since more basic limitations may inhere in the warranty itself, it does not follow that removing privity barriers attributable to the sale would automatically generate a warranty obligation benefiting the consumer.

Does calling the warranty obligation "tort" rather than "contract" improve the consumer's position? A representation made to the immediate vendee is of no greater help to the consumer than a promise to the immediate vendee.[13] Conversely, if a representation directly to the consumer can be "implied," so can a promise. Merely adopting the analogy of deceit (representation instead of promise) leaves the problem exactly where it was. The crucial question is whether a liability directly to the consumer is justifiable.

§2.4. Bridging the privity gap — The direct liability approach. If the law can impose a uniform liability in particular situation-types involving direct seller-buyer relationships, regardless of (or transcending) the actual intentions of the parties, it can impose uniform liability in appropriate situation-types where original seller and ultimate buyer do not deal directly with each other. The typical manufacturer knows or should know that the act of

[13] See Waite, Sales 200 (2d ed. 1938).

selling goods will directly affect the lives of persons beyond the immediate buyer just as fully as, if not more than, the immediate purchaser himself. He knows or should know that if affected they will be affected by the very factors that would make him liable were he selling to them directly. From a policy standpoint, a direct legal connection between manufacturer and consumer is called for here as fully as in the negligence situation dealt with in *MacPherson* v. *Buick Motor Co.*

Liability imposed on this basis can be considered, with equal appropriateness, as resting on quasi-promise or quasi-tort (quasi-deceit).[1] It can be imposed *as if* the manufacturer had made a promise or representation[2] directly to the consumer and *as if* the consumer had accepted the supposed promise or relied on the supposed representation. In either case, the fiction transcends the actual contract made between the manufacturer and his immediate vendee, and establishes a clean-cut legal bond directly between manufacturer and consumer. Privity of contract is no longer a consideration.[3]

Theories of third party beneficiaries, warranties running with the goods, and consumers' purchasing agents are unsatisfactory not because they are based on fictions but because they are based on inadequate fictions.[4] (It is not

§2.4. [1] See cases cited in Note, 22 Wash. U.L.Q. 406, 419 n.82 (1937).

[2] This approach seems to be preferred in Note, 42 Harv. L. Rev. 414 (1929).

[3] The possibility of imposing liability on the basis of quasi-tort in the form of quasi-negligence (which is outside the field of warranty) is discussed in §2.18.

[4] Many writers apparently stigmatize fictions as such. *E.g.*, Note, 29 B.U.L. Rev. 107, 114 (1949); Note, 21 Minn. L. Rev. 315, 324 (1937). *Cf.* Fuller, "Legal Fictions," 25 Ill. L. Rev. 363, 365 (1930); Ihering, Geist des römischen Rechts, iii,[1] 310 n.425 (1888) ("the bogey of the fiction revenges itself often bitterly on those who would track it down!" (Fuller's translation)).

enough merely to allow the consumer crumbs from a table set for the wholesaler.) Even courts that verbally accept these approaches repudiate them in practice by ignoring the existence and nature of the implied warranties, if any, actually raised between the manufacturer and the wholesaler.

The simplest approach is to create a direct liability to the consumer without fiction or analogy. Because the situation it deals with arises normally as a result of a sale by the manufacturer, this kind of liability is likewise appropriately, though not necessarily, incorporated into the miscegenous [5] household of "warranty." The characterization of its various aspects as "contract" or "tort" could follow in due time without making these processes necessary steps in the generation of the obligation. Few courts have been so bold.[6]

§2.5. Privity under the Uniform Sales Act. Where the Uniform Sales Act is in effect, there are additional complications. Section 15 says that there is no implied warranty as to quality for any particular purpose except as provided by that section. The implied warranties specifically named in Section 15 seem to be raised in the first instance as between seller and buyer. This is certainly true of the warranty of fitness of Section 15 (1). In the cases under discussion, the manufacturer is not seller to the consumer; and the consumer, if a buyer, is a buyer from the retailer in a separate sale. The word "buyer" does not appear in Section 15 (2), dealing with the warranty of merchantability, but the tenor of the language and the context of the section strongly suggest that Section 15 (2) has no wider

[5] So characterized in Note, 42 Harv. L. Rev. 414 (1929).

[6] *E.g.*, Jackson Coca-Cola Bottling Co. v. Chapman, 106 Miss. 864, 64 So. 791 (1914). A lower Pennsylvania court has recently taken the novel view that manufacturers' direct accountability may be founded squarely on the old retail food warranty. Sincavage v. Armour & Co., 41 Luz. Leg. Reg. 183 (Pa. C.P. 1950).

range than Section 15 (1). Section 69, providing remedies for breach of warranty, undoubtedly uses the terms "seller" and "buyer" to refer to persons who occupy those positions in the same transaction.[1]

Accordingly, it has been said that "The implication of any warranty directly by manufacturer to consumer flouts the plain meaning of the act." [2] At the same time, since the Act clearly raises a warranty of wholesomeness between the manufacturer and his purchaser, "merely failing in section 69 to trace its subsequent application, its inurement to the consumer might well be engrafted on the terms of section 15 without undue violence to legislative intent." [2] Under this rationale, the protection of the consumer depends upon a transaction between the manufacturer and his immediate purchaser. To the hazards of disclaimer and possible want of reliance by the distributor in sales not "by description" must be added the difficulty the consumer would have in proving a transaction he was not party to.

There is some talk that the Uniform Sales Act, which deals only with seller-buyer relationships, leaves it to the common law to adjust the rights, if any, of third parties.[3] The generally accepted view appears to repudiate this result.[4]

Another possible escape for the consumer from the apparent restrictions of the Uniform Sales Act lies in the words "particular purpose." If, as used in Section 15 (4) (barring a warranty of fitness for any *particular* purpose in a sale under

§2.5. [1] Smith v. Salem Coca-Cola Bottling Company, Inc., 92 N.H. 97, 98, 25 A.2d 125, 127 (1942).

[2] Note, 25 Wash. U.L.Q. 293, 295 n.13 (1940).

[3] Comment, 33 Col. L. Rev. 868 (1933); Note, 42 Harv. L. Rev. 414, 415 n.10 (1929).

[4] *E.g.*, Smith v. Salem Coca-Cola Bottling Company, Inc., 92 N.H. 97, 98, 25 A.2d 125, 127 (1942); Note, 40 Harv. L. Rev. 886, 887 n.3 (1927).

a trade name), these words do not rule out a warranty of fitness for a *general* purpose under Section 15 (2) (warranty of merchantability), the phrase "there is no implied warranty or condition as to the quality or fitness for any *particular* purpose" (italics added), in the opening clause of Section 15, would not necessarily preclude an implied warranty of fitness for a *general* purpose. For food, where the particular purpose and the general purpose are ordinarily the same, this might close the gap.

In the light of the reported cases, however, this speculation is academic. Considerations of public health have apparently outweighed the technical misgivings, if any, in the minds of the courts that have dropped privity requirements. Most Sales Act states that dispense with privity impose liability in disregard of or in spite of the Uniform Sales Act.

What is so far unique, though not necessarily unjustified, is the approach of the California Supreme Court. This rests recovery squarely on Section 15 (1) of the Uniform Sales Act.[5] Such an approach, in protecting the consumer by a warranty between manufacturer and distributor, leaves "at least theoretical chinks in the consumer's armor." [6] The chinks will probably remain theoretical.

§2.6. Procedural devices for lessening the effects of the privity gap where it cannot be bridged. In states that have by statute adopted the "third party action," the manufacturer is indirectly reachable in warranty through a procedural device,[1] even though want of privity may pre-

[5] Klein v. Duchess Sandwich Co., 14 Cal. 2d 272, 93 P.2d 799 (1939). *Contra:* Smith v. Salem Coca-Cola Bottling Co., Inc., 92 N.H. 97, 25 A.2d 125 (1942).

[6] Note, 25 Wash. U.L.Q. 293, 295 (1940).

§2.6. [1] *E.g.*, N.Y. Civil Practice Act §193–a (Laws 1946, c. 971). Cases under the earlier impleader procedure include McSpedon v. Kunz, 271 N.Y. 131, 137, 2 N.E.2d 513, 515 (1936); Linn v. Radio Center

vent the consumer from reaching him directly. The consumer sues the retailer in warranty. The retailer impleads his wholesaler, and so on, until the manufacturer, if available, is brought in on the basis of his vendee's claim over.[2] The consumer joins the manufacturer on a negligence count. Even though the consumer gets judgment against both, the retailer is entitled to his judgment over against the wholesaler, and so on, so that no matter who the consumer collects from, the manufacturer (if responsible) ultimately pays.[3]

Unfortunately, this procedure works only where the third party is within the jurisdiction of the state. Outside of New York and the federal courts, it is rarely used in food products liability cases, probably because of the interstate character of the great bulk of the food industry.

The common law rule which under certain conditions enables the defendant to make adverse findings binding on persons against whom he has a claim over, by giving notice and an opportunity to defend, has doubtful applicability in suits for breach of warranty of quality.[4] It has apparently never been used in suits by the food consumer.[5] It would

---

Delicatessen, 169 Misc. 879, 9 N.Y.S.2d 110 (1939); and cases cited in the following note.

[2] Occhipinti v. Buscemi, 267 App. Div. 874, 46 N.Y.S.2d 292 (2d Dept. 1944); Weiner v. Mager & Throne, 167 Misc. 338, 3 N.Y.S.2d 918 (1938); Cohen v. Dugan Bros., 134 Misc. 155, 235 N.Y. Supp. 118 (1929); Barker v. Weingarten Riverside Co., Inc., 232 S.W.2d 692 (Tex. Civ. App. 1950).

[3] Cohen v. Dugan Bros., 134 Misc. 155, 157, 235 N.Y. Supp. 118, 120 (1929).

[4] Freeman, Judgments 978 (5th ed. 1925); 50 C.J.S. 361; 30 Am. Jur. 969. Held applicable: Carleton v. Lombard, Ayres & Co., 149 N.Y. 137, 43 N.E. 422 (1896). Held inapplicable: Smith v. Moore, 7 S.C. 209 (1875); Morgan v. Winston, 2 Swan 472 (Tenn. 1852). And see Booth v. Scheer, 105 Kan. 643, 185 Pac. 898 (1919).

[5] The possibility, however, was envisaged in Martin v. Great Atlantic & Pacific Tea Co., 301 Ky. 429, 434, 192 S.W.2d 201, 203 (1946).

probably be less effective than the third party action in reaching the manufacturer in warranty, because it requires a later and separate suit by the defendant against the third party. Were this doctrine put to effective use, however, it would provide some inducement to the manufacturer voluntarily to expose himself in the consumer's action.

§2.7. Express representations. A famous automobile case, *Baxter* v. *Ford Motor Co.*,[1] caused a flurry of speculation as to whether advertisements and other express representations by the manufacturer might not furnish a valuable additional basis for holding him accountable directly to the consumer.[2] However, the course of history since that decision suggests that, for food at least, it remains grist for academic mills. Only an infinitesimal amount of food is marketed by manufacturers under a solid representation to the consumer.[3] Besides, the doctrine of the *Baxter* case appears to be limited to defects common to the product. This excludes the only kind of food defect that is likely to be

§2.7. [1] 168 Wash. 456, 12 P.2d 409 (1932).

[2] Comment, 33 Col. L. Rev. 868, 877 (1933); Note, 18 Corn. L.Q. 445 (1933); Note, 25 Minn. L. Rev. 83, 92 (1940) (suggesting that the approach of the Baxter case is the true solution to protecting the consumer); Note, 22 Wash. U.L.Q. 406, 424 (1937) (suggesting that the basis of the Baxter case was "negligent advertising"); Note, 7 Wash. L. Rev. 351 (1932). Compare the manufacturer's representation as express warranty and as ground for a negligence suit. See §2.18 *infra*, note 2.

[3] The courts are reluctant to find an express warranty against specific defects. Davis v. Van Camp Packing Co., 189 Iowa 775, 787, 176 N.W. 382, 387 (1920) (can of beans was marked "sanitary"; label said goods had been "inspected and passed" and were "ready for the table"); Scruggins v. Jones, 207 Ky. 636, 296 S.W. 743 (1925) (retailer said that manufacturer was "reliable"); Pelletier v. Dupont, 124 Me. 269, 276, 128 Atl. 186, 189 (1925) (label: "Purity Nutrition Cleanliness absolutely applies to Edgeworth Bread"); Alpine v. Friend Bros., Inc., 244 Mass. 164, 167, 138 N.E. 553, 554 (1923) (advertisement: "sweet, healthful and tasty bread"); Newhall v. Ward Baking Co., 240 Mass. 434, 437, 134 N.E. 625, 626 (1922) (label: "This bread is 100% pure . . . a healthful and nutritious food"); Handler, "False and Misleading Advertising," 39 Yale L.J. 22, 23 (1929).

the subject of a civil suit. A few courts have flirted with the idea of basing liability on direct advertising appeals but they find almost as much comfort in simple labels and trademarks.[4] Comfort such as this depends more on fiction than on fact.

§2.8. Causation. Even though he solves the problem of privity, the plaintiff who sues the manufacturer for breach of warranty must also solve the problem of causation.[1] This means showing that the plaintiff's injury is somehow attributable to the defendant. Because there have been, in warranty suits on the one hand, a general preoccupation with the problems of privity and, in the more numerous negligence suits on the other, a tendency to identify the problem of causation with that of fault, most of the detailed analyses of the causation problem relate to suits for negligence. Since causation as such presents the same problems in both kinds of suits, the principles outlined in the following Topic, insofar as they relate to causation as an independent requirement, apply equally here.

TOPIC B. *Liability of the Manufacturer for Negligence*

§2.9. The problem of proof. Because of privity pitfalls, the theory of action most frequently used against the manufacturer is that of tort for negligence. It has been exploited not so much for its inherent appropriateness as for its being the least undesirable of locally available alternatives.

Privity of contract was once required even here, largely

[4] *E.g.*, Curtiss Candy Co. v. Johnson, 163 Miss. 426, 141 So. 762 (1932). See Anderson v. Tyler, 223 Iowa 1033, 1037, 274 N.W. 48, 50 (1937).

§2.8. [1] As in Strawn v. Coca-Cola Bottling Co. of Missouri, 234 S.W.2d 223 (Kan. City Ct. of App., Mo. 1950).

because of dicta in *Winterbottom* v. *Wright*,[1] but an exception grew up for articles intended to affect human life, which were "imminently dangerous," first in their natural state,[2] finally in their defective condition.[3] Because something that injures is likely to be found dangerous, the exception has bid fair to swallow the rule. Though the requirement has not wholly disappeared, it may be ignored so far as food is concerned because defective food has long been considered "imminently dangerous." [4]

Even if it avoids privity problems and other intricacies of the law of sales, the negligence action as applied to the consumer's action against the food manufacturer has complications of its own.

The difficulty is this: Liability in negligence assumes that the plaintiff's injury is traceable to specific conduct of

§2.9. [1] 10 M. & W. 109, 152 Eng. Rep. 402 (1842).

[2] Huset v. J. I. Case Threshing Mach. Co., 120 Fed. 865 (C.C.A. 8th, 1903).

[3] MacPherson v. Buick Motor Co., 217 N.Y. 382, 111 N.E. 1050 (1916). The Scottish Court of Session has refused to go so far. Mullen v. A. G. Barr & Co., Ltd., [1929] S.C. 461, 470 (Ct. Sess.)

[4] *E.g.*, Drury v. Armour & Co., 140 Ark. 371, 216 S.W. 40 (1919); Freeman v. Schultz Bread Co., 100 Misc. 528, 530, 163 N.Y. Supp. 396, 397 (1916). See cases cited in Comment, 4 Ford. L. Rev. 295, 296 n.7 (1935). On the general question of privity in tort cases, see Bohlen, "Liability of Manufacturers to Persons Other than Their Immediate Vendees," 45 L.Q. Rev. 343 (1929); Feezer, "Tort Liability of Manufacturers," 10 Minn. L. Rev. 1 (1925), 19 Minn. L. Rev. 752 (1935); Jeanblanc, "Manufacturers' Liability to Persons Other than Their Immediate Vendees," 24 Va. L. Rev. 134 (1937); Russell, "Manufacturers' Liability to the Ultimate Consumer," 21 Ky. L.J. 388 (1933); Seefeld, "Tort Liability of Manufacturers to Users of Their Goods," 25 Marq. L. Rev. 173 (1941); Note, 21 Minn. L. Rev. 315 (1937).

Bohlen, *id.* at 356, suggests that tort food liability stood on its own feet and did not develop merely as part of the doctrines of the Huset and Winchester cases.

A milestone in English law was M'Alister (or Donoghue) v. Stevenson, [1932] A.C. 562, [1932] S.C. (H.L.) 31, 48 L.T.R. 494, 101 L.J.P.C. 119, discussed in Pollock, "The Snail in the Bottle, and Thereafter," 49 L.Q. Rev. 22, 24 (1933).

the defendant that falls below the legal minimum standard of care. In the typical food injury case, the precise cause of the defect is forever a mystery.[5] Unless the defect is common to the product or a particular, identifiable batch, both parties necessarily rely on circumstantial evidence that is, in most cases, far from conclusive.

There is frequently evidence tending to show that the injury was caused by a defect traceable to the defendant and sometimes evidence that the defendant's general program of care is inadequate.[6] Beyond this, there is usually nothing to show that the defendant was careless in the particular instance. If carelessness is to be inferred or presumed, therefore, it must ordinarily rest on the facts (1) that the defendant either created the condition or refrained from removing it and (2) that creation or nonremoval is usually the result of carelessness. For his part, the most the defendant can ordinarily hope to show is that he maintains an establishment in which he has adopted all reasonable precautions, or that the plaintiff got his injury somewhere else.

Usually there is little difficulty in showing that the plaintiff was injured. The plaintiff meets his first serious

[5] Guiher and Morris, "Handling Food Products Liability Cases," 1 Food Drug Cosmetic L.Q. 109, 126 (1946); King, "Evidence and Presumptions in Food Products Liability," 5 Food Drug Cosmetic L.J. 513, 514 (1950).

[6] Collins Baking Co. v. Savage, 227 Ala. 408, 150 So. 336 (1933) (inadequate inspection of certain ingredients); Arena v. John P. Squire Co., 321 Mass. 423, 73 N.E.2d 836 (1947) (improper inspection for trichinae); Catalanello v. Cudahy Packing Co., 264 App. Div. 723, 34 N.Y.S.2d 37 (2d Dept. 1942) (improper processing of salami to intercept trichinae); Jones v. Mercer Pie Co., 187 Tenn. 322, 214 S.W.2d 46 (1948) (plant generally dirty); Lockhart v. Barr, [1941] S.C. 578 (Ct. Sess.) (washing and filling operations too close together); M'Alister (or Donoghue) v. Stevenson, [1932] A.C. 562, [1932] S.C. (H.L.) 31, 48 L.T.R. 494, 101 L.J.P.C. 119 (improper storage of empty bottles and inadequate inspection); Kirby v. Burke & Holloway, [1944] Ir. R. 207 (inadequate supervision of capping process).

problem of proof when he begins to trace the causal sequence back to the defendant.

§2.10. The problem of proof — The foreign substance in the sealed container. The plaintiff finds the going easiest where he has been injured by a readily ascertainable foreign object found in food that has been packed and purchased in a sealed container. Where he has suffered an immediate reaction or injury the only problems likely to cause trouble are those of showing that the object was in the package when it was opened and that there was no reasonable possibility of tampering by intermediate handlers. With respect to the first problem, the plaintiff must exclude the possibility that the defect entered the product after he opened the package, especially where the defendant's product was combined with other ingredients. In these cases, direct evidence of how the food was prepared and consumed is usually available, with occasional help from the nature of the defect. If the bolt in the can of tomatoes is like those used on the defendant's machinery, the plaintiff's chances of success are good. Quite the opposite, if the lead soldier found in the bottle of milk matches several in Junior's toy chest.

The tampering point has not proved difficult for most products, since canned goods and other foods in sealed containers generally speak for themselves. If the reported cases are a reliable index, the soft-drink bottle cap has been the only significant source of uncertainty. Even here it has apparently not caused real difficulty outside of Tennessee and several other states.[1] Most courts seem satisfied with

§2.10. [1] Coca-Cola Bottling Works v. Sullivan, 178 Tenn. 405, 158 S.W.2d 721 (1942); Harbin v. F. A. Weigel & Sons, CCH Food Drug Cosmetic Law Rep. ¶22,129 (Tenn. App. 1947); Dungy v. Coca-Cola Bottling Works, CCH Food Drug Cosmetic Law Serv. ¶18,246 (Tenn. App. 1942); Coca-Cola Bottling Co. v. Rowland, 16 Tenn. App. 184, 66

evidence that the bottle and contents had a normal appearance or, at most, with evidence showing the usual way in which the bottles are distributed and handled.[2] The real burden of persuasion on this point seems to be on the defendant.[3] Even so, it seems a wise precaution for the plaintiff

S.W.2d 272 (1933); Jordan v. Coca Cola Bottling Co. of Utah, — Utah —, 218 P.2d 660 (1950); Todd v. Coca Cola Bottling Co. of Puerto Rico, 88 F. Supp. 870 (D.C. Puerto Rico, 1950).

[2] Sufficient evidence of no tampering was found in Dr. Pepper Co. v. Brittain, 234 Ala. 548, 176 So. 286 (1937); Claxton Coca Cola Bottling Co. v. Coleman, 68 Ga. App. 302, 22 S.E.2d 768 (1942); Duval v. Coca-Cola Bottling Co. of Chicago, 329 Ill. App. 290, 68 N.E.2d 479 (1946); Coca Cola Bottling Works of Evansville, Inc. v. Williams, 111 Ind. App. 502, 37 N.E.2d 702 (1941); Glasgow Coca-Cola Bottling Works, Inc. v. Reed, 312 Ky. 731, 229 S.W.2d 438 (1950) (facts appear in 230 S.W.2d 106, 107); Seale v. Coca Cola Bottling Works of Lexington, 297 Ky. 450, 179 S.W.2d 598 (1944); Underhill v. Anciaux, — Nev. —, 226 P.2d 794 (1951); Sullivan v. Henry, CCH Food Drug Cosmetic Law Serv. ¶18,195 (Tenn. App. 1940); Beaumont Coca-Cola Bottling Co. v. Guillot, 222 S.W.2d 141 (Tex. Civ. App. 1949); Texas Coca-Cola Bottling Co. v. Wimberley, 108 S.W.2d 860 (Tex. Civ. App. 1937); Coca Cola Bottling Co. v. Kerlee, CCH Food Drug Cosmetic Law Serv. ¶18,194 (Tex. 2d Jud. Dist. 1940); Mathews v. Coca-Cola Co. of Canada, [1944] 2 D.L.R. 355, O.R. 207, O.W.N. 159, *aff'd*, [1945] 1 D.L.R. 1.

Insufficient evidence of no tampering was found in East Kentucky Beverage Co. v. Stumbo, 313 Ky. 66, 230 S.W.2d 106 (1950); Nichols v. Louisiana Coca-Cola Bottling Co., 46 So.2d 695 (La. App. 1950).

In several cases instructions permitting the jury to find negligence from the mere presence of the foreign object in the bottle have been overturned on the ground that they deprived the defendant of the defense that the object may have intruded after the bottle left his hands. Newport News Coca-Cola Bottling Co. v. Babb, 190 Va. 360, 366, 57 S.E.2d 41, 44 (1950); Pepsi-Cola Bottling Co. of Norfolk, Inc. v. McCullers, 189 Va. 89, 95, 52 S.E.2d 257, 259 (1949). And see Amarillo Coca-Cola Bottling Co., Inc. v. Loudder, 207 S.W.2d 632, 634 (Tex. Civ. App. 1947) (based presumably on breach of warranty).

[3] *E.g.*, Middlesboro Coca Cola Bottling Works, Inc. v. Campbell, 179 Va. 693, 20 S.E.2d 479 (1942) (soap and caustic soda in Coca-Cola); Norfolk Coca-Cola Bottling Works, Inc. v. Krausse, 162 Va. 107, 173 S.E. 497 (1934) (glass in Coca-Cola). A less persuasive application of this view appears in Cloverland Farms Dairy, Inc. v. Ellin, 75 A.2d 116 (Md. App. 1950) (involving a non-airtight and easily removable soft-drink cap).

Since it relates to the problem of causation, the reasonable possibility

to secure all the evidence on the point that he reasonably can.

In the much less frequent case where the plaintiff's reaction to the foreign object is delayed illness, there is the additional problem of relating the illness to the defective product. Here he relies on a chemical analysis or circumstantial evidence. He may be able to show, for instance, that others in his family or party who ate the suspected food also got sick, while those who ate only other foods did not.[4]

In the foreign-object-sealed-container cases the plaintiff has had his least difficulty in tracing his injury to the defendant and in this area he has enjoyed a high degree of success.[5]

---

of tampering is equally a problem in suits for breach of warranty. Strawn v. Coca Cola Bottling Co. of Missouri, 234 S.W.2d 223, 225 (Kan. City Ct. of App., Mo. 1950).

[4] *E.g.*, Jonesboro Coca-Cola Bottling Co. v. Young, 198 Ark. 1032, 132 S.W.2d 382 (1939) (plaintiff lost because he couldn't connect illness with bottle of Coca-Cola); and cases in which plaintiff lost cited in note 5 *infra*. The problem here is the same as that faced in the cases cited in §2.11 *infra*, note 3.

[5] *Alabama:* Dr. Pepper Co. v. Brittain, 234 Ala. 548, 176 So. 286 (1937) (glass in Coca-Cola); Magic City Bottling Co. v. Tolbert, 41 So.2d 619 (Ala. App. 1949) (worm in Zimba Kola); Birmingham Coca-Cola Bottling Co. v. Sellers, 39 So.2d 706 (Ala. App. 1949) (roach in Coca-Cola); Alabama Coca-Cola Bottling Co. v. Causey, 180 So. 588 (Ala. App. 1938) (safety pin in Coca-Cola).

Arizona: Southwestern Coca Cola Bottling Co. v. Northern, 65 Ariz. 172, 177 P.2d 219 (1947) (decomposed flesh in Coca-Cola).

Arkansas: Coca-Cola Bottling Co. of Fort Smith v. Reeves, 211 Ark. 452, 200 S.W.2d 811 (1947) (glass in Coca-Cola); Coca-Cola Bottling Co. v. Cromwell, 203 Ark. 933, 159 S.W.2d 744 (1942) (spider in Coca-Cola); Coca Cola Bottling Co. of Arkansas v. Morrison, 194 Ark. 248, 106 S.W.2d 601 (1937) (spider in Coca-Cola); Coca Cola Bottling Co. v. McBride, 180 Ark. 193, 20 S.W.2d 862 (1929) (safety pin in Coca-Cola).

California: Medeiros v. Coca Cola Bottling Co. of Turlock, Ltd., 57 Cal. App. 2d 707, 135 P.2d 676 (1943) (cleaning brush in Coca-Cola); Klein v. Duchess Sandwich Co., 14 Cal. 2d 272, 93 P.2d 799 (1939) (mag-

§2.10, note 5 (*Continued*)

gots in packaged ham sandwich; plaintiff showed that restaurateur held goods only an hour).

Connecticut: Bagre v. Daggett Chocolate Co., 126 Conn. 659, 13 A.2d 757 (1940) (tooth filling in candy).

Georgia: Dalton Coca-Cola Bottling Co. v. Watkins, 70 Ga. App. 790, 29 S.E.2d 281 (1944) (safety pin in Coca-Cola); Claxton Coca Cola Bottling Co. v. Coleman, 68 Ga. App. 302, 22 S.E.2d 768 (1942) (kerosene in Coca-Cola).

Illinois: Patargias v. Coca-Cola Bottling Co. of Chicago, 332 Ill. App. 117, 74 N.E.2d 162 (1947) (mouse in Coca-Cola); Duval v. Coca-Cola Bottling Co. of Chicago, 329 Ill. App. 290, 68 N.E.2d 479 (1946) (mouse in Coca-Cola); Paolinelli v. Dainty Foods Manufacturers, Inc., 322 Ill. App. 586, 54 N.E.2d 759 (1944) (foreign object in packaged soup mix); Sullivan v. Coca-Cola Bottling Co. of Chicago, Inc., 313 Ill. App. 517, 40 N.E.2d 579 (1942) (electric light bulb base in Coca-Cola).

Indiana: Coca Cola Bottling Works of Evansville, Inc. v. Williams, 111 Ind. App. 502, 37 N.E.2d 702 (1941) (concrete in Coca-Cola).

Kentucky: Glasgow Coca-Cola Bottling Works, Inc. v. Reed, 312 Ky. 731, 229 S.W.2d 438 (1950) (mouse in Coca-Cola) (facts appear in 230 S.W.2d 106, 107); Seale v. Coca Cola Bottling Works of Lexington, 297 Ky. 450, 179 S.W.2d 598 (1944) (glass in Coca-Cola); Nehi Beverage Co. v. Hall, 295 Ky. 353, 174 S.W.2d 509 (1943).

Louisiana: Mayerhefer v. Louisiana Coca-Cola Bottling Co., Ltd., 45 So.2d 442 (La. App. 1950) (iodine in Coca-Cola); Dye v. American Beverage Co., 194 So. 438 (La. App. 1940) (foreign substance in Royal Crown Cola).

Maryland: Coca Cola Bottling Works, Inc. v. Catron, 186 Md. 156, 46 A.2d 303 (1946) (mouse in Coca-Cola).

Mississippi: Coca Cola Bottling Works, Inc., of Columbus v. Petty, 190 Miss. 631, 200 So. 128 (1941) (animal matter in Coca-Cola); Delta Nehi Bottling Co. v. Lucas, 184 Miss. 693, 185 So. 561 (1939) (paper clip in soft drink).

Missouri: Norman v. Jefferson City Coca-Cola Bottling Co., 211 S.W. 2d 552 (Kan. City Ct. of App., Mo. 1948); Hutchison v. Moerschel Products Co., 234 Mo. App. 518, 133 S.W.2d 701 (1939) (mouse in Coca-Cola).

Nevada: Underhill v. Anciaux, — Nev. —, 226 P.2d 794 (1951) (slimy matter in Coca-Cola).

New Jersey: Lewis v. V. La Rosa & Sons, Inc., 128 N.J.L. 474, 26 A.2d 879 (1942) (bolt in macaroni); Nadel v. Boller Beverages, Inc., CCH Food Drug Cosmetic Law Rep. ¶22,236 (N.J. Super. 1950) (deleterious matter in raspberry soda); Wilson v. Coca Cola Bottling Company of New York, Inc., 65 A.2d 630 (N.J. Super. 1948) (rusted Coca-Cola cap in Coca-Cola).

New York: Tyrrell v. Lay, 195 Misc. 403. 91 N.Y.S.2d 680 (1949) (wire in bread).

§2.10, note 5 (*Continued*)

North Carolina: Breece v. Asheville Coca-Cola Bottling Co., 212 N.C. 388, 193 S.E. 269 (1937) (glass in Coca-Cola).

Pennsylvania: Smith v. Coca Cola Bottling Co. of Pennsylvania, 152 Pa. Super. 445, 33 A.2d 488 (1943) (spider in Coca-Cola); Stein v. Woodlawn Farm Dairy Co., 50 Lack. Jur. 1 (Pa. C.P. 1949) (glass in milk).

South Carolina: Floyd v. Florence Nehi Bottling Co., 188 S.C. 98, 198 S.E. 161 (1938) (flies in Orange Crush).

Tennessee: Sullivan v. Henry, CCH Food Drug Cosmetic Law Serv. ¶18,195 (Tenn. App. 1940) (glass in Coca-Cola).

Texas: Coca Cola Bottling Co. of Fort Worth v. Tannahill, 235 S.W.2d 224 (Tex. Civ. App. 1950) (cigar in Coca-Cola); Beaumont v. Coca Cola Bottling Co. v. Guillot, 222 S.W.2d 141 (Tex. Civ. App. 1949) (rag in Coca-Cola); Texas Coca-Cola Bottling Co. v. Kubena, 109 S.W.2d 1098 (Tex. Civ. App. 1937) (mouse in Coca-Cola); Texas Coca-Cola Bottling Co. v. Wimberley, 108 S.W.2d 860 (Tex. Civ. App. 1937) (glass in Coca-Cola); Coca Cola Bottling Co. v. Kerlee, CCH Food Drug Cosmetic Law Serv. ¶18,194 (Tex. 2d Jud. Dist. 1940) (spider in Coca-Cola).

Virginia: Middlesboro Coca Cola Bottling Works, Inc. v. Campbell, 179 Va. 693, 20 S.E.2d 479 (1942) (soap and caustic soda in Coca-Cola); Norfolk Coca-Cola Bottling Works, Inc. v. Krausse, 162 Va. 107, 173 S.E. 497 (1934) (glass in Coca-Cola); Pepsi-Cola Bottling Company of Norfolk, Inc. v. McCullers, 189 Va. 89, 52 S.E.2d 257 (1949) (mouse in Pepsi-Cola); Norfolk Coca-Cola Bottling Works, Inc. v. Land, CCH Food Drug Cosmetic Law Rep. ¶22,165 (Va. App. 1949) (worm in Coca-Cola).

West Virginia: Blevins v. Raleigh Coca-Cola Bottling Works, 121 W. Va. 427, 3 S.E.2d 627 (1939) (rotten meat in Coca-Cola); Parr v. Coca-Cola Bottling Works of Charleston, 121 W. Va. 314, 3 S.E.2d 499 (1939) (maggots in Coca-Cola).

Federal: Houston Coca-Cola Bottling Co. v. Kelley, 131 F.2d 627 (C.C.A. 5th, 1942) (glass in Coca-Cola); Fisher v. Washington Coca-Cola Bottling Works, Inc., 84 F.2d 261 (App. D.C. 1936) ("noxious substance" in Coca-Cola); Gray v. Pet Milk Co., 108 F.2d 974 (C.C.A. 7th, 1940).

England: M'Alister (or Donoghue) v. Stevenson, [1932] A.C. 562, [1932] S.C. (H.L.) 31, 48 L.T.R. 494, 101 L.J.P.C. 119 (snail in ginger beer).

Canada: Mathews v. Coca Cola Co. of Canada, [1944] 2 D.L.R. 355, O.R. 207, O.W.N. 159, *aff'd*, [1945] 1 D.L.R. 1 (mouse in Coca-Cola); Compagnie des Liqueurs Corona Soft Drinks Co., Ltd. v. Champagne, 64 Que. K.B. (1937) (brass chain in Coca-Cola).

See Whitehorn v. Nash-Finch Co., 67 S.D. 465, 293 N.W. 859 (1940).

The above list of authorities is representative rather than exhaustive.

The plaintiff lost in the following cases.

Alabama: Chero-Cola Bottling Co. v. Watford, 31 Ala. App. 493, 19

§2.10, note 5 (*Continued*)

So.2d 77 (1944) (cigarette package in Royal Crown Cola; plaintiff's sickness attributed to other causes).

Arkansas: Jonesboro Coca-Cola Bottling Co. v. Hambrooke, 206 Ark. 385, 175 S.W.2d 387 (1943) (bobby pin in Coca-Cola; plaintiff's sickness was not immediate, may have resulted from prior stomach trouble).

Georgia: Miller v. Gerber Products Co., 207 Ga. 385, 62 S.E.2d 174 (1950) (glass in strained peas; no direct evidence that glass came from jar); Sox v. Carrollton Coca-Cola Bottling Co., 59 Ga. App. 367, 1 S.E.2d 42 (1939) ("foreign substance" in Coca-Cola; plaintiff failed to show that defendant was the bottler).

Kentucky: East Kentucky Beverage Co. v. Stumbo, 313 Ky. 66, 230 S.W.2d 106 (1950) (contraceptive rubber in Pepsi-Cola; possibility of tampering).

Louisiana: Stewart v. Natchitoches Coca Cola Bottling Co., 34 So.2d 281 (La. App. 1948) (slimy object in Coca-Cola; evidence was insufficient to show causation); Basile v. World Bottling Co., 17 So.2d 734 (La. App. 1944) (oil in bottle of Jumbo; plaintiff failed to show that contents made her sick); Jenkins v. Bogalusa Coca Cola Bottling Co., Ltd., 1 So.2d 426 (La. App. 1941) (spider in Coca-Cola; plaintiff failed to show that contents made her sick); Gunter v. Alexandria Coca-Cola Bottling Co., 197 So. 159 (La. App. 1940) (glass alleged to be in Coca-Cola; plaintiff was probably injured by chip from bottle top broken when it was opened); Freeman v. Louisiana Coca-Cola Bottling Co., Ltd., 179 So. 621 (La. App. 1938) (glass in Coca-Cola; plaintiff's story doubted).

Minnesota: Swenson v. Purity Baking Co., 183 Minn. 289, 236 N.W. 310 (1931) (moth larvae in bread; plaintiff failed to show negligence and possibly causation).

Mississippi: Neely v. Jackson Coca Cola Co., 183 Miss. 635, 184 So. 467 (1938) (flies in Coca-Cola; defendant not shown to be the bottler).

New Hampshire: Smith v. Salem Coca-Cola Bottling Co., Inc., 92 N.H. 97, 25 A.2d 125 (1942) (glass in Coca-Cola; plaintiff failed to show negligence).

Rhode Island: Murray v. P. Ballantine & Sons, 75 R.I. 13, 62 A.2d 895 (1948), 63 A.2d 730 (1949) (foreign substance in beer; no evidence of causation).

South Carolina: Welsh v. Gibbons, 211 S.C. 516, 46 S.E.2d 147 (1948) (lye in Coca-Cola; cause remanded because certain evidence reflecting on plaintiff had been excluded).

Tennessee: Coca-Cola Bottling Works v. Sullivan, 178 Tenn. 405, 158 S.W.2d 721 (1942) (glass in Coca-Cola; bottle may have been tampered with after it left defendant); Dungy v. Coca-Cola Bottling Works, Inc., CCH Food Drug Cosmetic Law Serv. ¶18,246 (Tenn. App. 1942) (glass in Coca-Cola; bottle may have been tampered with after it left defendant); Creswell v. William Gerst Brewing Co., CCH Food Drug Cosmetic Law Serv. ¶18,173 (Tenn. App. 1940) (roach in beer; defendant's general care negatived negligence); Coca-Cola Bottling Co. v. Rowland, 16

§2.11. The problem of proof — The foreign substance not in a sealed container. Where the foreign object is traced to an item not marketed in a sealed container,[1] the problems of proof for the plaintiff differ only with respect to the second of the two difficulties just discussed: the possibility that the defect is attributable solely to intermediate handlers. Here the plaintiff is frequently helped by the nature of the object or its location when discovered. The position of a piece of wire in a loaf of bread, for instance, usually indicates whether the wire intruded during baking or afterwards.[2] In the former contingency, the plaintiff easily convinces the jury that the defect was caused by the manufacturer's negligence, and recovery usually follows.[3]

Tenn. App. 184, 66 S.W.2d 272 (1933) (mouse in Coca-Cola; plaintiff's general due care negatived negligence and probably causation).

England: Mullen v. A. G. Barr & Co., Ltd., [1929] S.C. 461 (Ct. Sess.) (mouse in ginger beer; defendant's general care negatived negligence).

Canada: Saddlemire v. Coca Cola Co. of Canada, [1941] 4 D.L.R. 614, O.W.N. 392 (mouse in Coca-Cola; contributory negligence and failure to establish causation); Ferstenfeld v. Kik Co., 77 Que. S.C. 165 (1939) (glass in bottled drink; possible that glass got in after cap was removed).

§2.11. [1] This category includes cases where the plaintiff is served packaged foods in a restaurant, the contents having been removed in the kitchen by the restaurant keeper, not at the table by the patron.

The dichotomy used here between sealed container cases and non-sealed container cases is very loose. The line is actually undiscernible. For goods in "sealed containers" there are important differences in degree between different types of containers with respect to the extent to which they protect their contents from later deterioration and tampering. Goods not in "sealed containers," though in general more susceptible, likewise show their susceptibility in differing degrees. Even so, for present purposes the distinction seems useful to illustrate general tendencies while avoiding unnecessarily detailed gradations. In a particular controversy, of course, the court looks at the specific type of container.

[2] See Danker v. Fischer Baking Co., 5 N.J. Super. 248, 68 A.2d 774 (1949); Tyrrell v. Lay, 195 Misc. 403, 91 N.Y.S. 2d 680 (1949); Sell v. Spaulding Bakeries, Inc., 66 Mont. Co. L. Rep. 103 (Pa. C.P. 1949).

[3] Collins Baking Co. v. Savage, 227 Ala. 408, 150 So. 336 (1933) (tacks and wire in bread); Dryden v. Continental Baking Co., 11 Cal. 2d 33, 77

§2.12. The problem of proof — The latent defect in the sealed container. A third type of situation (the converse of the second) is that of the latent defect imputed to food packed and purchased in a sealed container. The main problem here is to trace the plaintiff's injury to the unopened package. This is frequently difficult where there was a substantial lapse of time between eating and recognition of injury. In the absence of a sample available for chemical analysis, circumstantial evidence implicating the defendant's product is, once more, usually necessary. For a plaintiff who can trace his injuries to a latent defect in the defendant's product, however, recovery for negligence is almost always allowed.[1]

P.2d 833 (1938) (glass in bread); Bagre v. Daggett Chocolate Co., 126 Conn. 659, 13 A.2d 757 (1940) (tooth filling in candy); Curtiss Candy Co. v. Johnson, 60 Ga. App. 268, 3 S.E.2d 777 (1939) (glass in Baby Ruth bar); Flynn v. First National Stores, Inc., 296 Mass. 521, 6 N.E.2d 814 (1937) (wire in hamburg steak); Tonsman v. Greenglass, 248 Mass. 275, 142 N.E. 756 (1924) (metal in bread); McKittrick v. Dugan Bros., 119 N.J.L. 605, 197 Atl. 905 (1938), *aff'd*, 121 N.J.L. 49, 1 A.2d 331 (1938) (glass in muffin); Cohen v. Dugan Bros., 134 Misc. 155, 235 N.Y. Supp. 118 (1929) (nail in bread); Freeman v. Schultz Bread Co., 100 Misc. 528, 163 N.Y. Supp. 396 (1916) (nail in bread); Ward Baking Co. v. Trizzino, 27 Ohio App. 475, 161 N.E. 557 (1920) (needle in cake); Menaker v. Supplee-Wills-Jones Milk Co., 125 Pa. Super. 76, 189 Atl. 714 (1937) (half mouse in ice-cream cone); Bissonette v. National Biscuit Co., 100 F.2d 1003 (C.C.A. 2d, 1939) (glass in bread); Newcomb v. Armour & Co., 39 F. Supp. 716 (M.D. Pa. 1941) (wire in frankfurter); Quinn v. Swift & Co., 20 F. Supp. 234 (M.D. Pa. 1937) (metal in sausage); Arendale v. Canada Bread Co., Ltd., [1941] 2 D.L.R. 41, O.W.N. 69 (glass in bread); Buckley v. Mott, 50 D.L.R. 408 (Nova Scotia, 1919) (glass in chocolate bar). See Irick v. Peoples Baking Co., 187 S.C. 238, 242, 196 S.E. 887, 888 (1938) (glass in cake); Chaproniere v. Mason, [1905] 21 T.L.R. 633 (stone in bun). The plaintiff lost in Levine v. Wilson & Co., 16 Conn. Supp. 404 (C.P. 1950) (fly in bacon); Piazza v. Fischer Baking Co., 197 Misc. 418, 98 N.Y.S.2d 508 (screw in bread); Canton Provision Co. v. Gauder, 130 Ohio St. 43, 196 N.E. 634 (1935) (rat ordure in liver pudding; misjoinder of parties); Nichols v. Continental Baking Co., 34 F.2d 141 (C.C.A. 3d, 1929) (cockroach in bread).

§2.12. [1] Ballard & Ballard Co. v. Jones, 246 Ala. 478, 21 So.2d 327

§2.13. The problem of proof — The latent defect not in a sealed container. The plaintiff has his hardest case where a latent defect is imputed to food sold by the defendant other than in a sealed container. Here the plaintiff may find it hard either to implicate the defendant's product or to trace a defect in the product back to the defendant. The problems of proof are those already discussed. Here they appear in combination. The plaintiff's chances of recovery

---

(1945) (calcium arsenic in branded flour found by chemical analysis); Swift & Co. v. Mabry, 203 Ark. 818, 159 S.W.2d 61 (1942) (tainted sausage-in-oil; three who ate substantial amount got sick, others who did not escaped); Criswell Baking Co. v. Milligan, 77 Ga. App. 861, 50 S.E.2d 136 (1948) (unwholesome pie packed in paper box); Armour & Co. v. Roberts, 63 Ga. App. 846, 12 S.E.2d 376 (1940) (unfit dried beef); Cloverland Farms Dairy, Inc. v. Ellin, 75 A.2d 116 (Md. App. 1950) (kerosene in orange juice product); Piscatore v. V. La Rosa & Sons, Inc., 121 N.J.L. 288, 2 A.2d 328 (1938) (unwholesome macaroni; plaintiff was the only one who ate macaroni and the only one who got sick); McAteer v. Sheffield Farms Co., Inc., 9 N.J. Misc. 33, 152 Atl. 469 (1930) (unfit milk sold, presumably, in closed bottle); Lockhart v. Barr, [1941] S.C. 578 (Ct. Sess.) (phenol in "aerated water"); Kirby v. Burke & Holloway, [1944] Ir. R. 207 (only those in family who ate jam got sick).

The plaintiff lost in H. J. Heinz Co. v. Fortson, 62 Ga. App. 130, 8 S.E.2d 443 (1940) (unwholesome canned soup; defendant's general care negatived negligence); Armour & Co. v. Gulley, 61 Ga. App. 414, 6 S.E.2d 165 (1939) (tainted canned meat; plaintiff failed to show that the meat was defective); Comforto v. Cloverland Dairy Products Co., Inc., 194 So. 43 (La. App. 1940) (allegedly unwholesome milk; plaintiff failed to prove allegation); Kohlman v. Jefferson Bottling Co., 192 So. 113 (La. App. 1939) (caustic soda allegedly in "Tom Collins, Jr."; plaintiff's story that drink was unwholesome and caused his illness held implausible); Johnson v. Swift & Co., Inc., 186 Miss. 803, 191 So. 423 (1939) (unwholesome sausage-in-oil; insufficient evidence that produce was unwholesome); Walker v. Hickory Packing Co., 220 N.C. 158, 16 S.E.2d 668 (1941) (unwholesome lard; plaintiff retailer was contributorily negligent, failed to show causation or negligence); Walraven v. Sprague, Warner & Co., 235 Wis. 259, 292 N.W. 883 (1940) (contaminated tuna fish and crabmeat; plaintiff failed to show that contamination was not caused after the can was opened); Daniels v. R. White & Sons, Ltd., [1938] 4 All E.R. 258 (K.B.) (carbolic acid in lemonade; defendant's general care negatived negligence); Willis v. Coca Cola Co. of Canada, Ltd., 47 Brit. Col. 481 (1933) (caustic soda in Coca-Cola; defendant's general care negatived negligence).

are correspondingly less, but if he surmounts the difficult causation hurdle he is likely to succeed.[1]

§2.14. Negligence out of causation. It is plain from the reported cases that on evidence tending to show causation, without more, the plaintiff is entitled at least to go to the jury on the issue of negligence.[1] Some courts go farther and recognize a presumption of negligence in the plaintiff's favor, without, however, shifting the burden of proof. Others recognize a presumption and place the burden of proof on the defendant to show that he was careful. (There are also differences respecting the technical effect on the plaintiff's case of the defendant's introduction of evidence of due care.)

The doctrine of *res ipsa loquitur* [2] is invoked in the plain-

§2.13. [1] Parks v. G. C. Yost Pie Co., 93 Kans. 334, 144 Pac. 202 (1914) (ptomaines in pie); Arena v. John P. Squire Co., 321 Mass. 423, 73 N.E.2d 836 (1947) (trichinae in pork); Amabile v. Kramps, 121 N.J.L. 219, 2 A.2d 178 (1938) (unwholesome creamcakes); Hollis v. Armour & Co., 190 S.C. 170, 2 S.E.2d 681 (1939) (contaminated sausage-in-oil; original can opened by retailer). The plaintiff lost in Wilson v. Moore, 159 So. 399 (La. App. 1935) (unwholesome pie; condition attributed to restaurateur's handling); Johnson v. Stoddard, 310 Mass. 232, 37 N.E.2d 505 (1941) (paratyphoid "B" in cream puff; no evidence of negligence); Cudahy Packing Co. v. Baskin, 170 Miss. 834, 155 So. 217 (1934) (unwholesome sausage, carelessly handled by retailer); Sonenthal v. Harry Weinstein & Son, 14 N.J. Misc. 368, 185 Atl. 917 (1936) (poisoned whitefish; the fault may well have been the retailer's); Steinberg v. Bloom, 5 N.Y.S.2d 774 (N.Y.S. Ct. 1938) (unwholesome ice cream; the fault may well have been the retailer's); Mercer v. Rogers, CCH Food Drug Cosmetic Law Serv. ¶18,330 (Tenn. App. 1945) (contaminated chocolate custard pie; the fault may well have been the restaurateur's); Joynes v. Jones Fine Bread Co., 147 S.W.2d 1112 (Tex. Civ. App. 1941) (allegedly unwholesome bread; no negligence found, and no competent evidence that bread was unwholesome).

§2.14. [1] *E.g.*, Watkins v. Dalton Coca-Cola Bottling Co., 66 Ga. App. 848, 19 S.E.2d 316 (1942); Bergantino v. General Baking Co., 298 Mass. 106, 108, 9 N.E.2d 521, 522 (1937) (green scum in pie). For the trichinosis cases, see §2.17 *infra*, note 2.

[2] For the general doctrine of *res ipsa loquitur*, see Carpenter, "The Doc-

tiff's favor in many states but, except for the confusion this heterogeneous Latinism normally injects into any analysis, it adds nothing of substance to what has already been said.[3] In each of the categories described, courts can be found acting under the auspices of *res ipsa loquitur.*[4]

In food cases against the manufacturer, differences in kind of defect have had little effect on the plaintiff's chances of getting to the jury. Human toes in chewing tobacco lift eyebrows higher than do cigarette butts in a soft-drink bottle, but once causation is established, negligence is inferred almost as readily in the latter case as it is in the

---

trine of Res Ipsa Loquitur," 1 U. of Chi. L. Rev. 519 (1934); Heckel and Harper, "Effect of Doctrine of Res Ipsa Loquitur," 22 Ill. L. Rev. 724 (1928); Prosser, "The Procedural Effect of Res Ipsa Loquitur," 20 Minn. L. Rev. 241 (1936); Schneider, "The Presumptive Rule of Negligence or When Do the Facts Speak," 13 B.U.L. Rev. 50 (1933). For the doctrine as applied to suits against the food manufacturer, see King, "Evidence and Presumptions in Food Products Liability," 5 Food Drug Cosmetic L.J. 513, 514 (1950); Note, 23 Ky. L.J. 535 (1935); Comment, 3 Miami L.Q. 613 (1949).

[3] ". . . the Latin tag should be consigned to the legal dustbin." Prosser, *id.* at 271. "The only question normally involved in the cases is as to the weight of evidence. The circumstances may be such that a reasonable man could not draw an inference of negligence or of causation; or that reasonable men could properly either draw or not draw such an inference; or that such an inference is required if no further evidence is introduced. *There is nothing peculiar in the situations in which the phrase is used except the paucity of evidence.*" (Italics added.) Seavey, "Res Ipsa Loquitur: Tabula in Naufragio," 63 Harv. L. Rev. 643 (1950).

[4] Note, 23 Ky. L.J. 535 (1935). One of the strange features of the negligence cases invoking the doctrine of *res ipsa loquitur* is that they rarely indicate expressly what is being established by its application. Presumably it is the defendant's negligence. If the courts are applying the doctrine to arrive at negligence but not to arrive at the intermediate fact of causation, they are proceeding from direct fact A to inferred conclusion X by the device of simple inference, and proceeding the rest of the way to inferred conclusion Y by the magic device of *res ipsa loquitur.* If, on the other hand, they are applying the doctrine to cover the causation point as well, and thus to bridge the whole gap between direct evidence and defendant's liability, why not do the same in the warranty cases? *Cf.* Amarillo Coca-Cola Bottling Co., Inc. v. Loudder, 207 S.W.2d 632, 634 (Tex. Civ. App. 1947).

former. Only the trichinosis and typhoid cases raise a real question here.[5]

§2.15. Negligence and warranty compared. On the basis of the preceding section, it may be asked, what is the essential difference, if any, between suing the manufacturer for negligence and suing him for breach of warranty?

With respect to what the plaintiff has to do to get to the jury, there appears to be no practical difference. In a negligence case the defect must theoretically be such that it would not ordinarily happen except as a result of a negligent act. But in food cases the courts either take this for granted or draw their own conclusions from the nature of the defect without requiring the plaintiff to produce evidence on the point Accordingly, if the defendant puts in no evidence, the plaintiff can expect about the same degree of success whether suing for negligence or breach of warranty. A jury that will find causation between the plaintiff's injury and the defendant's enterprise will as readily make the additional inference of negligence.

The difference, if any, lies in what the defendant can do affirmatively to defeat the plaintiff's case. This is considered in the next section.

§2.16. Evidence of the defendant's due care. One of the commonest defenses is to introduce evidence showing the care the defendant uses in making the product. This evidence is, theoretically, of two kinds. The first kind relates to the specific article causing the plaintiff's injury. Unfortunately, the defendant is almost never able to give an account of what happened in the particular case.[1] Like the

[5] See §2.17 *infra*, note 2.

§2.16. [1] Exception: Johnson v. Stoddard, 310 Mass. 232, 37 N.E.2d 505 (1941) (paratyphoid "B" in cream puff). See also Lovich v. Salvation Army, Inc., 81 Ohio App. 317, 75 N.E.2d 459 (1947) (typhoid germs in orange juice).

plaintiff, he must fall back on circumstantial evidence. The second kind relates to the general program of precautions taken with respect to the product to guard against the kind of injury suffered by the plaintiff. Here the defendant elaborately describes his methods of manufacture (including technological devices for intercepting defects), his inspection programs, and his housekeeping methods.

Evidence such as this may be used, inferentially, to show (1) that the defect could not have occurred at the defendant's plant, or (2) that, even if it did, there was no negligence.

If the evidence is persuasive for the first purpose the defendant wins; but on this basis he would win as readily in a suit pressed on the theory of warranty. It is only if the defendant can win on the basis of the second use that a substantive difference can be made out between the suit in negligence and the suit in warranty. (No significant difference can be spelled out with respect to the effect of the plaintiff's fault.)[2]

The courts are not agreed on the weight they should give a showing of general due care. Suppose this situation: The plaintiff has shown that he was cut by glass fragments while drinking from the defendant's soft-drink bottle. The defendant has shown that he has the most modern bottling plant, that it has every known precautionary device, that he has an elaborate and rigorous program of inspection. Who wins here?

In most cases approximating this situation, the court is willing to let the case go to the jury, and the jury almost always finds for the plaintiff.[3] (Where the jury finds for the

[2] See Chapter I, Topic G.

[3] *E.g.*, Dr. Pepper Co. v. Brittain, 234 Ala. 548, 176 So. 286 (1937); Southwestern Coca Cola Bottling Co. v. Northern, 65 Ariz. 172, 177 P.2d 219 (1947); Coca-Cola Bottling Co. v. Cromwell, 203 Ark. 933, 159 S.W.2d 744 (1942); Coca Cola Bottling Co. of Arkansas v. Morrison, 194

defendant, it is usually because the plaintiff is not telling the truth [4] or was injured from another cause.) [5] Part of this rests on the natural prejudice of juries against presumably rich manufacturers. Part of it rests on good sense.

If the plaintiff has jumped the causation hurdle, it must be assumed that the defect existed at the defendant's factory despite the highest general care which he could exercise. From this, negligence in the particular case may normally be inferred or presumed.[6]

Ark. 248, 106 S.W.2d 601 (1937); Claxton Coca Cola Bottling Co. v. Coleman, 68 Ga. App. 302, 22 S.E.2d 768 (1942); Curtiss Candy Co. v. Johnson, 60 Ga. App. 268, 3 S.E.2d 777 (1939); Duval v. Coca Cola Bottling Co. of Chicago, 329 Ill. App. 290, 68 N.E.2d 479 (1946); Rost v. Kee & Chapell Dairy Co., 216 Ill. App. 497 (1920); Camp v. Homer Coca-Cola Bottling Co., Inc., 20 So.2d 186 (La. App. 1944); Norfolk Coca-Cola Bottling Works v. Krausse, 162 Va. 107, 173 S.E. 497 (1934); Blevins v. Raleigh Coca-Cola Bottling Works, 121 W. Va. 427, 3 S.E.2d 627 (1939); Parr v. Coca-Cola Bottling Works of Charleston, 121 W. Va. 314, 3 S.E.2d 499 (1939); Bissonette v. National Biscuit Co., 100 F.2d 1003 (C.C.A. 2d, 1939); and cases cited in notes 8 and 9 *infra*.

The plaintiff lost in H. J. Heinz Co. v. Fortson, 62 Ga. App. 130, 8 S.E.2d 443 (1940); Stewart v. Natchitoches Coca-Cola Bottling Co., 34 So.2d 281 (La. App. 1948); Swenson v. Purity Baking Co., 183 Minn. 289, 236 N.W. 310 (1931); Smith v. Salem Coca-Cola Bottling Co., Inc., 92 N.H. 97, 25 A.2d 125 (1942); Creswell v. William Gerst Brewing Co., CCH Food Drug Cosmetic Law Serv. ¶18,173 (Tenn. App. 1940); Rogers v. Coca-Cola Bottling Co., 156 S.W.2d 325 (Tex. Civ. App. 1941); Nichols v. Continental Baking Co., 34 F.2d 141 (C.C.A. 3d, 1929); Daniels v. R. White & Sons, Ltd., [1938] 4 All E.R. 258 (K.B.); Mullen v. A. G. Barr & Co., Ltd., [1929] S.C. 461, 467 (Ct. Sess.); Willis v. Coca Cola Co. of Canada, Ltd., 47 Brit. Col. 481 (1933).

[4] The court was suspicious of the plaintiff's story in Moore v. Natchitoches Coca-Cola Bottling Co., 32 So.2d 347 (La. App. 1947); Basile v. World Bottling Co., 17 So.2d 734 (La. App. 1944); Kohlman v. Jefferson Bottling Co., 192 So. 113 (La. App. 1939); Freeman v. Louisiana Coca-Cola Bottling Co., Ltd., 179 So. 621 (La. App. 1938); Eppy v. Chattanooga Coca-Cola Bottling Co., CCH Food Drug Cosmetic Law Serv. ¶18,137 (Tenn. App. 1939).

[5] *E.g.*, Comforto v. Cloverland Dairy Products, 194 So. 43 (La. App. 1940); Coca-Cola Bottling Co. v. Rowland, 16 Tenn. App. 184, 66 S.W.2d 272 (1933); Rogers v. Coca Cola Bottling Co., 156 S.W.2d 325 (Tex. Civ. App. 1941).

[6] Comment, 22 Wash. U.L.Q. 406, 414 (1937), explains a trichinosis

Most of the confusion at this point [7] arises from a failure to distinguish between the general care the defendant exercises over a period of time and over a wide range of operations, and the care he used at the particular time and place. There is also some tendency to forget the normal principles of *respondeat superior*.

The issue is not what happens generally in the defendant's plant but what happened in the particular instance. Evidence that the defendant had installed the most perfect system human ingenuity can devise does not mean that a specific negligent act was not the cause of the plaintiff's injury.[8] Also, the fact that the defendant's management was above reproach does not mean that one of the plant employees did not fall below the legal standard of reasonable conduct in the particular situation.[9]

---

case as going to the defendant because of his showing of general due care. *Quaere* whether the true basis for this decision isn't the fact that trichinae do not ordinarily result from negligence and that, therefore, no negligence is to be inferred from their presence.

[7] *E.g.*, Swenson v. Purity Baking Co., 183 Minn. 289, 236 N.W. 310 (1931); Smith v. Salem Coca-Cola Bottling Co., Inc., 92 N.H. 97, 25 A.2d 125 (1942); Creswell v. William Gerst Brewing Co., CCH Food Drug Cosmetic Law Serv. ¶18,173 (Tenn. App. 1940); Nichols v. Continental Baking Co., 34 F.2d 141 (C.C.A.3d 1929); Daniels v. R. White & Sons, Ltd., [1938] 4 All E.R. 258 (K.B.).

[8] Chaproniere v. Mason, [1905] 21 T.L.R. 633. Some cases go so far as to say that the defendant's proof of general due care, in the light of the fact that the defect somehow got into the product in the particular case, fortifies the inference of negligence. Alabama Coca Cola Bottling Co. v. Causey, 180 So. 588, 590 (Ala. App. 1938), *cert. denied*, 235 Ala. 570, 180 So. 590; Richenbacher v. California Packing Corporation, 250 Mass. 198, 145 N.E. 281 (1924). But *cf.* Mullen v. A. G. Barr & Co., Ltd., [1929] S.C. 461, 467–469 (Ct. Sess.).

[9] Alabama Coca-Cola Bottling Co. v. Causey, 180 So. 588, 590 (Ala. App. 1938), *cert. denied*, 235 Ala. 570, 180 So. 590; Dryden v. Continental Baking Co., 11 Cal. 2d 33, 77 P. 2d 833 (1938); Bagre v. Daggett Chocolate Co., 126 Conn. 659, 13 A.2d 757 (1940); Albany Coca-Cola Bottling Co. v. Shiver, 67 Ga. App. 359, 20 S.E.2d 181 (1942); Rozumailski v. Philadelphia Coca Cola Bottling Co., 296 Pa. 114, 145 Atl. 700 (1929); Newcomb v. Armour & Co., 39 F. Supp. 716 (M.D. Pa. 1941); Lock-

Whose inference is the stronger? Clearly the plaintiff's.[10] If workers are careful most of the time, some probability may exist that they were careful in a particular instance. However, such a probability dissolves when (1) the employees are known to be careless occasionally, and (2) there is evidence that one of them was careless in the particular case. Moreover, no claim that a technological process is 99.99 per cent perfect in excluding defects relates in any significant sense to the cause of defects falling within the .01 per cent area of tolerance. Once causation has been established and the particular event is thus assumed to fall within the area of tolerance inherent in any system, the fact that the area of tolerance is extremely small is irrelevant to the question of what specific forces were at play within that area.[11]

It is commonly said that the food manufacturer is held to a higher standard of care than other manufacturers. As a statement of law with respect to the actions of particular employees in particular situations, it is difficult to evaluate since it is almost never known in what particular respect and to what extent the employee, for whose acts the manufacturer is vicariously accountable, fell below legal minimum standards. As a description of substantive results, it is probably understatement. The jury is normally permitted

hart v. Barr, [1941] S.C. 578 (Ct. Sess.); Mathews v. Coca-Cola Co. of Canada, [1944] 2 D.L.R. 355, O.R. 207, O.W.N. 159, *aff'd*, [1945] 1 D.L.R. 1.

[10] See Minutilla v. Providence Ice Cream Co., 50 R.I. 43, 144 Atl. 884 (1929); Chaproniere v. Mason, [1905] 21 T.L.R. 633; Carpenter, "The Doctrine of Res Ipsa Loquitur," 1 U. of Chi. L. Rev. 519, 534 (1934); Prosser, "The Procedural Effect of Res Ipsa Loquitur," 20 Minn. L. Rev. 241, 269 (1936).

[11] See Davis v. Van Camp Packing Co., 189 Iowa 775, 801, 176 N.W. 382, 392 (1920); Parks v. G. C. Yost Pie Co., 93 Kan. 334, 337, 144 Pac. 202, 203 (1914); Bissonette v. National Biscuit Co., 100 F.2d 1003, 1004 (C.C.A. 2d, 1939).

to, and normally does, infer "negligence" from direct evidence tending to show causation, without regard to the question whether in the particular instance the peculiar circumstances surrounding the defect may, in the light of experience, suggest that that kind of defect is more often the result of culpability than it is the result of pure accident.[12]

The defendant's chances of refuting the general assumption of negligence are best in a trichinosis or typhoid case. Neither defect is ordinarily generated directly by the carelessness of the manufacturer; at best, he can be expected only to take limited precautionary or warning measures.

The main line of attack normally open to the manufacturer is confined to refuting the plaintiff's contention that the defect is physically traceable to the defendant's factory. Apart from privity considerations, this is also his main defense to a warranty action.[13]

§2.17. Proof of negligence, and absolute liability. If the foregoing analysis is correct, any court that raises a causation-based presumption of negligence in the plaintiff's favor is in practical effect creating absolute liability, because even with a wholly logical jury rebuttal is practically impossible. As for the states that raise only a permissible inference, any significant difference between a presumption and permissible inference is fully compensated for by the sympathies of the typical jury.

The proof of the pudding is that the plaintiff who establishes a legal defect plus causation rarely loses. That the

[12] It is sometimes said that the plaintiff must also show that if anyone was negligent it was more probably the defendant than anyone else. Comment, 33 Col. L. Rev. 868, 874 n.36 (1933). But this is ordinarily taken care of by the causation point. The kind of defect also shows it, indirectly, by helping to establish causation. Except as it helps to show causation, the kind of defect is usually ignored.

[13] *E.g.*, see Strawn v. Coca-Cola Bottling Co. of Missouri, 234 S.W.2d 223 (Kan. City Ct. of App., Mo. 1950). See §2.8 *supra*.

courts are imposing virtual absolute liability upon the manufacturer, packer, and processor, while paying lip service to rules of negligence, appears equally from an examination of the cases in which the plaintiff has been unsuccessful. Aside from those in which he loses (or a new trial is granted) for procedural reasons, the plaintiff finds that the crucial point of his case is the establishment not of negligence but of a chain of causation between his stomach and the defendant.

North Carolina purports to require a showing of actual negligence accomplished (in the absence of other evidence) by introducing one or more similar instances of defective products traceable to the defendant.[1] Unless significant in number or closely bunched, these instances have no real probative force on the issue of negligence because even the most perfect care will not exclude all defects, and to show that the area of tolerance permits more than one defect in a given period of time proves nothing about carelessness in the specific case. The requirement is believed to be not only unhelpful but unfortunately onerous because it imposes on otherwise deserving plaintiffs a burden of proof heavier than they can ordinarily sustain.

Outside of North Carolina only a few reported cases have denied recovery solely because actual negligence has not been proved.[2] Cases like *Curtis* v. *Akron Coca-Cola Bottling*

§2.17. [1] *E.g.*, Thompson v. Dr. Pepper Bottlers Corp., 217 N.C. 795, 8 S.E.2d 234 (1940); Evans v. Charlotte Pepsi-Cola Bottling Co., 216 N.C. 716, 6 S.E.2d 510 (1940); Tickle v. Hobgood, 216 N.C. 221, 4 S.E.2d 444 (1939); Smith v. Coca-Cola Bottling Co. of Henderson, 213 N.C. 544, 196 S.E. 822 (1938); Breece v. Asheville Coca-Cola Bottling Co., 212 N.C. 388, 193 S.E. 269 (1937); Coca-Cola Bottling Co. of Henderson v. Munn, 99 F.2d 190 (C.C.A. 4th, 1938). See Note, 40 Mich. L. Rev. 928 (1942). But *cf.* Parsonnet v. Keil's Newark Bakery, Inc., 119 N.J.L. 301, 196 Atl. 661 (1938).

On "safety history" generally, see Morris, "Proof of Safety History in Negligence Cases," 61 Harv. L. Rev. 205, 225 (1948).

[2] The clearest case involving a manufacturer seems to be Nichols v. Continental Baking Co., 34 F.2d 141 (C.C.A. 3d, 1929) (cockroach in

Co., [8] holding that the mere fact of the plaintiff's injury from a defect in the defendant's product proves nothing in itself, go off as readily on the ground that the plaintiff has failed to show that the defect was in the product when it left the defendant's control.

---

bread). Here the court apparently took for granted that the cockroach was baked into the bread by the defendant, but in view of the general high standards maintained by the defendant it held that there was insufficient evidence of negligence to go to the jury. To like effect: Creswell v. William Gerst Brewing Co., CCH Food Drug Cosmetic Law Serv. ¶18,173 (Tenn. App. 1940).

In Smith v. Salem Coca Cola Bottling Co., Inc., 92 N.H. 97, 25 A.2d 125 (1942) (glass in Coca-Cola), the court held that on the basis of the defendant's deposition with respect to its program of general care no inference of negligence could be drawn. The case is not clean-cut because it is not clear that causation had been made out.

Johnson v. Stoddard, 310 Mass. 232, 37 N.E.2d 505 (1941) (paratyphoid "B" in cream puff), is almost unique in that the defendant was able to show the specific source of the difficulty, establishing that the particular carrier was not discovered until after the plaintiff's infection. And see Lovich v. Salvation Army, Inc., 81 Ohio App. 317, 75 N.E.2d 459 (1947).

In the two following cases the courts talked in terms of no showing of negligence, but in indicating that the source of defect was a mystery suggested that they were as much troubled by the question of causation. Swenson v. Purity Baking Co., 183 Minn. 289, 236 N.W. 310 (1931); Walker v. Hickory Packing Co., 220 N.C. 158, 16 S.E.2d 668 (1941).

The following cases are inconclusive because they also rest on the ground that the plaintiff failed to make out a case of causation (want of causation is enough in itself to negative negligence). Coca-Cola Bottling Co. v. Rowland, 16 Tenn. App. 184, 66 S.W.2d 272 (1933); Joynes v. Jones Fine Bread Co., 147 S.W.2d 1112 (Tex. Civ. App. 1941).

The trichinosis cases are *sui generis*. The following cases barred recovery because the plaintiff failed to show negligence. However, the results can also be rationalized on the ground that there is no causation in such cases, the trichinae having entered the hogs before they reached the defendant. Cheli v. Cudahy Bros. Co., 267 Mich. 690, 255 N.W. 414 (1934) (trichinae in sausage); Lucey v. Harstedt, 270 App. Div. 900, 61 N.Y.S.2d 157 (2d Dept. 1946) (trichinae in fresh pork); Tavani v. Swift & Co., 262 Pa. 184, 105 Atl. 55 (1918) (trichinae in pork); Ketterer v. Armour & Co. 247 Fed. 921 (C.C.A. 2d, 1917) (trichinae in lachshinken); Yachetti v. John Duff & Sons Ltd., [1943] 1 D.L.R. 194, [1942] O.R. 682, [1942] O.W.N. 639 (trichinae in sausage). For a general discussion of trichinae, see Chapter IV, Topic B.

[8] CCH Food Drug Cosmetic Law Serv. ¶18,102 (Ohio App., 9th Jud. Dist. 1939).

§2.18. Absolute liability under a fiction of negligence. So far, this discussion has dealt with courts that have handled the matter as a true negligence problem. To be contrasted is the occasional court that apparently imposes absolute liability under cover of a fiction of negligence.[1] The practical results are usually the same, but the legal approach is different. The former attempts to litigate actual negligence. The latter is absolute liability *as if* negligence were present (quasi-negligence). The difference lies in keeping the door open to the defendant to use whatever rare opportunity he can discover to show that the specific defect was accidental or that that kind of defect is usually accidental. Even here the practical difference is narrowed by any prejudice the jury may have against manufacturers.

The line between absolute liability and liability based on culpability is hard to draw. Liability for injuries incurred is absolute with respect to a particular kind of defect when it is made to depend solely on the existence of the defect. It is based on culpability when it is made to depend upon the defendant's failure to meet an accepted or prescribed standard of conduct which is reasonably attainable and which, if attained, normally intercepts the defect. When the presence of the defect is defined in terms of a reasonably attainable standard of conduct of the defendant, or vice versa, the two concepts merge. The right of the defendant to rely on the plaintiff's meeting a reasonably attainable standard of conduct is a related factor.

Public policy must ultimately determine whether the food manufacturer is to be legally responsible for particular kinds

§2.18. [1] Parks v. G. C. Yost Pie Co., 93 Kan. 334, 144 Pac. 202, 203 (1914); Jackson Coca-Cola Bottling Co. v. Chapman, 106 Miss. 864, 64 So. 791 (1914). *Cf.*: Escola v. Coca Cola Bottling Co. of Fresno, 24 Cal. 2d 453, 150 P.2d 436 (1944) (concurring opinion of Traynor, J.); Darks v. Scudder-Gale Grocer Co., 146 Mo. App. 246, 130 S.W. 430 (1910).

of defects (such as trichinae in pork) which he can neither prevent nor discover, or which he can prevent or discover only by taking extraordinary or unreasonable precautions. If such a responsibility is to be imposed, absolute liability (whether naked or dressed as "promise," "representation," or "negligence") is necessarily adopted without restriction. If such a responsibility is not to be imposed, the result is attained either by (1) applying the orthodox theory of negligence (which leaves the door only slightly ajar), or (2), as a possible alternative, adopting absolute liability as a general theory but defining "defect" so as to exclude these kinds of defects. The latter approach washes out the fatuous trying of issues relating to what happened in particular cases while protecting the manufacturer in the situation supposed.[2]

§2.19. Violation of pure food law. Where the defendant's action in selling food violates a pure food statute, the plaintiff's burden of establishing liability on the basis of "negligence" is theoretically eased.[1] Whether or not a

[2] It has been suggested that another basis for calling the manufacturer to account, in some cases, is negligent advertising. Note, 22 Wash. U.L.Q. 406, 410 (1937). Cases using this approach include Crist v. Art Metal Works, 230 App. Div. 114, 243 N.Y. Supp. 496 (1st Dept. 1930) ("absolutely harmless" toy gun); Henry v. Crook, 202 App. Div. 19, 195 N.Y. Supp. 642 (3d Dept. 1922) ("harmless" sparklers); Rosenbusch v. Ambrosia Milk Corp., 181 App. Div. 97, 168 N.Y. Supp. 505 (1st Dept. 1917) ("absolutely safe" dried milk product); Marsh v. Usk Hardware Co., 73 Wash. 543, 132 Pac. 241 (1913) ("absolutely safe" explosive). See E. I. DuPont de Nemours v. Baridon, 73 F.2d 26 (C.C.A. 8th, 1934) (plant disinfectant). However, these cases deal only with the negligent misrepresentation of the inherent characteristics of the product. Presumably they have no bearing on exceptional lapses from wholesomeness not common to the product or brand.

§2.19. [1] Criswell Baking Co. v. Milligan, 77 Ga. App. 861, 50 S.E.2d 136 (1948); Shindelus v. Sevcik, 211 Minn. 432, 1 N.W.2d 399 (1941); Meshbesher v. Channellene Oil & Manufacturing Co., 107 Minn. 104, 119 N.W. 428 (1909); Catalanello v. Cudahy Packing Co., 264 App. Div. 723, 34 N.Y.S.2d 37 (2d Dept. 1942); McKenzie v. Peoples Baking Co., 205 S.C. 149, 31 S.E.2d 154 (1944); Caines v. Marion Coca-Cola Bot-

given sale by a manufacturer violates the local pure food law depends of course upon the nature of the proscribed defects and whether or not knowledge of the defect is a prerequisite. The application of the doctrine of negligence per se to the manufacturer probably offers no complications that are not involved also in the case of the retailer.[2]

TOPIC C. *Some Considerations of Public Policy Relating to Manufacturers' Responsibility*

§2.20. Arguments for absolute liability. States that require privity of contract in warranty actions do so on technical legal grounds, ordinarily without the buttressing of "public policy" considerations. Recovery in negligence, resting on orthodox theories of culpability, likewise calls for little policy discussion, even though the results approach absolute accountability. The few states that have done away with privity have done so partly because privity is not

---

tling Co., 198 S.C. 204, 17 S.E.2d 315 (1941); Haley v. Swift & Co., 152 Wis. 570, 140 N.W. 292 (1913). See Gray v. Pet Milk Co., 108 F.2d 974 (C.C.A. 7th, 1940). But *cf.* Cheli v. Cudahy Bros. Co., 267 Mich. 690, 255 N.W. 414 (1934); Square v. Model Farm Dairies (Bournemouth), Ltd., [1939] 2 K.B. 365, 1 All E.R. 259, 55 T.L.R. 384, 83 Sol. J. 152; Yachetti v. John Duff & Sons Ltd., [1943] 1 D.L.R. 194, [1942] O.R. 682, [1942] O.W.N. 639.

The plaintiff lost in Pierce v. City Baking Co., 28 Ohio L. Abs. 503 (Ohio App., 9th Jud. Dist. 1938) (roach in bread; plaintiff failed to show that bread was deleterious to the health of persons generally); Leonardi v. A. Habermann Provision Co., 143 Ohio St. 623, 56 N.E.2d 232 (1944) (trichinae in pork butt; plaintiff contributorily negligent).

[2] The doctrine is discussed in Note, 15 B.U.L. Rev. 851 (1935); Comment, 4 Ford. L. Rev. 520 (1935); Note, 14 St. John's L. Rev. 110, 119 (1939); Note, 10 St. John's L. Rev. 336 (1936); Note, 22 Wash. U.L.Q. 405, 412 (1937). The New York Agriculture and Markets Law is discussed in Wolfram, "Proof of Manufacturer's Care in Food Products Liability Cases in New York," 122 N.Y.L.J. 1786, 1802 (1949).

technically or historically necessary but largely because policy considerations are said to require absolute liability. However, most of the policy considerations relating to the liability of the food [1] manufacturer have been outlined, not in the reported cases, but in the texts and law reviews.

There appear to be two of these policy considerations: (1) Manufacturers' liability tends to correct the evil at its source. (2) Such a liability provides a kind of consumer insurance whereby the aggregate of people consuming the particular product, by paying slightly higher prices, share the financial burdens caused by defective food products.[2] This is commonly called "spreading" the risk or loss.

The liability of the manufacturer has also received a strong practical boost from the general assumption that manufacturers as a class are financially well-heeled. For the most part, this is an extralegal consideration but it has helped, at least in jury cases, to produce a large number of substantial judgments. Legally, the financial standing of manufacturers-in-general is relevant only as it signifies the economic capacity of this group to accomplish either of these two objectives.[3]

The existing case law indicates that only a few courts are willing openly to espouse absolute liability, but most text and law-review writers agree that, for one or both of the

§2.20. [1] There has been some discussion as to whether food is properly treated as a category apart. *E.g.*, Llewellyn, "On Warranty of Quality, and Society, II," 37 Col. L. Rev. 341, 404 (1937); Comment, 4 Ford. L. Rev. 295, 304, 306 (1935); Note, 21 Minn. L. Rev. 315, 317 n.11 (1937).

[2] Llewellyn, Cases and Materials on the Law of Sales 341 n.5 (1930); Note, 7 Wash. L. Rev. 351 (1932). See also Feezer, "Tort Liability of Manufacturers," 10 Minn. L. Rev. 1, 5 (1925).

[3] This is what Feezer apparently means by "capacity to bear loss." Feezer, "Capacity to Bear Loss as a Factor in the Decision of Certain Types of Tort Cases," 78 U. of Pa. L. Rev. 805, 811 (1930). Feezer's phrase is misleading since "bearing loss" normally connotes absorption of the loss, not passing it on.

reasons stated, absolute manufacturer liability is desirable in food cases.[4]

There are two separate issues here: (1) Should the manufacturer bear the final burden of liability where the defect is traceable to the product in his hands? (2) If so, should the manufacturer be *directly* liable to the consumer?

It is possible to impose absolute liability on the manufacturer with the ultimate legal benefit accruing to the injured consumer without doing away with privity.[5] This is by a chain of buyer-seller actions against the retailer, the respective intermediate distributors, and the manufacturer. Because such a result can be reached by orthodox methods without referring to public policy considerations, most policy arguments for holding the manufacturer absolutely accountable have been advanced as part of the groundwork for doing away with the privity requirement.

The argument against privity, of course, is that the courts should avoid circuity of action where the manufacturer is in fact accessible to the consumer.[6] Unnecessary circuity wastes time and money. Besides, a broken link means a broken chain.[7]

Most of the arguments on both points have been rudimentary. For example, on the first point Perkins says, "Since he [the manufacturer] is in a much better position to know the condition of his food and to guard against impurities than is the ordinary dealer, the liability without fault imposed upon the latter for the protection of lives and health

[4] Most writers like the implied warranty theory (minus privity requirements). An exception is Clark, who plumps for absolute tort liability à la squib. "Let the Maker Beware," 19 St. John's L. Rev. 85, 93 (1945).

[5] Even the privity states admit that the manufacturer should be liable, at least when they apply the sealed container exception to the retailer. Note, 7 Wash. L. Rev. 351, 358 (1932).

[6] Comment, 33 Col. L. Rev. 868, 869 n.7 (1933).

[7] Note, 42 Harv. L. Rev. 414, 418 (1929).

of the public, may with greater reason be extended to the former."[8] On the second he says, ". . . it would be a reproach to the law if the one ultimately answerable could not be held directly responsible by the person injured . . ."[9]

Most writers do not distinguish between avoidable and unavoidable defects. If a defect is avoidable, at least in the sense that vigilance will help to reduce the risk, it seems reasonable to assume that liability furnishes an incentive to be vigilant. What about pure accidents, or defects (like trichinae in pork) that are probably unavoidable, at least by the manufacturer? Besides the trichinosis (and possibly the typhoid) cases, there are very few defects that can be put into classes that do not also include avoidable or reducible risks. Even where such categories do exist, the other rationale can be brought into play: The financial burden of unavoidable injuries can be shared by consumers by the device of spreading the risk or loss through increased manufacturer's prices. Besides, risks that are unavoidable as a class (by the manufacturer) are usually attributable to the manufacturer's suppliers, employees, or other third parties he deals with. Here liability tends to result in pressure by the manufacturer on the person ultimately at the root of the trouble.

Although the phrases "spreading the risk" and "spreading the loss" are often used interchangeably, there are two different ideas here. "Spreading the risk" seems the better description where the manufacturer raises (or refrains from lowering) prices to pay for the cost of improving the product or adopting precautionary devices. That is, it relates to spreading the cost of prevention. "Spreading the loss,"

[8] Perkins, "Unwholesome Food as a Source of Liability," 5 Iowa L. Bull. 86, 95 (1920).
[9] *Id.* at 87.

on the other hand, seems more apt where the manufacturer raises (or refrains from lowering) prices to cover liability losses or insurance premiums.[10] Prevention and risk-spreading are concomitant objectives, but prevention and loss-spreading tend to be alternative. The incentive to improve, flowing from liability, is the incentive to increase or maintain profits. Liability threatens profits only where its cost cannot be passed on in the form of higher prices. Therefore, to the extent that there is incentive to improve, there tends to be no loss-spreading. Conversely, to the extent that there is loss-spreading, there tends to be no incentive to improve.[11]

In the abstract, prevention is naturally to be preferred to indemnification, even where the costs of indemnification are widely distributed. This notion is undoubtedly shared by manufacturers. But how a manufacturer reacts to a specific situation depends for the most part upon the relative costs

[10] Compare the approach of Douglas, "Vicarious Liability and the Administration of Risk," 38 Yale L.J. 584, 720 (1929), where risk administration is broken down into four basic concepts. Douglas distinguishes "risk avoidance" (not undertaking the activity) from "risk prevention" (undertaking it but with precautions against injury). In contrast, the text lumps the two under the single tag "prevention," since to separate out avoidance serves no purpose here. He uses the term "risk shifting" to cover any arrangement, such as insurance, by which the seller gets another person to assume the risk of financial loss from personal injury, whereas, on the assumption that this is of secondary importance and not necessarily desirable, the text talks simply about buying insurance. He uses the term "risk distribution" to cover what the text calls "spreading the loss" (distributing liability losses or insurance costs). Douglas apparently ignores what the text calls "spreading the risk" (distributing the cost of preventive measures). This is surprising because he is careful to include distributing the cost of insurance protection under "risk distribution." However, the omission does no real harm since risks and losses are spread through the same people, in the same way, and frequently in the same transactions.

[11] The tendency, however, is not fully realized. If the manufacturer insures, his insurer will ordinarily encourage him to take all reasonable precautions.

of incurring the liability and adopting improved manufacturing and housekeeping methods, taking into account such factors as the effect on good will. Presumably a manufacturer will not adopt costly precautionary measures unless their cost is offset by the sum of the following: (1) the anticipated savings in products liability claims (or insurance premiums), (2) the increase in returns anticipated from reasonably attainable price increases, and (3) the increase in returns anticipated from increased physical volume, with its accompanying savings in per-unit indirect costs. However, since the manufacturer's ability to increase prices is the same whether or not liability is imposed, no real financial incentive exists unless the cost of the precautionary measures is substantially less than the sum of (1) and (3) alone. In any event, the higher the potential liability risk, the more the manufacturer is financially prodded to adopt improved methods.

§2.21. Arguments against absolute liability. Taking an affirmative stand against absolute liability is the great body of authority that requires privity of contract and imposes liability under the guise of orthodox negligence. The maintenance of the *status quo* has made it unnecessary to appeal to considerations of public policy. Even so, several such considerations have been advanced against openly espousing absolute liability directly to the consumer.

One argument against absolute liability has been the danger of encouraging fraudulent claims.[1] (The same argument would also apply to the absolute liability of the

§2.21. [1] *E.g.*, Condon, "The Practical Impact of the Proposed Uniform Commercial Code on Food Poisoning Cases," 5 Food Drug Cosmetic L.J. 213, 229 (1950); Comment, 33 Col. L. Rev. 868, 869 n.7 (1933); Comment, 4 Ford. L. Rev. 295, 306 (1935).

On the other hand, it has been said that "There appears to be no more litigation on this subject in jurisdictions that have dispensed with privity." Comment, 23 Calif. L. Rev. 621, 626 (1935). This observation,

retailer.) Not significantly persuasive to the courts, this argument has received only passing attention in the texts and law reviews and in most cases it has been given small weight. Its merits are discussed in Chapter V, Section 5.14.

Also occasionally met is the argument that improvement in quality standards is better handled by direct government regulation in the form of tighter food laws, direct government inspection, and enforcement sanctions. This view received classic expression by Judge Augustus Hand in *Valeri* v. *Pullman Co.*[2] It does not necessarily deny the efficacy of the civil action for preventive purposes but it relegates it to a secondary place and thus removes much of the incentive for doing away with privity requirements or for otherwise changing the *status quo.* It has been widely criticized.[3]

Pound has attacked absolute tort liability for the manufacturer as a civil "welfare" measure, a form of social control that would be better handled by direct government action under adequate legislation. This kind of court-made "humanitarianism," he says, assumes that "losses and injuries without fault of anyone, which are part of the ordinary experience of life in society, will be borne ultimately by society through imposing liability for damages upon those able

---

made by a student editor, was apparently more of a visceral reaction than a scientific conclusion.

"The problem is not the strictness of liability, but the age-old one of distinguishing truth from falsehood." King, "Evidence and Presumptions in Food Products Liability," 5 Food Drug Cosmetic L.J. 513, 528 (1950).

[2] 218 Fed. 519 (S.D.N.Y. 1914).

[3] *E.g.*, Wasserman, "Commentary on Diners' Protection," 61 N.J.L.J. 57, 59 (1938). See also authorities cited §1.28 *supra*, note 24. Agreement with Hand is found in Condon, "The Practical Impact of the Proposed Uniform Commercial Code on Food Poisoning Cases," 5 Food Drug Cosmetic L.J. 213, 218–221 (1950).

immediately to bear them and to recoup them from the public . . . through including them in prices charged for manufactured products." [4]

But the kind of absolute liability described here is not being imposed by the courts, and no one has even urged that it be imposed.[5] It omits the important condition that the defendant must have caused the defect [6] and gives no weight

[4] "Newer Ideas of Liability," 123 N.Y.L.J. 523, 524 (1950). Pound dismisses the idea that the costs of absolute liability are actually passed along to the consumer, but his supporting reasons relate only to public utilities. These views are restated by Pound in "Law in the Service State: Freedom *versus* Equality," 36 A.B.A.J. 977, 981 (1950).

[5] Pound apparently attributes such a position to the concurring opinion of Traynor, J., in Escola v. Coca Cola Bottling Co. of Fresno, 24 Cal. 2d. 453, 150 P.2d 436 (1944). The context suggests, however, that the judge was preoccupied with dispensing with negligence and not with dispensing with causation as well.

Even if I have misinterpreted Pound, there is a recent tendency to identify absolute liability with absolute liability for defects caused by later handlers. Note 6 *infra* and see Mintener, "Report on 1950 Developments in Product Liability Law," 6 Food Drug Cosmetic L.J. 225, 227–228 (1951).

[6] One recent writer believes that he has found confirmation of Pound's views in certain medical experience with meat poisoning. Condon, "The Practical Impact of the Proposed Uniform Commercial Code on Food Poisoning Cases," 5 Food Drug Cosmetic L.J. 213, 229 (1950). The great bulk of this is said to be traceable to staphylococcus bacteria. The fact that dangerous propagation of this kind normally results from exposing cooked food to the air at medium room temperatures suggests that, for packaged foods at least, the particular trouble results more often from the careless distributor or consumer than from the careless manufacturer. However, experience with a limited class of food defects is hardly a reliable basis for conclusions respecting unwholesome food generally. Moreover, if manufacturers (who for the most part are already subject to absolute liability) are being harassed by spurious staphylococcus claims, the fact does not appear from the reported court cases, since civil cases expressly involving staphylococcus are extremely rare. If, on the other hand, many or most of the reported cases that involve a latent food defect are in fact staphylococcus cases, the fact more plausibly suggests that the real difficulty lies with defense counsel who are remiss in educating the courts on the causes and avoidance of food poisoning. Certainly, no responsible authority contends that the manufacturer should stand a loss that is attributable solely to later handlers.

Further indication of the high incidence of staphylococcus is found in

to the idea that liability so restricted helps to prevent or lessen defects.

If Pound's contentions are apt, they should apply also to warranty suits. Possibly to avoid inconsistency, he dismisses as historically and analytically unsound the devices courts have built to bridge the privity gap. But the problem of privity, which is simply the problem of circuity, must not be confused with the more fundamental question whether, privity or no privity, the manufacturer should bear the ultimate burden of liability for defects of which he is the innocent author. Even under the most conservative approaches to warranty, the manufacturer has long been absolutely accountable to the consumer; directly, when he acts also as retailer, and indirectly, through a chain of actions, when the goods reach the consumer through intermediate handlers. Absolute liability of the manufacturer, therefore, cannot be treated simply as a new and abnormal outgrowth of tort law divorced from warranty.

Topic D. *Liability of the Wholesaler* *

§2.22. Special position of the wholesaler. Of all the sellers the consumer might want to reach, the wholesaler is the most elusive. Since he does not deal directly with the consumer he is protected from conventional warranty actions by the lack of privity.[1] Since he does not create the

---

Ranz, "The Liability of Manufacturers in and the Defense of Food Poisoning Cases," 23 Ohio Bar 371, 373 (1950).

* There is a general discussion of this topic in Comment, 7 J.B.A. Kan. 183 (1938). In this section the term "wholesaler" will be used loosely to refer to any distributor who does not sell directly to the consumer.

§2.22. [1] De Gouveia v. H. D. Lee Mercantile Co., 231 Mo. App. 447, 100 S.W.2d 336 (1937); Howson v. Foster Beef Co., 87 N.H. 200, 177 Atl. 656 (1935); Cornelius v. B. Filippone & Co., Inc., 119 N.J.L. 540,

product, which is usually packaged, he is relatively immune from an action for negligence.[2] Briefly, the wholesaler is almost invulnerable to suit by the consumer so long as he remains purely a distributor.

§2.23. The wholesaler in the shoes of the manufacturer. If the wholesaler passes off a product as having been made by him, the courts treat him as if he were the manufacturer.[1] Here there is vicarious liability founded on representation. The problem is raised by wholesalers who sell, under their own private brand names, goods made by others. Most branding wholesalers show on the label that they are distributors by prefacing their names with "Packed for," adding the description "Distributors," or including similar material. (The manufacturer's name is almost never mentioned.) The question arises as to when such language is sufficient to preserve the seller's position as wholesaler.

In *Swift & Co.* v. *Blackwell*,[2] the Swift company was held liable in negligence for defective food packed for it by Libby. The word "Distributor" followed the Swift name in small letters but elsewhere on the can and in the advertising the

---

197 Atl. 647 (1938); Hopkins v. Amtorg Trading Corp., 265 App. Div. 278, 38 N.Y.S.2d 788 (1st Dept. 1942).

The defendant was apparently a wholesaler in Mellace v. John P. Squire Co., 306 Mass. 515, 29 N.E.2d 26 (1940). If so, this case also is in point.

[2] Flaccomio v. Eysink, 129 Md. 367, 100 Atl. 510 (1916); Elmore v. Grenada Grocery Co., 189 Miss. 370, 197 So. 761 (1940); Cornelius v. B. Filippone & Co., Inc., 119 N.J.L. 540, 197 Atl. 647 (1938); Hopkins v. Amtorg Trading Corp., 265 App. Div. 278, 38 N.Y.S.2d 788 (1st Dept. 1942); Singer v. Zabelin, 24 N.Y.S.2d 962 (N.Y. City Ct. 1941).

§2.23. [1] Restatement, Torts §400 (1934) provides: "One who puts out as his own product a chattel manufactured by another is subject to the same liability as though he were its manufacturer." See Thornhill v. Carpenter-Morton Co., 270 Mass. 593, 108 N.E. 474 (1915) (nonfood case); Darks v. Scudders-Gale Grocer Co., 146 Mo. App. 246, 130 S.W. 430 (1910).

[2] 84 F.2d 130 (C.C.A. 4th, 1936).

word "Swift" was played up to give what the court felt was an over-all impression that the product was a Swift product and therefore manufactured by it. Accordingly, where the wholesaler's name is used as the brand name, it is generally held that the defendant stands in the shoes of the manufacturer, even though he describes himself as "Distributor" on the package.[3] Whether the words "Packed for" are a better protection to the seller is not clear.[4]

The identification of the wholesaler with the particular product is less obvious where the name of the brand is not the name of the wholesaler. In *Slavin* v. *Francis H. Leggett & Co.*,[5] the trade name was "Premier." The can also bore the defendant's name and the description "Distributor." The court apparently assumed that the ownership of the brand name was thereby plainly shown on the face of the can. On the ground that the description "Distributor" did not rule out manufacture by the defendant, the court held the defendant liable for the manufacturer's negligence. In *Fleetwood* v. *Swift & Co.*,[6] a Georgia court reached the oppo-

[3] Burkhardt v. Armour & Co., 115 Conn. 249, 161 Atl. 385 (1932) (negligence); Swift & Co. v. Hawkins, 174 Miss. 253, 164 So. 231 (1935) (negligence); Hunter v. Derby Foods, Inc., CCH Food Drug Cosmetic Law Serv. ¶18,077 (S.D.N.Y. 1938) (negligence), *aff'd*, 110 F.2d 970 (C.C.A. 2d, 1940).

[4] In Armour & Co. v. Leasure, 177 Md. 393, 9 A.2d 572 (1940), the wholesaler was held liable in negligence. On the other hand, in De Gouveia v. H. D. Lee Mercantile Co., 231 Mo. App. 447, 450, 100 S.W.2d 336, 338 (1937), the wholesaler was excused. The court distinguished the Slavin and Hawkins cases on the ground that the present suit was for breach of warranty, not negligence. It said that Section 400 of the Restatement of Torts did not apply because the words "packed for" negatived the idea that the defendant was the packer. The distinction between warranty and negligence does not seem to be relevant under Section 400. See Walker v. Great Atlantic & Pacific Tea Co., 131 Tex. 57, 112 S.W.2d 170 (1938) (branding retailer held in warranty).

[5] 114 N.J.L. 421, 177 Atl. 120 (1935), *aff'd*, 117 N.J.L. 101, 186 Atl. 832 (1936).

[6] 27 Ga. App. 502, 506, 108 S.E. 909, 911 (1921).

site result because the evidence did not show that the brand was the defendant's. Even so, it granted the plaintiff a new trial, saying that it was up to the defendant "to exculpate itself" by showing that it had bought from a reputable manufacturer, since there was nothing on the package to indicate who, as manufacturer, was responsible.

Theoretically, putting the wholesaler in the shoes of the manufacturer has no legal consequences unless the manufacturer himself is shown to be responsible. In warranty cases causation is a problem, and in negligence cases the plaintiff also has the burden of showing culpability. Where the manufacturer is in Argentina the task of establishing this responsibility might seem formidable. Practically, it has not been so. An Ohio plaintiff by-passed the Argentina problem altogether by showing the wholesaler's own "negligence" from a violation of the pure food law.[7] Two cases inferred the manufacturer's negligence from the fact of causation.[8] Three others simply ignored the problem.[9] In net result the difference between negligence and breach of warranty is, once more, hardly discernible.

The foregoing cases rest largely on estoppel or misrepresentation. If this is the sole test for dealing with the branding wholesaler, difficult problems arise where the ownership of the brand name, on which the representation of manufacture is based, can be established only by extrinsic factors. Suppose, for example, the package carries the brand name "Premier" without further identification. Here the buying public would be unlikely to associate the brand name with

[7] Hunter v. Derby Foods, Inc., 110 F.2d 970 (C.C.A. 2d, 1940).

[8] Armour & Co. v. Leasure, 177 Md. 393, 9 A.2d 572 (1940); Swift & Co. v. Blackwell, 84 F.2d 130 (C.C.A. 4th, 1936).

[9] Burkhardt v. Armour & Co., 115 Conn. 249, 161 Atl. 385 (1932); Swift & Co. v. Hawkins, 174 Miss. 253, 164 So. 231 (1935); Slavin v. Francis H. Leggett & Co., 114 N.J.L. 421, 177 Atl. 120 (1935), *aff'd*, 117 N.J.L. 101, 186 Atl. 832 (1936).

the wholesaler, because it generally thinks of the sponsor of a brand name (however anonymous) as being its manufacturer. It is doubtful that a misrepresentation or estoppel could be spelled out here. So far, no reported food case has dealt with this situation. Branded food products that carry no sponsor's name are, fortunately, very rare.

The situation just supposed raises the general question whether the estoppel or misrepresentation approach is sufficiently broad to explain all the cases. A suggestion that it may not be is found in cases that rest liability, at least in part, on the fact that the branding wholesaler has suppressed the identity of the manufacturer.[10] Here the emphasis is on considerations other than passing off.

§2.24. The wholesaler as brand owner. There is some talk that mere ownership of the brand should be enough to support liability. This is based on the relatively sophisticated assumption that

> The large wholesaler who brands the products of various small manufacturers and sells them as his own, is in a position to gain market control through the integration of manufacturing with marketing. Such a wholesaler is very apt to control production and may even maintain an inspector at the establishment of the manufacturer.[1]

Such a view puts the same economic evaluation on a branding wholesaler as it does on a manufacturer. It assumes that there is a substantial correlation between brand ownership and economic domination of the channels of manufacturing and distribution. It implies that in these situations liability should ultimately rest on the wholesaler,

[10] Burkhardt v. Armour & Co., 115 Conn. 249, 161 Atl. 385 (1932). See Comment, 7 J.B.A. Kan. 183, 186 (1938).

§2.24. [1] Note, 2 Mo. L. Rev. 235, 238 (1937).

not the offending manufacturer. No court has rested liability on this ground.

§2.25. The wholesaler as wholesaler. Even where the wholesaler neither claims to be the manufacturer nor owns the brand, there is an incipient realization that he may be a useful object of liability in making the manufacturer more accessible to the consumer. The wholesaler short cut reduces circuity of action and, to the same extent, removes the risk that intermediate financial irresponsibility or physical remoteness will break the chain of actual accountability.

In *Swengel* v. *F. & E. Wholesale Grocery Co.*,[1] the Kansas Supreme Court held a wholesaler liable directly to a consumer for breach of warranty of sauer kraut juice despite the facts that the product was packed by Libby, the label was Libby's and not the defendant's, there was no privity of contract between the defendant and the consumer, and the product was packed in an uninspectable sealed container. This was the most drastic liability ever imposed in a consumer case. The court said:

> . . . it seems illogical to hold that the injured consumer might maintain an action against the immediate seller or the manufacturer or packer, but not against the intermediate purchasers and sellers of the articles of food. To so hold would mean that if the immediate seller were financially irresponsible, and the packer, for instance, were located in a foreign country, the injured consumer would, from a practical standpoint, be without remedy.

The way had been paved by an earlier Kansas case whose implications might have been even more sensational had the warranty issues been raised more directly. In *Challis* v. *Hartloff*,[2] a consumer sued a retailer, a "broker," and a manufacturer. The court held that the plaintiff's suit against

§2.25. [1] 147 Kan. 555, 561, 77 P.2d 930, 935 (1938).
[2] 136 Kan. 823, 18 P.2d 199 (1933).

the manufacturer was barred by the statute of limitations. In reaching this result it said that the warranty obligations of the retailer and "broker" (against whom the action was timely) were separate from the warranty obligation of the manufacturer (against whom the action was not timely) and could not be used as a basis for sustaining the suit against the manufacturer. One interesting feature of the case is that it seems to say that even a food broker is accountable directly to the consumer. A broker is normally agent of the seller, without title to the goods. To hold such a seller liable in warranty, especially where there is no privity of contract, would extend the consumer's civil protection about as far as it could go. However, the statement of facts says that the "broker" had purchased the goods from the manufacturer and sold them to the retailer. This suggests that he may have been a distributor in the more orthodox sense.

Despite these cases, the weight of authority supports the privity requirement.[3] Missouri is unique in that although a lower court has dropped privity as against the manufacturer,[4] it has retained it as against the wholesaler.[5] Whether other courts now dispensing with privity as against the manufacturer will follow the Kansas court or the Missouri court, when dealing with the wholesaler, remains to be seen.

TOPIC E. *The Problem of Classification*

§2.26. Who are "manufacturers" or "distributors"? The foregoing discussion has presumed a sharp dichotomy

[3] See §2.1 *supra*, note 3.

[4] Madouros v. Kansas City Coca-Cola Bottling Co., 230 Mo. App. 275, 90 S.W.2d 445 (Kansas City Ct. of App. 1936).

[5] De Gouveia v. H. D. Lee Mercantile Co., 231 Mo. App. 447, 100 S.W.2d 336 (1937).

between the concepts of "maker" and "distributor." The former is the person who created the product; the latter, a person who, like the relay runner, merely passed on the baton as he received it. Whether a seller deals directly or indirectly with the consumer, the nature of his liability for qualitative defects depends in most states upon which class he falls into. This is certainly the result in the privity states, where "negligence" will stick against the manufacturer but not against a distributor. It is also true in a lower Missouri court which, though it has knocked out the privity requirement in suits against the manufacturer, has retained it in suits against the wholesaler.

From the reported decisions it appears that the difference between making and distributing is a difference in kind, with little or no attention within either category to differences, if any, in degree.

The conventional view of the manufacturer tacitly accepted for the purposes of food products liability law is that he is a person of formidable financial standing whose sole function is to operate factories at which he converts raw materials into finished products. It is generally assumed that such a person has knowledge and control sufficient to eliminate or minimize the danger of injury to the consumer from defects that are traceable to the condition of the goods as they left his factory. His knowledge and control are assumed to be denied the distributor.

For the purposes of food products liability law, a person is to be characterized in terms of, not his over-all operations, but his operations relating to the particular kind of product that caused the plaintiff's injury. For instance, some sellers manufacture some of the products they sell and purchase the rest. In some of these cases the predominant pattern is distribution; in others, manufacture. Even with respect to a single product and brand, some companies make part and buy part. Thus, a particular seller may, in the same breath, be appropriately called a "distributor" on the basis of his over-all operations, and a "manufacturer" on the basis of his operations with respect to a particular product (or particular batch of the product). The converse situation is also common. Between the extremes of all-manufacturer and all-distributor is every combination of making and distributing.

In administering the price control program of World War II, the Office of Price Administration found it necessary for the most part to determine prices product by product and to classify sellers, not on the basis of their over-all operations, but on the basis of their relationships to particular products. The same approach is appropriate here. Except as his over-all operations may tend to show his economic strength and position, the manufacturer's activities with respect to the particular product are generally the only useful object of study.[1]

Measured in terms of a particular food product, what are the marks of a manufacturer? Popular usage suggests two: (1) a processing operation in some manner affecting the character of the end product, and (2) a factory and machinery. These are separate criteria, because not every operation involving the use of a factory and machinery affects the character of the product, and not everything that a seller may do to affect the character of the product involves a factory and machinery. Thus, one who merely packages or repackages goods has a manufacturing operation that does not affect the character of the product itself. Conversely, a butcher who grinds hamburger in a local meat

§2.26. [1] Tangible recognition of the principle is found in the proposed Uniform Commercial Code — Sales (1951): Section 2–314(1) raises a warranty of merchantability "if the seller is a merchant *with respect to goods of that kind*." (Italics added.) Uniform Commercial Code (1951).

market is not considered as having a factory and machinery in the sense usually associated with manufacturing. Is either of these a food manufacturer? Or must both factors conjoin to have manufacturer's liability as distinct from distributor's liability?

Close examination will show that "manufacturer" and "distributor" are hardly discrete compartments. Rather, with all delicate shadings of degree, the two concepts flow together.

Consider the following sellers:

(1) The seller who makes a relatively complicated food product which combines a large number of ingredients and which differs from any of them. Examples are bakery products, canned soups, and candy bars.

(2) The seller who makes a food product which is closely identified with one of its ingredients, and to which the other ingredients are added primarily for the purpose of processing the main ingredient. Examples are canned or frozen fruits and vegetables, commercially smoked ham, and salted peanuts.

(3) The seller who produces a product by processing a single ingredient. Examples are canned concentrated tomato juice (unseasoned), refined sugar, and sliced fresh apples (for sale to bakeries).

(4) The seller who performs only the simplest assembling operation, such as mixing two ingredients manufactured or produced by others, combined with the operation of packaging. The foremost example is the bottling of most soft drinks.

(5) The seller whose product has not been processed (in the sense of changing its character or structure) but has been subjected to a mechanical "process" such as cleaning or sorting. Dry edible beans are an example.

(6) The seller who performs only a packaging operation.

An example is maraschino cherries bought in barrels and without further processing packed in consumer-size bottles for sale to wholesalers.

(7) The seller who buys food products in large quantities for sale, after warehousing, in smaller quantities. An example is canned goods as handled by wholesalers, primary distributors (wholesalers' wholesalers), or chain retailers.

(8) The seller who buys and resells food products without physically handling or even seeing the goods. A typical example is fresh fruits and vegetables as handled by carlot distributors.

The list is not exhaustive. There are many intermediate situations. Even so, it shows that there is no sharp breaking point between "manufacturer" and "distributor."

There are not only degrees of processing or affecting the character of the end product, or otherwise handling it, but also degrees of what constitutes a factory. At the one extreme is the large and intricate plant usually associated with assembly-line mass production. At the other is the equipment of the small retail butcher who makes his own sausage.

Most discussions of food products liability seem to assume that all manufacturers fall into the first two classes described, even when dealing with situations that clearly fall into the intermediate categories such as No. (4), which, incidentally, is that most frequently met in food products liability litigation. They also seem to assume that all distributors fall into the last two. In other words, it is generally assumed that manufacturers always create their products in a rather complete sense, while distributors have little intimate contact with products they sell or at least with the defects that cause consumers injury.

If the courts are to differentiate kinds of liability by the type of seller involved, it is questionable, in view of the absence of discrete compartments, whether they should not resort to criteria other than the simple test of whether the seller is a "manufacturer" or a "distributor." The differences in kind of liability imposed should presumably bear a reasonable relationship to the specific differences that mark the separate classifications.

Liability is imposed on the creator of a product either because he was actually culpable in the particular case (which can rarely be shown) or because he bears a special relationship to the product. For present purposes only the latter concerns us.

The special relationships which the manufacturer bears to a product made by him may consist of one or more of the following: (1) his ability to control the character of the end product; (2) his ability to know the character of the end product (and thus warn the consumer of defects he cannot remove); and (3) his ability to spread the risk or loss among the persons who consume the end product.

Here again the differences between the various kinds of sellers listed vary more in degree than in kind. The typical soft-drink bottler, for example, is an assembler of two ingredients, carbonated water and syrup, both of which he buys from others. So far as foreign objects that presumably entered the drink during the mixing and bottling process are concerned, the defect is a direct result of the manufacturing operation, and it makes sense to impose liability on the seller in his capacity as maker of the end product.

But what about defects in the purchased ingredients? Several reported cases appear in which the manufacturer has been held liable for damage caused by such defects. Is this "manufacturer's liability" or "distributor's liability"?[2] If the former, what is the difference between the two kinds of liability? What is the difference, for example, between a soft-drink bottler whose end product is adulterated by the arsenic that hides in the syrup he bought from a supposedly reliable syrup manufacturer, and a wholesaler who handles syrup that is similarly adulterated? In both cases the defect is latent and in neither case did it enter the product as a result of any defect in the handling or processing operation of the seller. In both cases it is traceable to an earlier seller who was presumably reliable. This being so, is there any greater reason to hold the manufacturer than the distributor? Assuming equal financial standing and bargaining strength, each has the same opportunity to choose his suppliers and to submit samples for laboratory test.

In the supposed situation it might be useful to distinguish the ingredient from the end product. Thus, although with respect to the end product one seller is a "manufacturer"

[2] The tendency of courts to reason in discrete, oversimplified compartments results in contrasts such as this: If the distributor of a defective product represents that he is its manufacturer, by selling under his private brand name, he is held vicariously liable for the negligence of the manufacturer (Thornhill v. Carpenter-Morton Co., 270 Mass. 593, 108 N.E. 474 (1915)), even though he is otherwise blameless. If the manufacturer of the product represents that he is the manufacturer of a defective part, by incorporating it in the end product, he is not vicariously liable for the negligence of the manufacturer of the part. (Martin v. Studebaker Corp., 102 N.J.L. 612, 133 Atl. 384 (1926)). Including an unlabeled part in a product otherwise manufactured by the seller would seem to be at least as strong a representation of the manufacturer as merely attaching a private brand name as "Distributor." Why, therefore, shouldn't the principle of the Restatement of Torts §400 (see §2.23 *supra*, note 1), eliminate the culpability issue in manufacturer cases such as MacPherson v. Buick Motor Co., 217 N.Y. 382, 111 N.E. 1050 (1916), as it does in wholesaler cases such as Swift & Co. v. Hawkins, 174 Miss. 253, 164 So. 231 (1935)? The reluctance of manufacturers to warrant accessories made by others is noted in Bogert and Fink, "Business Practices Regarding Warranties in the Sale of Goods," 25 Ill. L. Rev. 400, 412 (1930).

and the other a "distributor," both are "distributors" in almost the same sense with respect to any purchased ingredient.

If this analysis is correct it suggests that whatever rule of liability is appropriate in such a case to the manufacturer is equally appropriate to the distributor. Conversely, if it is considered inappropriate to hold the distributor in such a case, the same rationale would serve to free the manufacturer. In the latter case, the absolute liability of the manufacturer would then be a liability guaranteeing only against defects or lapses in the *seller's own operations;* there would be no guarantee that there was no defect traceable to an earlier supplier.

Suppose, instead of arsenic, the syrup contained broken glass. Here, unless the distributor was also a rebottler, the defect would be equally latent so far as he is concerned since he would have no occasion to open the containers. In this type of situation, however, there would be a possible basis for holding the manufacturer liable while excusing the distributor. The manufacturer must open the container, and a failure to intercept a defect for which the manufacturer would be held if the broken glass were introduced during the mixing and bottling operations might well be considered a defect in his own operations.

Everything that has been said of the manufacturer who processes may be said of the manufacturer who merely repackages.

Consider the converse case of the distributor. If his operations include warehousing and other physical handling of the goods, and if, through no fault of his own, the food he stores becomes infested with rats, why should he not guarantee his own operations to be free of defects as fully as the manufacturer or repackager guarantees his?

This suggests that any attempted differentiation between manufacturer's liability and distributor's liability, if carried to its logical conclusion in the situations that actually exist (instead of those involving all-or-nothing concepts of "manufacturer" and "distributor"), resolves itself into a distinction between guaranteeing the seller's own operations (except the operation of selecting a supplier) and guaranteeing his own operations plus the operations of his suppliers.

Such an approach avoids deciding cases on the basis of the seller's over-all relationship to the product (whether he is "manufacturer," "wholesaler," or "retailer") and looks at the type of defect and the way it entered, or generally enters, the product. Questions of public policy should not deal with "manufacturer" and "wholesaler" in general but with the question whether sellers performing that type of operation at the place in the production and marketing scheme should be expected to exclude the particular kind of defect from entering (or remaining) in the end product sold.

The fundamental policy question, of course, is the extent to which a seller should be responsible for nondiscoverable defects traceable to his supplier. The argument that a retailer should have this responsibility in order to provide a practical conduit by which the consumer can indirectly reach the manufacturer argues that every seller, whether manufacturer or distributor, should guarantee all his operations with respect to the product, including the operation of selecting his suppliers. Such an approach, if adopted, removes any occasion for distinguishing, for policy reasons, between manufacturers and distributors.

CHAPTER III

Responsibility of the Restaurant Keeper for Unwholesome Food

General References

For general discussions of this topic, see Friend v. Childs Dining Hall Co., 231 Mass. 64, 120 N.E. 407 (1918); Ford v. Waldorf System, Inc., 57 R.I. 131, 188 Atl. 633 (1936); Cushing v. Rodman, 82 F.2d 864 (App. D.C. 1936); Melick, The Sale of Food and Drink 162–263 (1936); Williston, Sales §242b (3d ed. 1948); Perkins, "Unwholesome Food as a Source of Liability," 5 Iowa L. Bull. 86, 96 (1920); Wasserman, "Commentary on Diners' Protection," 61 N.J.L.J. 57 (1938); Note, 20 Minn. L. Rev. 527 (1936); Note, 14 Notre Dame Law. 318 (1939); Comment, 10 So. Calif. L. Rev. 188 (1937); Comment, 66 U.S.L. Rev. 581 (1932).

CHAPTER III

Responsibility of the Restaurant Keeper for Unwholesome Food *

TOPIC A. *Liability for Breach of Warranty*

§3.1. Sale or service? In 1699, in the case of *Parker* v. *Flint*,[1] the Court of King's Bench had to decide whether the plaintiff's establishment at which he entertained boarders and lodgers at a specified price for each item of food or service was an inn in which soldiers could be quartered under the statute of 4 & 5 William and Mary, c. 13, p. 18, "An Act for Carrying on War with France." The court held that it was not. Appended by the reporter is the remark of the defeated counsel that "an innkeeper, as such cannot be bankrupt, because he does not sell but utters his provision."

In 1896, in the case of *Sheffer* v. *Willoughby*,[2] the Illinois Supreme Court excused a restaurant keeper from liability in a suit for negligence on the ground that the allegation of negligence had not been sustained. The court said that to

* Problems of contributory fault are considered in Chapter I, Topic G; problems of privity, in Chapter I, Topic E, and Chapter II, Topic A.

§3.1. [1] 12 Mod. 254, 88 Eng. Rep. 1303. Also reported as Parkhurst v. Foster, 1 Salk. 387, 91 Eng. Rep. 337; Carth. 417, 90 Eng. Rep. 842; 1 Ld. Raym. 479, 91 Eng. Rep. 1219; and as Parkhouse v. Forster, 5 Mod. 427, 87 Eng. Rep. 746. Several versions must be read to get the full picture.

[2] 163 Ill. 518, 45 N.E. 253 (1896).

hold the restaurant keeper as insurer would be incorrect on principle and, so far as it had been advised, such a rule had not been sustained by any respectable authority.

On the strength of these cases Beale, in his treatise Innkeepers and Hotels,[3] concluded that an innkeeper is not an insurer of his food, and that the patron's only recourse is to an action for negligence. From this has come a substantial body of authority relieving the restaurant keeper of absolute responsibility. No warranty of wholesomeness attaches because there is no sale for it to attach to. This is the law in Alabama, Connecticut, Delaware, Georgia, Maryland, New Hampshire, New Jersey, and Tennessee.[4]

[3] Section 169 (1906).

[4] McCarley v. Wood Drugs, Inc., 228 Ala. 226, 227, 153 So. 446, 448 (1934); C. C. Hooper Cafe Co. v. Henderson, 223 Ala. 579, 137 So. 419 (1931); Steele-Smith Dry Goods Co. v. Blythe, 208 Ala. 288, 94 So. 281 (1922); Albrecht v. Rubinstein, 135 Conn. 243, 63 A.2d 158 (1948); Lynch v. Hotel Bond Co., 117 Conn. 128, 132, 167 Atl. 99, 100 (1933); Merrill v. Hodson, 88 Conn. 314, 91 Atl. 533 (1914); Pappa v. F. W. Woolworth Co. 33 A.2d 310 (Del. S. Ct. 1943); Rowe v. Louisville & N.R.R., 29 Ga. App. 151, 113 S.E. 823 (1922); Childs Dining Hall v. Swingler, 173 Md. 490, 197 Atl. 105 (1938); Kenny v. Wong Len, 81 N.H. 427, 436, 128 Atl. 343, 348 (1925); Rickner v. Ritz Restaurant Co., 13 N.J. Misc. 818, 181 Atl. 398 (1935); Corin v. S. S. Kresge, 110 N.J.L. 378, 166 Atl. 291 (1933); Nisky v. Childs Co., 103 N.J.L. 464, 468, 135 Atl. 805, 806 (1927); Petrucelli v. Green, MS. opinion, Tenn. S. Ct. (1925), cited in Bell v. Bowers Stores, 3 Tenn. App. 590, 598 (1926); F. W. Woolworth Co. v. Wilson, 74 F.2d 439, 441 (C.C.A. 5th, 1934); Horn & Hardart Baking Co. v. Lieber (C.C.A. 3d, 1928). See Greenwood Cafe v. Lovinggood, 197 Ala. 34, 72 So. 354 (1916); Pantaze v. West, 7 Ala. App. 599, 61 So. 42 (1913); Stell v. Townsend's California Glace Fruits Inc., 138 Cal. App. 777, 28 P.2d 1077 (1934); Roseberry v. Wachter, 3 Harr. 253, 138 Atl. 273 (Del. 1925) (dictum of Superior Court judge in charge to jury); Sheffer v. Willoughby, 163 Ill. 518, 45 N.E. 253 (1896) (dictum repudiated by later Illinois cases).

One of the rare expressions of agreement in the secondary authorities appears in Note, 22 Ky. L.J. 452, 453 (1934).

The following case turned, at least in part, on the peculiarities of the local pure food statute. Loucks v. Morley, 39 Cal. App. 570, 179 Pac. 529 (1919). In Valeri v. Pullman Co., 218 Fed. 519 (S.D.N.Y. 1914), the court admitted that a sale might take place but refused to find liability in warranty.

The conclusion reached by these cases has been widely criticized. One approach questions Beale's conclusion regarding the liability of innkeepers, principally by attacking his authorities.[5] It points out that *Sheffer* v. *Willoughby* involved a restaurant, not an inn, and the suit was for negligence, not breach of warranty. *Parker* v. *Flint*, insofar as it had legal force, was irrelevant and, insofar as it was relevant, had no legal force.

However, *Crisp* v. *Pratt*[6] and *Saunderson* v. *Rowles*,[7] cited by the reporter of *Parker* v. *Flint* (though not by Beale), lend apparent strength to Beale's proposition. In the former case, an ejectment suit, it was relevant to determine whether an innkeeper could be a bankrupt under the bankruptcy statutes. The court said:

> . . . an innholder doth not get his living by buying and selling; for although he buy provision to be spent in his house, he doth not properly sell it, but utters it at such rates as he thinks reasonable gains, and the guests do not take it at a certain price, but they may have it or refuse it if they will.

Beale's use of this distinction between "sell" and "utter" to show that the innkeeper does not pass title to the food he serves assumes that "utter" does not carry with it the aspects of sale upon which a warranty can be hung. As normally used, the concepts of uttering and sale were probably not exclusive. "Uttering," in its market context, appears to have covered the general idea of commercial dissemination

[5] *E.g.*, Melick, The Sale of Food and Drink 166–169, 176–178 (1936).

[6] Cro. Car. 549, 79 Eng. Rep. 1072 (1640); also reported as Crisp v. Prat, March N.C. 34, 82 Eng. Rep. 399.

[7] 4 Burr. 2064, 98 Eng. Rep. 77 (1767). Mansfield said of the innkeeper: "He makes no particular contract, like a trader. He cannot be said to make his living by buying and selling, as a trader does. He buys, only to spend in his house; and when he utters it again, it is attended with many circumstances additional to the mere selling price. He can not be considered as a trader at large."

and thus included, rather than excluded, the notion of sale.[8] As used in special contrast to "sale," however, it was probably meant to cover the commercial supplying of goods under an arrangement not involving contracts for separate items at separate prices. Conversely, as used in special contrast to "uttering," the term "sale" was confined to its most conventional sense of separate items individually requested and obtained at separate prices. If so, the distinction is between two special concepts whose contours were shaped by the peculiarities of English statutory law covering bankruptcy.[9] Only persons whose trade was buying and selling could be bankrupts. *Crisp* v. *Pratt* and fellow cases [10] holding that innkeepers did not do the kind of buying and selling contemplated by the bankruptcy laws hardly related to the question whether they might be buying and selling in any other significant sense. As authority for Beale's proposition, they had little force.[11]

Melick suggests that even innkeepers were absolutely liable under the early English law, at least when they furnished food on an à la carte basis,[12] but he gives no evidence that relates directly to inns as distinct from other types of establishments where food is eaten on the premises.

[8] See Newton v. Trigg, 3 Mod. 327, 87 Eng. Rep. 217; 1 Show. 96, 268, 89 Eng. Rep. 474, 566; 1 Salk. 109, 91 Eng. Rep. 100; 3 Lev. 309, 83 Eng. Rep. 704; Comb. 181, 90 Eng. Rep. 417; Carth. 149, 90 Eng. Rep. 692 (1691), where other tradesmen were said to "utter" their goods.

[9] 13 Eliz. c. 7 (1570), 1 Jac. 1, c. 15 (1604), 21 Jac. 1, c. 19 (1623).

[10] Newton v. Trigg (full citation appears in note 8 *supra*); Saunderson v. Rowles, 4 Burr. 2064, 98 Eng. Rep. 77 (1767); Buscall v. Hogg, 3 Wils. 146, 95 Eng. Rep. 982 (1770).

[11] Perkins says that the English cases that excluded "the inn-keeper from the bankruptcy statutes seem to have been influenced in no small degree by the notion that this person has so many peculiar burdens that he may reasonably be excused from involuntary bankruptcy." "Unwholesome Food as a Source of Liability," 5 Iowa L. Bull. 86, 100 (1920).

[12] Melick, The Sale of Food and Drink 175 (1936). See also Friend v. Childs Dining Hall Co., 231 Mass. 65, 70, 120 N.E. 407, 408 (1918).

In a second line of attack on the view that no warranty attaches to food served by a restaurant keeper, it has been pointed out that today's restaurant corresponds to the early "tavern," an institution different from the common law inn.[13] Although Lord Mansfield disagreed,[14] the bankruptcy cases headed by *Crisp* v. *Pratt*[15] treated the taverner differently from the innkeeper. Certainly an institution in which the supplying of food was the main if not the sole object of the transaction could legitimately be distinguished from one in which it was only one of many services.[16] But whatever the status of the innkeeper, under modern tax, liquor, game, and pure food statutes the transactions of restaurants are usually considered sales;[17] and if under the early English law the retail food dealer was absolutely liable

[13] Barrington v. Hotel Astor, 184 App. Div. 317, 171 N.Y. Supp. 840 (1st Dept. 1918); Ford v. Waldorf System, Inc., 57 R.I. 131, 134, 188 Atl. 633, 635 (1936); Melick, *id.* at 169 n.20, 170–176. Beale conceded this. Innkeepers and Hotels §15 (1906).

[14] Saunderson v. Rowles, 4 Burr. 2064, 98 Eng. Rep. 77 (1767).

[15] See notes 6 and 10 *supra*. In Patman v. Vaughn, 1 T.R. 572, 99 Eng. Rep. 1257 (K.B. 1787), it was held that even an innkeeper was subject to the bankruptcy laws where he sold liquor to anyone who asked for it.

[16] It is particularly easy to find a sale where the meal is dispensed à la carte. See Valeri v. Pullman Co., 218 Fed. 519, 521 (S.D.N.Y. 1914).

[17] *E.g.*, Pappanastos v. State Tax Commission, 235 Ala. 50, 177 So. 138 (1937) (sales tax); Liggett Drug Co. v. Lee, 126 Fla. 359, 171 So. 326 (1937) (gross receipts tax); Brevoort Hotel Co. v. Ames, 360 Ill. 485, 196 N.E. 461 (1935) (retailers' occupation tax); Commonwealth v. Phoenix Hotel Co., 157 Ky. 180, 162 S.W. 823 (1914) (game sold out of season); Commonwealth v. Warren, 160 Mass. 533, 36 N.E. 308 (1894) (sale of substandard milk); Commonwealth v. Worcester, 126 Mass. 256 (1879) (illegal sale of liquor); People v. Clair, 221 N.Y. 108, 116 N.E. 868 (1917) (illegal sale of game); Commonwealth v. Penn-Harris Hotel Co., 21 D. & C. 460 (Pa. 1934) (sales tax); Commonwealth v. Miller, 131 Pa. St. 118, 18 Atl. 938 (1890) (illegal sale of oleomargarine); State v. Lotti, 72 Vt. 115, 47 Atl. 392 (1900) (illegal sale of liquor); State v. Grays Harbor Commercial Co., 124 Wash. 227, 214 Pac. 13 (1923) (sale of unwholesome food); and cases cited *infra* §3.7, note 2. *Cf.* San Francisco v. Larsen, 165 Cal. 179, 181, 131 Pac. 366, 367 (1913). Many of these cases are summarized in Note, 24 Marq. L. Rev. 155 (1940).

for the food he served, there is evidence that the restaurant keeper had a similar responsibility.[18] There is little warrant, therefore, for applying Beale's conclusion to the ordinary restaurant, however appropriate it may have been to the common law inn.

The doctrinal reticence of many courts to find a sale, at least in the case of inns, can be traced to three factors. The first is the lumping of the food itself with the attendant services and with other commodities and services needed by the patron. But why including food in a larger aggregate should be an insuperable barrier to the existence of a sale has not been satisfactorily explained. A sale of an aggregate of commodities is no less a sale of the component items because there is no breakdown and allocation of the total price. Why shouldn't the same be true of combinations of goods and services? [19]

The second factor is the problem created when a commodity is furnished as a mere incident of rendering a service. An example is the wax a filling station uses when simonizing a customer's car. But even if the simonize contract is mainly one for work and labor, where title to incidental materials is acquired by gradual accession and not by sale, to say of a restaurant transaction that the food is only incidental is to let the tail wag the dog. Food is hardly incidental to the services of preparing and bringing it to the table; nor is it merely incidental in the operation of an American-plan hotel. It is a major object of the bargain.

The third factor is the destruction of the product, allegedly in the process of acquiring it. This has made it difficult for some authorities to see how the passage of title consid-

[18] Y.B. 9 Hen. VI, f. 53B, pl. 37 (1431). See Topic A of Chapter I.

[19] See Wasserman, "Commentary on Diners' Protection," 61 N.J.L.J. 57, 59 (1938). But *cf.* Note, 22 Ky. L.J. 452, 453–454 (1934).

ered necessary to a sale could take place.[20] (Title by accession, too, does not fit.) This kind of misgiving puts the problem in a setting of medieval metaphysics. It forecloses the question by taking for granted a concept of sale that precludes another result. But even those who find the destruction of goods in the act of receiving them incompatible with a sale may find comfort in the possibility that title passes when the food is put on the table.

Beale's tacit assumption that title does not pass at that time rests on the notion that the patron is entitled only to what he can eat at that sitting and that he has no right to the remainder. This not-necessarily-fatal [21] notion has been criticized as unrealistic under modern conditions. Today it is generally assumed that the restaurant keeper consigns the food he serves to the full command of his patron and that it is a matter of indifference what the patron chooses to eat, what he chooses to take away, and what he chooses to abandon.[22]

Williston and others have indicated that the sale issue

[20] *E.g.*, Merrill v. Hodson, 88 Conn. 314, 318, 91 Atl. 533, 534 (1914); Beale, Innkeepers and Hotels §196 (1906).

[21] See Temple v. Keeler, 238 N.Y. 344, 144 N.E. 635 (1924); Comment, 10 So. Calif. L. Rev. 188, 190 (1937); Comment, 27 Yale L.J. 1068 (1918).

[22] *E.g.*, Wasserman, "Commentary on Diners' Protection," 61 N.J.L.J 57, 59 (1938); Note, 32 Harv. L. Rev. 71, 72 (1918).

"It can hardly be said that the parties intended a transaction which would make the customer guilty of a tort or a crime if he removed the uneaten food." Note, 2 U. of Chi. L. Rev. 653 (1935). The assumption noted in the text is not so clear for (1) sugar and condiments put on the table for continued and general use, (2) potato chips or popcorn placed on the bar in a saloon, (3) smörgåsbord meals provided on an "all you can eat for eighty-five cents" basis. However, in Yochem v. Gloria, Inc., 134 Ohio St. 427, 429, 17 N.E.2d 731, 733 (1938), the court said that salt and pepper were part of the sale and concluded that the same is true of drinking water served. (An à la carte approach to such a case might prove embarrassing.) Warranty protection was extended to a glass of water in Sartin v. Blackwell, 200 Miss. 579, 28 So.2d 222 (1946).

may well be a legal red herring, because there is no persuasive reason for confining the benefits of warranty to transactions technically qualifying as sales.[23] In line with this thought, several cases have said that they would impose a warranty obligation even if no sale were involved.[24] An important consideration is the disparity that would otherwise exist between the responsibility of the restaurant keeper and the responsibility of the retailer.[25]

If the foregoing analysis is correct, there is little need to distinguish between à la carte and table d'hôte meals; between service restaurants, cafeterias, automats, lunch wagons, caterers, restaurants with curb service, food concessionaires, and lunch peddlers; between restaurants serving food to be eaten off the premises [26] or on or off according to the wishes of the customer; and between European- and American-plan hotels. Whatever the early common law rule as to inns, there is little warrant for putting even that institution in a separate class.

[23] "A sale is not the only transaction in which a warranty may be implied." Williston, Sales §242b (3d ed. 1948), quoted with approval in Sartin v. Blackwell, 200 Miss. 579, 583, 28 So.2d 222, 223 (1946). See also Vold, Sales §153, p. 477 (1931); Note, 17 Minn. L. Rev. 210 (1933).

[24] Stanfield v. F. W. Woolworth Co., 143 Kan. 117, 123, 53 P.2d 878, 882 (1936); Friend v. Childs Dining Hall Co., 231 Mass. 65, 75, 120 N.E. 407, 411 (1918); Cushing v. Rodman, 82 F.2d 864, 867–868 (App. D.C. 1936).

[25] In Friend v. Childs Dining Hall Co., 231 Mass. 65, 72, 120 N.E. 407, 409 (1918), the court said: "It would be an incongruity in the law amounting at least to an inconsistency to hold with reference to many keepers of restaurants who conduct the business both of supplying food to guests and of putting up lunches to be carried elsewhere and not eaten on the premises, that, in case of want of wholesomeness, there is liability to the purchaser of a lunch to be carried away founded on an implied condition of the contract, but that liability to the guest who eats a lunch at a table on the premises rests solely on negligence." See also Williston, Sales §242b (3d ed. 1948).

[26] Here there is a retail sale (with attendant warranties) regardless of the state's views on other types of restaurant transactions. Williams v. Elson, 218 N.C. 157, 10 S.E.2d 668 (1940) (glass in sandwich).

Whatever the intellectual difficulties, the weight of authority today holds the restaurateur absolutely liable for breach of implied warranty. This includes Arkansas, California, the District of Columbia, Florida, Illinois, Indiana, Kansas, Louisiana, Massachusetts, Minnesota, Mississippi, Missouri, New York, Ohio, Pennsylvania, Rhode Island, Texas, and England.[27] It is probably the rule also in

[27] Lewis v. Roescher, 193 Ark. 161, 98 S.W.2d 956 (1936); Jensen v. Berris, 31 Cal. App. 2d 537, 88 P.2d 220 (1939); Goetten v. Owl Drug Co., 6 Cal. 2d 683, 59 P.2d 142 (1936); Mix v. Ingersoll Candy Co., 83 Cal. App. 84, 49 P.2d 877 (1935), *rev'd* on other grounds, 6 Cal. 2d 674, 59 P.2d 145 (1936); Cliett v. Lauderdale Biltmore Corp., Inc., — Fla. —, 39 So.2d 476 (1949); Greenwood v. John R. Thompson Co., 213 Ill. App. 371, 379 (1919); Heise v. Gillette, 83 Ind. App. 551, 149 N.E. 182 (1925); Stanfield v. F. W. Woolworth Co., 143 Kan. 117, 53 P.2d 878 (1936); Ogden v. Rosedale Inn, 189 So. 162 (La. App. 1939); Doyle v. Fuerst & Kraemer, Ltd., 129 La. 838, 841, 56 So. 906, 907 (1911); Guthrie v. J. J. Newberry Co., 297 Mass. 245, 8 N.E.2d 774 (1937); Johnson v. Kanavos, 296 Mass. 373, 6 N.E.2d 434 (1937); Schuler v. Union News Co., 295 Mass. 350, 4 N.E.2d 465 (1936); Landfield v. Albiani Lunch Co., 268 Mass. 528, 168 N.E. 160 (1929); Smith v. Gerrish, 256 Mass. 183, 152 N.E. 318 (1926); Barringer v. Ocean S.S. Co. of Savannah, 240 Mass. 405, 134 N.E. 265 (1922); Friend v. Childs Dining Hall Co., 231 Mass. 65, 120 N.E. 407 (1918); Bark v. Dixson, 115 Minn. 172, 131 N.W. 1078 (1911); Sartin v. Blackwell, 200 Miss. 579, 28 So.2d 222 (1946); Bell v. S. S. Kresge Co., 129 S.W.2d 932 (Mo. 1939); Smith v. Carlos, 215 Mo. App. 488, 247 S.W. 468 (1922); Eisenbach v. Gimbel Bros., Inc., 281 N.Y. 474, 24 N.E.2d 131 (1939); Temple v. Keeler, 238 N.Y. 344, 144 N.E. 635 (1924); Race v. Krum, 222 N.Y. 410, 118 N.E. 853 (1918); De Coigne v. Ludlum Steel Co., 251 App. Div. 662, 297 N.Y. Supp. 636 (3d Dept. 1937); Meckler v. Silver's Lunch Stores, 246 App. Div. 806, 285 N.Y. Supp. 99 (1st Dept. 1936); Bernstein v. Queens County Jockey Club, 222 App. Div. 191, 225 N.Y. Supp. 449 (2d Dept. 1927); Muller v. Childs Co., 185 App. Div. 881, 171 N.Y. Supp. 541 (1st Dept. 1918); Barrington v. Hotel Astor, 184 App. Div. 319, 171 N.Y. Supp. 840 (1st Dept. 1918); Leahy v. Essex Co., 164 App. Div. 903, 148 N.Y. Supp. 1063 (3d Dept. 1914); Grossman v. Hotel Astor, 166 Misc. 80, 1 N.Y.S.2d 307 (1937); Tipple v. High Street Hotel Co., 41 N.E.2d 879 (Ohio App., Franklin Co. 1941); Yochem v. Gloria, Inc., 134 Ohio St. 427, 17 N.E.2d 731 (1938); West v. Katsafanas, 107 Pa. Super. 118, 162 Atl. 685 (1932); Ford v. Waldorf System, Inc., 57 R.I. 131, 188 Atl. 633 (1936); John B. Thompson Co. v. Smith, 8 Higgins 95 (Tenn. Civ. App. 1916), overruled by Petrucelli v. Green, MS. opinion, Tenn. S. Ct. (1925), cited in Bell v. Bowers Stores, 3 Tenn. App. 590, 598 (1926);

Iowa [28] and Maine.[29] In most instances the cases assume that a sale of food has taken place. Included are cases decided under the Uniform Sales Act. Inasmuch as few, if any, of the recent cases deal with the true inn, we cannot be sure that courts that hang liability on the peg of a sale would find a peg in that situation. However, there is little more doctrinal difficulty in finding a sale in the case of the inn than

---

Lohse v. Coffey, 32 A.2d 258 (D.C. Munic. App. 1943); Cushing v. Rodman, 82 F.2d 864 (App. D.C. 1936); Lockett v. A. & M. Charles, Ltd., 159 L.T.R. 547 (K.B. 1938), [1938] 55 T.L.R. 22, 4 All E.R. 170, 82 Sol. J. 951.

See Koplin v. Louis K. Liggett Co., 119 Pa. Super. 529, 181 Atl. 381 (1935), *rev'd* on other grounds, 322 Pa. 333, 185 Atl. 744 (1936); S. H. Kress & Co. v. Ferguson, 60 S.W.2d 817 (Tex. Civ. App. 1933) (stipulation that soda was "sold").

Travis v. Louisville & N.R.R., 183 Ala. 415, 62 So. 851 (1913), speaks of a "warranty" to use due care. See also C. C. Hooper Cafe Co. v. Henderson, 223 Ala. 579, 137 So. 419 (1931).

In the following cases the court assumed that a sale was involved but the plaintiff failed for other reasons. Blarjeske v. Thompson's Restaurant Co., 325 Ill. App. 189, 59 N.E.2d 320 (1945) (causation not proved); Goodwin v. Country Club of Peoria, 323 Ill. App. 1, 54 N.E.2d 612 (1944) (food not legally defective); Taylor v. F. W. Woolworth Co., 151 Kan. 233, 98 P.2d 114 (1940) (improper argument by counsel); Palmer v. Rosedale Catering Co., 195 So. 859 (La. App. 1940) (insufficient evidence of unwholesomeness); De Stefano v. Alpha Lunch Co., 308 Mass. 38, 30 N.E.2d 827 (1941) (remedy was under Workmen's Compensation Act); Miller v. W. T. Grant Co., 302 Mass. 429, 19 N.E.2d 704 (1939) (insufficient evidence of unwholesomeness); Savage v. Alpha Lunch Co. of Boston, 300 Mass. 520, 16 N.E.2d 38 (1938) (failure to give notice); Gracey v. Waldorf System, Inc., 251 Mass. 76, 146 N.E. 232 (1925); Marnelos v. Anastasovites, unreported, D.C. Springfield, Mass., App. Div. (Mar. 9, 1933) (food not legally defective); Stewart v. Martin, 353 Mo. 1, 181 S.W.2d 647 (1944) (insufficient evidence of unwholesomeness); Frank v. Justine Caterers, Inc., 271 App. Div. 980, 68 N.Y.S.2d 198 (2d Dept. 1947) (mental anguish alone insufficient); Frier v. Laube's Old Spain, 265 App. Div. 402, 39 N.Y.S.2d 794 (4th Dept. 1943) (no proof of foreign substance).

[28] Amdal v. F. W. Woolworth Co., 84 F. Supp. (N.D. Iowa, 1949).

[29] This seems a fair inference from the decision in Bigelow v. Maine Central R.R., 110 Me. 105, 85 Atl. 396 (1912), which applied the sealed container exception to canned asparagus served by the defendant.

in the case of the table d'hôte dinner or the "special" provided by a cafeteria.

§ 3.2. Some considerations of public policy. On the policy side, there is probably stronger reason to impose warranty liability on the restaurant keeper than on any other kind of food seller.[1]

The policy arguments for imposing strict liability on the retailer apply, for the most part, with even greater force to the restaurant keeper. The restaurant keeper deals directly with the consumer and he is as useful a conduit to earlier handlers, if involved, as the retailer. Besides, he receives additional compensation for performing the services of selection, preparation, and over-all vigilance that would otherwise fall to the consumer himself. The restaurant keeper has greater opportunities of interception and avoidance and is paid to exploit them.[2]

To the extent that the restaurant keeper has a greater

§3.2. [1] "On principle there can be no doubt that a person has greater opportunity to protect himself from unwholesome food which he prepares for his own table, than from that which is prepared for him in a hotel or restaurant. Hence the rule of law which is devised for the protection of the health and lives of the public, has greater reason to operate in the latter instance than in the former." Perkins, "Unwholesome Food as a Source of Liability," 5 Iowa L. Bull. 86, 101 (1920). Cliett v. Lauderdale Biltmore Corp., Inc., — Fla. —, 39 So.2d 476, 478 (1949). Section 2-314(1) of the proposed Uniform Commercial Code — Sales (1951), prepared by The American Law Institute and the National Conference of Commissioners on Uniform State Laws, would provide: "The serving for value of food or drink to be consumed either on the premises or elsewhere is a sale." Uniform Commercial Code (1951).

The policy considerations on both sides are well summarized in Cushing v. Rodman, 82 F.2d 864 (App. D.C. 1936). See also Wasserman, "Commentary on Diners' Protection," 61 N.J.L.J. 57, 59 (1938); Comment, 2 Md. L. Rev. 277 (1938); Note, 20 Minn. L. Rev. 527, 537 (1936); Note, 12 Neb. L. Bull. 163, 173-175 (1933). *Cf.* Note, 12 Corn. L.Q. 535 (1927); Note, 22 Ky. L.J. 452 (1934).

[2] Certainly the sealed container exception has no legitimate place here, whatever its dubious merits elsewhere. The Supreme Judicial Court of Maine, however, disagrees. Bigelow v. Maine Central R.R., 110 Me. 105, 85 Atl. 396 (1912).

opportunity than the retailer to control the quality of the food furnished, the consumer's opportunity to protect himself is correspondingly less; his reliance on his host, correspondingly greater. Certainly, the vigilance normally expected of the eater is low compared with that normally expected of the retail buyer and cook.[3]

Many of the arguments for imposing strict liability on the manufacturer apply also to the restaurant keeper. Although he is not generally so considered, the restaurateur is in a real sense a "manufacturer" of the meal served, because he often does a thorough-going job of fabricating the end product. It is true that to a substantial extent he is only an assembler of products fabricated by others, but the same is frequently true of the manufacturer. The important thing is that the opportunities for controlling the quality of what the consumer eats are almost as great in the one case as in the other. Whether the opportunities for spreading the risk or loss are as great is another question.

It is suspected that underlying the reluctance of many courts to hold the restaurant keeper to a standard of absolute accountability is the unexpressed assumption that the average restaurant keeper is small and economically weak in contrast to the supposedly large and economically strong average manufacturer. Even so, it is ironical that where the consumer's need for protection, on the one hand, and the seller's opportunities for fulfilling it, on the other, are so much greater the courts have been more reluctant to impose responsibility. Indeed, it would be hard to find in the law a rule with less justification than the rule, in force in eight states,[4] that the want of a sale precludes the absolute responsibility of the restaurant keeper.

[3] The standard of care expected of eaters is discussed in Topic G, Chapter I.

[4] Alabama, Connecticut, Delaware, Georgia, Maryland, New Hampshire, New Jersey, and Tennessee. See §3.1 *supra*, note 4.

Topic B. *Liability for Negligence*

§3.3. The problem of proof. The restaurant keeper has, independent of warranty, a duty of due care, and in those jurisdictions where he "utters" his food,[1] plaintiffs will be found framing their suits in tort for negligence.

But there is a serious problem of proof. As in the case of the retailer or the manufacturer it is usually difficult or impossible for the plaintiff to show specific acts of negligence, despite his direct contact with the defendant. In such a situation, matters of burden of proof, permissible inference, and presumption are all-important.

Generally speaking, mere proof of illness or injury following the eating of the defendant's food is insufficient to get the plaintiff to the jury. Normally it does not indicate negligence by the defendant and, at least in cases not involving foreign substances, it probably does not indicate even that the defendant's product caused the plaintiff's condition. The courts differ widely.

§3.4. The problem of proof — The foreign substance cases. In the cases involving readily ascertainable foreign substances, causation is usually taken for granted.[1] The central issue is culpability. The nature of the object and common experience with the causes of its intrusion, when known, help to point out the more probable sources. The mere presence of a foreign object in the food generally does not make out an issue of negligence for the jury,[2] unless the

§3.3. [1] See §3.1.

§3.4. [1] Unless the result is delayed illness. See Franklin v. Argyro, 211 Ala. 506, 100 So. 811 (1924) (centipede in soup). Or unless the food is sold on a "take out" basis. Hutton v. Gonzales, 15 So.2d 820 (La. App. 1943) (maggots in barbecued pork). Causation was apparently in doubt in Brett v. Holborn Restaurant Co., 3 T.L.R. 309 (1887) (needle in spinach).

[2] Smith v. McClary, 28 Cal. App. 2d 468, 82 P.2d 712 (1938) (cork in

court is willing to let the jury draw on its own experience to determine whether the particular kind of object usually intrudes as a result of improper handling or inadequate inspection by restaurant keepers.[3] If it will not, the plaintiff is put to it to produce evidence tending to establish that fact. In this respect he can frequently establish a prima facie case by showing the additional fact that the defendant prepared the particular food that served as immediate host to the intruding object.[4] (The plaintiff's permissible inference is

---

malted milk); McCabe v. Pennsylvania R.R., 311 Pa. 229, 166 Atl. 843 (1933) (glass in jelly omelet); Horn & Hardart Baking Co. v. Lieber, 25 F.2d 449 (C.C.A. 3d, 1928) (tack in strawberries). However, in Clark Restaurant Co. v. Rau, 41 Ohio App. 23, 26, 179 N.E. 196, 197 (1931), the court held that "the mere existence of particles of glass in the food [pie à la mode] furnished by the company to the defendant in error is evidence of negligence."

[3] *E.g.*, Louis Pizitz Dry Goods Co. v. Waldrop, 237 Ala. 208, 210, 186 So. 151, 152 (1939) (". . . so far as the court can see, the jury, from their experience as men of the world, may be warranted in thinking that an accident of this particular kind commonly does not happen except in consequence of negligence . . .")

[4] Steele-Smith Dry Goods Co. v. Blythe, 208 Ala. 288, 94 So. 281 (1922) ("ropy substance" in soup; judgment for plaintiff *rev'd* on other grounds); Bell v. S. S. Kresge Co., 129 S.W.2d 932 (Mo. 1939) (glass in soup; judgment for plaintiff *rev'd* on other grounds); Kenny v. Wong Len, 81 N.H. 427, 128 Atl. 343 (1925) (mouse in dressing); Panza v. Bickford's, Inc., of New Jersey, 129 N.J.L. 50, 28 A.2d 188 (1942) (metal slug in pie); Corin v. S. S. Kresge, 110 N.J.L. 378, 166 Atl. 291 (1933), *aff'g* 10 N.J. Misc. 489, 159 Atl. 799 (1932) (glass in coleslaw); Rosenswaike v. Interborough Rapid Transit Co., 175 N.Y. Supp. 828 (S. Ct., 1st Dept. 1919) (glass in potatoes); Black v. Child's Co. of Providence, 73 R.I. 516, 58 A.2d 115 (1948) (toothpicks in chicken croquettes); Chisholm v. S. S. Kresge Co., 55 R.I. 422, 182 Atl. 4 (1935) (pieces of wire in order of beef stew, coleslaw, and bread). *Contra:* Smith v. McClary, 28 Cal. App. 2d 468, 82 P.2d 712 (1938) (cork in malted milk prepared by defendant); O'Brien v. Louis K. Liggett Co., 255 Mass. 553, 152 N.E. 57 (1926) (glass in strawberry shortcake prepared by defendant); Jacobs v. Childs Co., 166 N.Y. Supp. 798 (N.Y. Munic. Ct. 1916) (nail in cake baked by defendant; the court said that because a nail is not a normal cake ingredient it might have been dropped in by an outsider).

sometimes awarded as an application of the doctrine of *res ipsa loquitur.*)[5]

This showing is, however, no guarantee of success. In *Ash* v. *Childs Dining Hall Co.*,[6] the plaintiff was injured by a tack imbedded in blueberry pie. Although the defendant had made the pie, the court said that it was as plausible to suppose that the tack accompanied the berries at the time of purchase as it was to suppose that it intruded because of the defendant's operations. Secondly, its dark color and small size removed any basis for inferring negligence from the fact that the defendant's inspection of the berries had failed to disclose it.

If such evidence fails to point more plausibly to the defendant, the plaintiff is vulnerable to a directed verdict unless he can show additional circumstances pointing to the defendant. He can greatly improve his chances by showing that the position of the object in the food made it discoverable upon reasonable inspection, that it is similar to nearby objects used in the defendant's kitchen,[7] or that there was a defective condition in the defendant's establishment.[8]

[5] See Smith v. McClary, 28 Cal. App. 2d 468, 82 P.2d 712 (1938); McPherson v. Capuano & Co., 31 Ga. App. 82, 121 S.E. 580 (1923); Costello v. Morrison Cafeteria Co. of Louisiana, Inc., 18 La. App. 40, 135 So. 245 (1931); King v. Davis, 296 Fed. 986 (App. D.C. 1924).

[6] 231 Mass. 86, 120 N.E. 396 (1918). To the same effect is O'Brien v. Louis K. Liggett Co., 255 Mass. 553, 152 N.E. 57 (1926) (glass in strawberry shortcake).

[7] O'Brien v. Louis K. Liggett Co., 282 Mass. 573, 185 N.E. 28 (1933) (glass in strawberry shortcake, prepared near glass and rubbish by defendant); Rickner v. Ritz Restaurant Co., 13 N.J. Misc. 818, 181 Atl. 398 (1935) (glass in corned beef sandwich, prepared near glass by defendant); Levy v. Horn & Hardart Baking Co., 103 Pa. Super. 282, 157 Atl. 369 (1931) (screw, in coffee prepared by defendant, similar to those in apparatus used by it); F. W. Woolworth Co. v. Wilson, 74 F.2d 439, 442 (C.C.A. 5th, 1934) (glass in ice-cream soda; cracked ice used was near counter where glasses were sometimes broken).

[8] In Sartin v. Blackwell, 200 Miss. 579, 28 So.2d 222 (1946), the jury was permitted to infer negligence from the fact that the plaintiff was

§3.5. The problem of proof — The latent defect cases. In the spoiled or diseased food cases, the greater hurdle appears to be that of causation. The mere fact of illness following the eating of the defendant's food does not implicate it, according to most courts.[1] Collateral circumstances must be shown. The possibilities here include showing (1) that others who ate the same food also got sick,[2] (2) that those in the same party who did not eat the same food did

served a water glass that was broken and contained glass fragments. In Ballas v. F. W. Woolworth Co., 90 N.H. 428, 10 A.2d 233 (1939), the plaintiff was injured by glass in ice cream. He established a prima facie case by showing that the arrangement of the defendant's fountain was possibly defective. He was aided by the fact that the manufacturer proved that it was highly improbable that glass entered during manufacture. In McCabe v. Pennsylvania R.R., 311 Pa. 229, 166 Atl. 843 (1933), the plaintiff, injured by glass slivers in jelly omelet, got a presumption in his favor when the defendant's witnesses admitted that the glass container from which the jelly was taken was broken at the top. The plaintiff's judgment was reversed on other grounds.

§3.5. [1] Green v. Wilson, 194 Ark. 165, 105 S.W.2d 1074 (1937) (unwholesome lemon pie); Lee v. Smith, 168 So. 727 (La. App. 1936) (unwholesome food); and see cases cited in notes 2, 3, 4, and 5 *infra*. *Contra*: McCarley v. Wood Drugs, Inc., 228 Ala. 226, 153 So. 446 (1934) (tainted food); Tipple v. High Street Hotel Co., 41 N.E.2d 879 (Ohio App., Franklin Co. 1941) (tainted sausage); Crocker v. Baltimore Dairy Lunch Co., 214 Mass. 177, 100 N.E. 1078 (1913) (tainted food). And see Yeo v. Pig & Whistle Sandwich Shops, 83 Ga. App. 91, 62 S.E.2d 668 (1950) (unwholesome meal).

[2] Louis Pizitz Dry Goods Co. v. Waldrop, 237 Ala. 208, 186 So. 151 (1939) (impure mayonnaise; seven persons sick); Greenwood Cafe v. Lovinggood, 197 Ala. 34, 72 So. 354 (1916) (plaintiff's companion also sick); Copeland v. Curtis, 36 Ga. App. 255, 136 S.E. 324 (1926) (another who ate similar food at same time also got sick); Sweany v. Walgreen Co., Inc., 323 Ill. App. 439, 55 N.E.2d 723 (1944) (both plaintiffs sick from same food); Doherty v. S. S. Kresge Co., 227 Wis. 254, 278 N.W. 437 (1938) (others who ate defendant's turkey got sick); Picard v. Smith, 40 F.2d 803 (App. D.C. 1930) (tainted oyster; three persons sick). See Palmer v. Rosedale Catering Co., 195 So. 859 (La. App. 1940) (tainted shrimp salad; four persons sick). The problem is the same in warranty cases. *E.g.*, Johnson v. Kanavos, 296 Mass. 373, 6 N.E.2d 434 (1937) (unwholesome frankfurter sandwich; three persons sick); Lohse v. Coffey, 32 A.2d 258 (D.C. Munic. App. 1943) (unwholesome food; another patron sick).

not get sick,[3] (3) that the food tasted, smelled, or looked bad,[4] and (4) that no other food (or, in the case of trichinosis, no other pork) was eaten during the period of probable exposure.[5] Helpful is testimony by the attending physician that the plaintiff's condition could well be the result of eating the defendant's product.[6] The problem of showing causation in the restaurant cases is not materially different from what the plaintiff faces when suing the retailer, wholesaler, or manufacturer,[7] or when suing the restaurateur for breach of warranty.[8]

[3] See Palmer v. Rosedale Catering Co., 195 So. 859 (La. App. 1940) (tainted shrimp salad; two of party of six who did not eat shrimp did not get sick).

[4] George's Restaurant v. Dukes, 216 Ala. 239, 113 So. 53 (1927) (tainted fish sandwich appeared decayed and was infected with maggots); Stell v. Townsend's California Glace Fruits, Inc., 138 Cal. App. 777, 28 P.2d 1077 (1934) (fish had peculiar taste). The problem is the same where the suit is for breach of warranty. *E.g.*, Johnson v. Kanavos, 296 Mass. 373, 375, 6 N.E.2d 434, 435 (1937) (frankfurter sandwich had a peculiar taste); Leahy v. Essex Co., 164 App. Div. 903, 148 N.Y. Supp. 1063 (3d Dept. 1914) (chocolate pie had peculiar taste and color). See, however, Blarjeske v. Thompson's Restaurant Co., 325 Ill. App. 189, 59 N.E.2d 320 (1945) (sickness of two plaintiffs and evidence that remaining beef had deep green fungus growth *held* insufficient where there was no analysis of the remainder of the sandwich and attending physician did not testify that there could have been a causal connection).

Compare the use of abnormal appearance, smell, or taste for the purpose of showing causation and its use for the purpose of showing negligence. See note 14 *infra*. In H. J. Heinz Co. v. Duke, 196 Ark. 180, 116 S.W.2d 1039 (1938), the fact that canned chili looked and tasted peculiar to the plaintiff did not mean that it did also to the restaurant keeper and hence there was no basis for inferring negligence.

[5] McPherson v. Capuano & Co., 31 Ga. App. 82, 121 S.E. 580 (1923) (unwholesome barbecued sandwich; nothing else eaten since lunch).

[6] Pantaze v. West, 7 Ala. App. 599, 603, 61 So. 42, 43 (1913). See Lohse v. Coffey, 32 A.2d 258 (D.C. Munic. App. 1943). At the same time, many courts exclude medical testimony that the defendant's product did in fact cause the plaintiff's illness. *E.g.*, Travis v. Louisville & N.R.R., 183 Ala. 415, 62 So. 851 (1913); Kenower v. Hotels Statler Company, Inc., 124 F.2d 658 (C.C.A. 6th, 1942). For a critical analysis of this view, see 2 Wigmore, Evidence §§672–680 (3d ed. 1940).

[7] See Topic B, Chapter II.

[8] *E.g.*, Miller v. W. T. Grant Co., 302 Mass. 429, 19 N.E.2d 704 (1939)

Once causation has been established, many courts appear ready to permit the inference that the defendant was negligent from the fact that the food is spoiled or diseased.[9] (A showing of general due care by the defendant has not been

---

(illness held to be only conjectural result of eating chop suey); Gracey v. Waldorf System, Inc., 251 Mass. 76, 146 N.E. 232 (1925) (no evidence of causation other than that illness followed eating in defendant's restaurant by three or four hours); Stewart v. Martin, 353 Mo. 1, 181 S.W.2d 647 (1944) (illness following eating of barbecued ham sandwich, without more, held insufficient evidence that sandwich was unwholesome); Blackman v. Lundy, 193 Misc. 745, 87 N.Y.S.2d 181 (1948) (illness not connected with defendant's food with reasonable certainty).

Sufficient evidence of causation was found in Ogden v. Rosedale Inn, 189 So. 162 (La. App. 1939) (of party of six, the four who ate defendant's shrimp got sick); Smith v. Gerrish, 256 Mass. 183, 152 N.E. 318 (1926) (unwholesome mackerel tasted unfit); Barringer v. Ocean S.S. Co. of Savannah, 240 Mass. 405, 134 N.E. 265 (1922) (food had peculiar taste; no other food eaten during probable incubation period); Tipple v. High Street Hotel Co., 41 N.E.2d 879 (Ohio App., Franklin Co. 1941) (tainted sausage).

[9] Louis Pizitz Dry Goods Co. v. Waldrop, 237 Ala. 208, 186 So. 151 (1939) (impure mayonnaise); Stell v. Townsend's California Glace Fruits, Inc., 138 Cal. App. 777, 28 P.2d 1077 (1934) (tainted fish); Beckham v. Jacobs Pharmacy Co., 25 Ga. App. 592, 103 S.E. 857 (1920) (deleterious Coca-Cola and celery drink); Sweany v. Walgreen Co., Inc., 323 Ill. App. 439, 55 N.E.2d 723 (1944) (unwholesome food); Picard v. Smith, 40 F.2d 803 (App. D.C. 1930) (tainted oysters; there was also evidence that the oysters were inadequately refrigerated). Under *res ipsa loquitur:* Copeland v. Curtis, 36 Ga. App. 255, 136 S.E. 324 (1926) (unwholesome food); McPherson v. Capuano & Co., 31 Ga. App. 82, 121 S.E. 580 (1923) (unwholesome barbecue sandwich). See Lee v. Smith, 168 So. 727 (La. App. 1936) (unwholesome food); Wilson v. Moore, 159 So. 399 (La. App. 1935) (manufacturer of pie absolved of negligence where spoiled pie had been held thirty-six hours by restaurant keeper); Costello v. Morrison Cafeteria Co. of Louisiana, Inc., 18 La. App. 40, 135 So. 245 (1931) (unwholesome cream cheese; general charge of negligence not demurrable). *Contra:* Sheffer v. Willoughby, 163 Ill. 518, 45 N.E. 253 (1896) (tainted oysters); Crocker v. Baltimore Dairy Lunch Co., 214 Mass. 177, 100 N.E. 1078 (1913) (tainted food; from plaintiff's illness the court was willing to permit an inference of causation but not of negligence); Goodwin v. Misticos, 207 Miss. 361, 379, 42 So.2d 397, 402 (1949) (unwholesome corned beef); Gill v. Ceases' Lunch System, Inc., 194 N.C. 803, 139 S.E. 925 (1927) ("unwholesome food"); Lamb v. Boyles, 192 N.C. 542, 135 S.E. 464 (1926) (unwholesome strawberry ale).

notably successful in combating this inference.)[10] However, in a specific case the nature of the particular defect ultimately controls. Thus the plaintiff is likely to win in a trichinosis case involving fresh pork, because, although undetectable, the condition is cured by customary restaurant cooking.[11] He is likely to lose where the trichinosis comes from a pork product, such as metwurst, which the restaurant keeper is not expected to cook.[12] He is also likely to lose in a typhoid case, or one involving a latent defect in food fabricated or produced by another.[13] On the other hand, he is likely to win in any case where the spoilage or taint is reasonably detectable because of abnormal color, taste, or smell,[14] or where there is some other evidence of negligence.[15]

[10] *E.g.*, Greenwood Cafe v. Lovinggood, 197 Ala. 34, 72 So. 354 (1916) (tainted food); Pantaze v. West, 7 Ala. App. 599, 61 So. 42 (1913) (tainted brains); Doyle v. Fuerst & Kraemer, Ltd., 129 La. 838, 840, 56 So. 906, 907 (1911) (unwholesome cakes and chocolate). But *cf.* Prinsen v. Russos, 194 Wis. 142, 215 N.W. 905 (1927) (proof by the defendant that he cooked pork at 137° F. or more tended to show that he was careful and that his product was not the source of the plaintiff's injury).

[11] Eisenbach v. Gimbel Bros., Inc., 281 N.Y. 474, 24 N.E.2d 131 (1939) (trichinae in pork tenderloin); Pantaze v. West, 7 Ala. App. 599, 603, 61 So. 42, 43 (1913) (the harmful effects of tainted brains often removed by proper cooking). But *cf.* Prinsen v. Russos, 194 Wis. 142, 215 N.W. 905 (1927).

[12] See Kenower v. Hotels Statler Co., Inc., 124 F.2d 658 (C.C.A. 6th, 1942) (typhoid-infected clams; plaintiff recovered in warranty but court found insufficient evidence of negligence).

[13] H. J. Heinz Co. v. Duke, 196 Ark. 180, 116 S.W.2d 1039 (1938) (unwholesome canned chili; goods had normal appearance when removed from can); Albrecht v. Rubinstein, 135 Conn. 243, 63 A.2d 158 (1948) (unwholesome corned-beef sandwich).

[14] C. C. Hooper Cafe Co. v. Henderson, 223 Ala. 579, 137 So. 419 (1931) (spoiled fish); Louisville & N.R.R. v. Travis, 192 Ala. 453, 68 So. 342 (1915) (tainted oysters); Pantaze v. West, 7 Ala. App. 599, 61 So. 42 (1913) (tainted brains); Bark v. Dixson, 115 Minn. 172, 131 N.W. 1078 (1911) (tainted meat); King v. Davis, 296 Fed. 986 (App. D.C. 1924) (tainted veal; expert testified that experienced person can ascertain its condition). But *cf.* H. J. Heinz Co. v. Duke, 196 Ark. 180, 116 S.W.2d 1039 (1938) (canned chili appeared peculiar to patron but not to defendant).

[15] Malone v. Jones, 91 Kans. 815, 139 Pac. 387 (1914), 92 Kans. 708,

It has been said,[16] with apparent accuracy, that where food is infected or spoiled (and causation has been established) the courts tend to raise a permissible inference or presumption of negligence more readily than where it contains a deleterious foreign substance. This is probably because mishandling or inadequate inspection by the restaurant keeper is more likely to be the significant factor in the case of such defects than it is in the case of foreign objects. If this analysis is correct, differences in result are to be attributed to differences in factual situation rather than in the legal principles applied. However, sound generalizations here can only relate to over-all tendencies, not clear-cut patterns.

§3.6. Restaurateurs and manufacturers compared. It has also been suggested [1] that the courts are less likely to apply the doctrine of *res ipsa loquitur* to the restaurant keeper than to the manufacturer. This, too, seems to be a correct generalization, and it applies equally to inferences and presumptions of negligence unadorned with Latin. Again the question arises as to whether the difference is attributable to differences in factual tendencies or to differences in the legal principles applied.

As fabricator, assembler, or distributor, the typical restaurant keeper probably draws more widely upon products fabricated or assembled by others than the typical manufacturer does. In view of the facts of manufacturers' liability for negligence already discussed, the courts are apparently placing a greater emphasis on the difference between

142 Pac. 274 (1914) (tainted beef, seen by defendant to have maggots); Picard v. Smith, 40 F.2d 803 (App. D.C. 1930) (tainted oysters, inadequately refrigerated).

[16] Note, 20 Minn. L. Rev. 527, 529–530 (1936).

§3.6. [1] Note, 13 Minn. L. Rev. 265 (1929).

the seller as fabricator and the seller as assembler or distributor in the case of the restaurateur than it does in the case of the manufacturer.[2]

Secondly, the opportunities of finding out what actually happened in a specific instance are substantially greater in restaurant cases than in those in which the defendant is a manufacturer. The food receives its final preparation for eating on the premises where the plaintiff is injured, usually just before he eats it. Closer access to the offending event makes it easier not only to show causation but to show a specific defective condition in the defendant's kitchen bearing a plausible relationship to the plaintiff's injury. Accordingly, the courts are able to come closer to trying a real negligence issue and there is less need to resort to the drastic inferences or presumptions which so often, in the case of the manufacturer, mean imposing what is in substance absolute liability. The irony here is twofold. The consumer's chances of recovery are less even though he needs protection more, and even though stronger evidence is available for showing actual fault.

As to whether the courts are holding the restaurant keeper to a lower standard of inspection, it would be hard to generalize significantly. The position of the Massachusetts court taken in *Ash* v. *Childs Dining Hall Co.*, noted in Section 3.4, contrasts with that taken in Ohio in *Clark Restaurant Co.* v. *Rau*,[3] where the mere existence of small glass fragments ("the size of half a pea") in ice cream made by another was held to be evidence of negligence.

§3.7. Violation of pure food law. Where there is an applicable pure food statute, the doctrine of negligence per se appears to apply as fully to the restaurateur as it does

[2] See Chapter II, Topics B and E.
[3] 41 Ohio App. 23, 24, 179 N.E. 196, 197 (1931).

to other kinds of food sellers. Any doubt that exists here apparently lies in the question whether the particular statute extends to this kind of seller.[1] As a matter of local statutory construction, the problem is of little significance here. If the statute applies, "negligence" usually follows from the defendant's violation as a matter of law.[2]

§3.7. [1] In Travis v. Louisville & N.R.R., 183 Ala. 415, 423, 62 So. 851, 853 (1913), the court said the Alabama statute forbidding butchers and other persons to sell tainted fish "is not *aimed at* but was passed for *the benefit of* hotels, restaurants, and public eating houses . . ."

[2] Greenwood v. John R. Thompson Co., 213 Ill. App. 371 (1919); Alphin v. La Salle Diners, Inc., 197 Misc. 415, 98 N.Y.S.2d 511 (1950); Yochem v. Gloria, Inc., 134 Ohio St. 427, 17 N.E.2d 731 (1938); Clark Restaurant Co. v. Simmons, 29 Ohio App. 220, 163 N.E. 210 (1927); Doherty v. S. S. Kresge Co., 227 Wis. 254, 278 N.W. 437 (1938) (construing the Minnesota pure food law); Hayes v. S. H. Kress and Co., CCH Food Drug Cosmetic Law Rep. ¶85,102 (W.D.S.C. 1947). See Mills Restaurant Co. v. Clark, 45 Ohio App. 25, 185 N.E. 470 (1933) (salmon salad; the plaintiff made out a case of causation but failed to show that the food was unwholesome to normal people generally). But *cf.* Christian v. Hotel Waldorf Astoria Corporation, 187 Misc. 516, 517, 67 N.Y.S.2d 281, 282 (1946) ("Merely because a condition or practice was objectionable to an investigator of the Department of Health would not establish negligence, unless there was a statute or ordinance violated, or customary methods were not followed, or the methods adopted would result in food not fit for use"). In Massachusetts, violation of a pure food law is only evidence of negligence. Schuler v. Union News Co., 295 Mass. 350, 4 N.E.2d 465 (1936). And see Chapter I, §1.24, and Chapter II, §2.19.

CHAPTER IV

What Is "Fit to Eat"?

CHAPTER IV

What Is "Fit to Eat"?

Topic A. *In General*

§4.1. The problem of wholesomeness. A stomach upset is not necessarily a cause of action, even where the seller has had something to do with it. The sufferer must show that his discomfort has been caused by something the law considers a defect. This is true whether the problem arises as one of "wholesomeness," "fitness," or "merchantability"; arises under the Uniform Sales Act or at common law; or arises in a suit for breach of warranty or common law negligence. For food the problem is single: Is what the seller delivers legally fit to eat?

The legal concept of wholesomeness is a concept of the quality of the goods delivered, but it is not a concept that what is delivered is good to eat in its existing condition. Packaged foods must be opened. Nonpackaged foods usually need trimming or washing. Packaged or not, most foods have to be heated, cooked, thawed, hydrated, combined with other ingredients, or otherwise processed before eating. When the seller says that his food is wholesome, he is not necessarily saying that you can eat it just as he hands it to you.

This does not mean that delivery time gives way to meal time as the true measuring stick. The seller is not responsible for all that happens after the product leaves his hands.

He is responsible for having it in such a condition at the time of delivery that if within a reasonable time certain things are done, it will then be good to eat. Thus the law calls for potential rather than immediate actual edibility. The problem is to determine the conditions under which the potentiality is to be realized.

The clearest case of legal defect is that of the generally unanticipated foreign object. Iron filings in canned tomatoes, pebbles in canned beans, and glass in bread are legal defects, even though removing them would make the remainder edible. Obviously, this is not the kind of potential edibility intended by the law. Similarly for botulinus and Malta fever germs. A different conclusion for maggots on sausage is hard to justify.[1]

§4.2. The test of "naturalness." It is common to say that the matter of legal defect turns on whether the condition involves something that is "natural" or "foreign" to the food. In *Mix* v. *Ingersoll Candy Co.*,[1] the California Supreme Court held as a matter of law that a chicken bone did not render a restaurant keeper's chicken pie defective. "Bones which are natural to the type of meat served cannot legitimately be called a foreign substance. . . ." The language was repeated by a lower court in *Silva* v. *F. W. Woolworth Co.*,[2] involving a turkey bone in dressing accompanying an order of roast turkey. The latter court was only slightly

§4.1. [1] Reese v. Smith, 9 Cal. 2d 324, 70 P.2d 933 (1937), holding for the defendant. See also Copeland v. F. W. Woolworth Co., 187 Misc. 456, 62 N.Y.S.2d 660 (1946) (nail in food). But *cf.* Medeiros v. Coca-Cola Bottling Co. of Turlock, Ltd., 57 Cal. App. 2d 707, 135 P.2d 676 (1943). Ordinarily, a foreign object is considered a legal defect. Whether or not the plaintiff actually recovers depends upon showing a breach of duty and proximate damage.

§4.2. [1] 6 Cal. 2d 674, 59 P.2d 145 (1936).
[2] 28 Cal. App. 2d 649, 83 P.2d 76 (1938).

bothered by the fact that the bone was in the dressing and not the turkey.[3] Upon the authority of these cases, the Iowa Supreme Court, in *Brown* v. *Nebiker*,[4] has since found a bone sliver compatible with a pork chop ("certainly small bones in a pork chop are not a foreign substance to the pork chop").

Insofar as these cases rest on the notion of "naturalness" in the sense that nothing that is an inherent part of the raw product itself can be a legal defect, they do not hold water. Sand is foreign to fresh spinach but not a legal defect. Conversely, salt crystals are natural to crab meat, oyster shells are natural to oysters, and yeast fermentation is natural to some soft drinks; and yet, as the next section shows, these substances have been treated as legal defects.

§4.3. The test of reasonable expectation. The better test of what is legally defective appears to be what consumers customarily expect and guard against. Canned foods are expected to be found already washed, cleaned, and trimmed, while the same foods in fresh form normally call for work of that sort by the consumer. Gravel, therefore, is a defect in canned spinach but not in fresh. Arsenic is a defect in canned apples but not (within the tolerance permitted by the food and drug laws) on fresh.

When frozen foods first appeared, no custom existed. Consumer expectations that frozen foods could be classed with canned rather than fresh foods in this respect were developed partly through advertising and newspaper and

[3] *Ibid.* ". . . we must look upon the service as one dish as delivered in which there was no substance not 'natural' to the type of meat served." Another case to the same effect is Frier v. Laube's Old Spain, Inc., 265 App. Div. 402, 39 N.Y.S.2d 794 (4th Dept. 1943). It is interesting to speculate on what the California court would have said had the bone been in the mashed potatoes, or had been in the mashed potatoes and served in a separate dish.

[4] 229 Iowa 1223, 1234, 296 N.W. 366, 371 (1941).

magazine publicity, but mostly through experience with the goods themselves. But the situation even with respect to "fresh" foods is subject to change. The development of prepackaged fresh fruits and vegetables for air transport, for example, suggests the increasingly greater reliance on the seller to provide a product that is nearer to actual edibility at the moment of sale.

The three cases already cited in the preceding section have adopted the consumer-expectation approach as a supporting rationale, possibly on the assumption that anything that is natural to the product is in fact anticipated by the consumer. At the same time, an Illinois appellate court has found a bone no undue threat to creamed chicken, on the basis of normal expectation, not what is natural or foreign.[1] Similarly for cherry pits in cherry pie in an unreported Massachusetts case,[2] and a bone in a barbecued pork sandwich in a recent Georgia case.[3]

The crucial situation, of course, is that where the alleged defect is natural but generally unanticipated. So far as is known, no court of last resort has held any such defect to exist as a matter of law, but at least two have left the question of wholesomeness to the jury.

In *Gimenez* v. *Great Atlantic & Pacific Tea Co.*,[4] the New York Court of Appeals upheld a judgment for the plaintiff where the defect was the presence in canned crab meat of natural salt crystals formed after canning from the natural juices of the meat. Whether this case was correctly decided

§4.3. [1] Goodwin v. Country Club of Peoria, 323 Ill. App. 1, 54 N.E.2d 612 (1944).

[2] Marnelos v. Anastasovites, unreported, D.C. Springfield, Mass., App. Div. (Mar. 9, 1933).

[3] Norris v. Pig'n Whistle Sandwich Shop, Inc., 53 S.E.2d 718 (Ga. App. 1949).

[4] 264 N.Y. 390, 191 N.E. 27 (1934).

would seem to depend upon what purchasers of crab meat normally anticipate and guard against. Melick, who was counsel for the defendant, says[5] that " . . . the record on appeal in this case discloses no direct evidence introduced by plaintiff to show the salt formed was deleterious or that it was customary for similar crab meat to be free from it . . ." The decision is perplexing because the question of wholesomeness was not fully discussed by the court and it is not clear what specific legal principles the court had in mind. It has since been interpreted by a lower New York court as holding that, however "natural," these salt crystals are legally deleterious.[6]

In *Bonenberger* v. *Pittsburgh Mercantile Co.*,[7] the Pennsylvania Supreme Court remanded a case in which there had been a directed verdict for the defendant. It said that whether oyster shells made canned oysters deleterious was a jury question. "We cannot say as a matter of law that the product furnished the plaintiffs was reasonably fit for human consumption." Couching the question only in general terms of what was "deleterious," the court did not say specifically that the jury's decision was to depend on what consumers-in-general anticipated. However, that is a fair inference, since the court clearly repudiated the natural-foreign test.

Although all the decisions cited rest at least partly on the normal-consumer-expectation approach, it is questionable whether several properly applied that doctrine. The *Gimenez* case, upholding liability, is probably the most doubtful. The *Silva* case, denying liability, is also questionable, not only on the basis of what the consumer may

[5] Melick, The Sale of Food and Drink 56 (1936).
[6] O'Hare v. Petersen, 174 Misc. 481, 21 N.Y.S.2d 487 (1940).
[7] 345 Pa. 559, 563, 28 A.2d 913, 915 (1942).

reasonably expect but also on the basis of what is "normal" to turkey dressing.

Chicken bones in chicken pie are near the borderline. If their true basis is reasonable consumer expectation, the matter would seem to be a proper jury question and not one of law for the court. The California court in the *Mix* case, in effect, took judicial notice of the frequency with which chicken bones appear in chicken pie.

> It is not necessary to go so far as to hold that chicken pies usually contain chicken bones. It is sufficient if it may be said that as a matter of common knowledge chicken pies occasionally contain chicken bones . . . a consumer who eats meat dishes ought to anticipate and be on his guard against the presence of such bones.[8]

In dispensing with "usual" and passing over "frequent" for "occasional," the court came dangerously close to saying that stones in baked beans are no defect because they are occasionally found there. Putting aside the fact that stones are not "natural" to baked beans (an irrelevant consideration at best), we may say that the only significant difference between stones and chicken bones is one of comparative frequency, sufficient to put the normal consumer on guard in one case and not in the other. Whether only an "occasional" object is sufficiently frequent to warn is open to question.

The cases denying liability cited above are restaurant cases. Although this apparently made no difference, the fact that the defendant was a restaurateur might well have been a relevant consideration in reaching the opposite result. The consumer is undoubtedly less vigilant in a restaurant than at home. In the former case he is on guard

[8] 6 Cal. 2d 674, 682, 59 P.2d 145, 148 (1936). In Paolinelli v. Dainty Foods Manufacturers, Inc., 322 Ill. App. 586, 54 N.E.2d 759 (1944), the plaintiff recovered for injuries caused by a chicken bone in chicken noodle soup. The question at issue was not discussed in the opinion.

only as eater; in the latter, first as one in control of preparation, then as eater. At least partly offsetting this would be any assumption that the standard of care generally expected of restaurateurs by consumers is lower than that generally expected of food manufacturers.

If the foregoing analysis is correct, nothing that prevents food from being edible is a legal defect if the normally expected processing by the consumer would anticipate and remove it. However, the converse proposition — that whatever prevents food from being edible is a legal defect if the normally expected processing by the consumer would not anticipate and remove it — is not necessarily true. Not everything that the consumer normally fails to intercept is attributable to culpable action or inaction by the defendant. The point is well illustrated by the trichinosis cases discussed in Topic B.[9]

Just as a barrier to immediate edibility existing when the goods are delivered is not necessarily a legal defect (at least where normal consumer precautions will remove it), the fact that the goods could be safely eaten at the time of sale does not mean that the goods are legally wholesome. The goods must be wholesome for a reasonable time after purchase. In the *Giminez* case the salt crystals developed after canning and could have developed even after purchase. In *White* v. *Coca-Cola Bottling Co.*,[10] the drink was wholesome

[9] An interesting problem was presented by Maddox Coffee Co. v. Collins, 46 Ga. App. 220, 167 S.E. 306 (1932). Here the plaintiff recovered for injuries caused by small particles of glass in a handful of the defendant's coffee beans which the plaintiff had consumed "raw." There was some indication that had the coffee been consumed in the normal way the glass risk might have been avoided. Recovery was allowed, however. The decision is probably correct, because the risk, which was properly attributable to the defendant, was not such as the usual modes of cookery are intended to prevent.

[10] 16 So.2d 579 (La. App. 1943).

when made, but improper sealing produced sugar fermentation and ultimately yeast. In *Rosenbusch* v. *Ambrosia Milk Corp.*,[11] a dried milk product deteriorated because of inherent characteristics. Whether deterioration occurred before or after purchase appears to have made no difference. In each case, since the food was eaten within a reasonable time, the product was defective because its condition when eaten showed that at the time of purchase and delivery it did not have the capacity for remaining edible which the law requires.

If goods deteriorate normally and the consumer is injured because he eats them beyond a reasonable time after *manufacture*, whether or not the goods were legally defective would presumably depend upon whether it was the seller or the consumer who held them too long.[12] If the former, the retailer would be responsible for having sold an unwholesome product. Whether earlier distributors and the manufacturer would also be accountable would depend upon who caused the delay. If the retailer was at fault, for example, earlier sellers would be free of negligence [13] and in both negligence and warranty suits they would have the defense of no causation.

Topic B. *The Trichinosis Cases* *

§4.4. The disease. Trichinosis is a disease that attacks the voluntary muscles. It temporarily cripples, usually has

[11] 181 App. Div. 97, 168 N.Y. Supp. 505 (1st Dept. 1917).

[12] *E.g.*, Barker v. Weingarten Riverside Co., Inc., 232 S.W.2d 692 (Tex. Civ. App. 1950).

[13] In Wilson v. Moore, 159 So. 399 (La. App. 1935), a pie manufacturer was absolved of negligence where the spoiled pie had been held thirty-six hours by the restaurant keeper.

* On trichinae generally, see Gould, Trichinosis (1945); Schwartz, "Trichinosis in Swine and Its Relationship to Public Health," Journal of

permanent results, and sometimes causes death. It is caused by the parasite, *Trichinella spiralis*, commonly called "trichina." Trichinae can be acquired and passed on only by a carnivorous or omnivorous animal. Human beings are infected by eating the infected muscle tissue of swine. Hogs acquire the disease at the farm, usually as a result of feeding conditions. For practical purposes, the presence of trichinae is undetectable.

§4.5. Trichinae as a problem of legal wholesomeness. Pork substantially infected with trichinae is plainly not good to eat in that condition. The question of legal wholesomeness is raised by the fact that, unlike the pasteurization of milk or the chlorination of water, removing the danger of trichinosis is normally practicable only *after* the goods have been turned over to the consumer. Trichinae can be killed by heating all parts of the meat to at least 137° F.,[1] by holding it at 5° F. or below for at least twenty days, or by using curing processes specially adapted to particular pork products. For the general run of pork it is not feasible for the seller to take any of these steps. On the other hand, it is feasible for the consumer to cook the product when he prepares it for eating.

All trichinous pork eaten by the consumer is in that condition when it passes over the retail counter. Is meat so delivered legally wholesome?

The argument for saying that it is runs sometimes like

---

the American Veterinary Medical Assn., Vol. XCII (N.S. 45) 317 (1938); Leaflet No. 34, U.S. Dept. of Agric. (rev. ed. May, 1946); Note, 21 Temp. L.Q. 80 (1941). For a discussion of the law, see Walker, "Liability of Packer or Retailer for Injuries Arising from the Consumption of Pork Containing Trichinae," 30 Ohio Opinions 18 (1945).

§4.5. [1] Schwartz, *id.* at 333, says that this is the correct temperature "for official purposes" but that studies by Ransom and Schwartz indicate that "the thermal death-point of trichinae is 131° F."

this: [2] Unless otherwise understood by the parties, pork is not ordinarily sold to be eaten raw; it can be assumed that the consumer will cook it. Properly cooked pork is safe. Therefore, pork may be legally wholesome even though it is infected with trichinae.

This approach resembles that already urged for food generally. But notice the jump from "cooking" to "proper cooking." The special twist in the trichinosis cases is the fact that, although the seller can rely on the consumer not to eat pork raw, it is not clear that he is justified in relying on the consumer to cook it sufficiently to kill all possible parasites.[3]

The difference between stating the seller's obligation in terms of common cooking practices and stating it in terms of "proper" (successful) cooking is the difference between a seller obligation with respect to quality and no obligation. Almost any food can be made edible if adequately processed, whatever its condition at the retail counter. Spinach and lettuce can be washed free of gravel, and glass can be removed from a soft drink bottle. The difference between gravel and glass is the difference between what is commonly accepted by the consumer as appropriate preparation for eating and what is not. It makes sense, therefore, only to phrase the seller's obligation in terms of the quality of the goods after *customary* consumer preparation.

Put on firmer ground, the cases that find no legal defect in trichinous pork are sound only if it can be assumed that commonly accepted cooking practices are adequate to intercept the parasite. That the presence of trichinae does not constitute a defect appears to have received some sup-

[2] *E.g.*, Feinstein v. Daniel Reeves, Inc., 14 F. Supp. 167, 168 (S.D.N.Y. 1936).

[3] *E.g.*, Holt v. Mann, 294 Mass. 21, 24–25, 200 N.E. 403, 405 (1936).

port in Illinois,[4] in Ontario,[5] and in one of the federal courts.[6]

§4.6. "Trichinous pork is unwholesome, but judgment for the defendant" — Contributory fault. The concept of what is fit to eat has been clouded in the trichinosis cases by the fact that most courts that have freed the defendant of responsibility have used alternative approaches that seem to imply, at least for the purposes of argument, that the presence of trichinae is a defect. In most of these cases the net result is the same or almost the same, but what such a court would do in the absence of the alternative is not always clear.

One approach is to say that since common cooking practice is adequate to kill trichinae, the fact that the plaintiff was injured means that the pork was not cooked according to accepted standards and, therefore, that the plaintiff is barred by his own fault.[1]

In negligence cases this approach fits the contributory negligence mold. It is more awkward where the suit is for

[4] Zorger v. Hillman's, 287 Ill. App. 357, 4 N.E.2d 900 (1936) (holding that Illinois' pure food statute requires only "that pork is fit for food when properly cooked"; that by "proper" the court meant "effective" is inferred from the fact that it approved an instruction that the plaintiff must show that the meat sold by the defendant was unfit for consumption after being heated to 137° F., an effective temperature). The assumption that customary cooking is proper cooking is also made in Nicketta v. National Tea Co., 338 Ill. App. 159, 87 N.E.2d 30 (1949).

[5] Yachetti v. John Duff & Sons Ltd., [1943] 1 D.L.R. 194, [1942] O.R. 682, [1942] O.W.N. 639.

[6] Feinstein v. Daniel Reeves, Inc., 14 F. Supp. 167, 168 (S.D.N.Y. 1936). "Having alleged the condition of the pork he ate, it was incumbent upon him to show that trichinae infected pork, when thoroughly cooked, would cause trichinosis. The evidence conclusively shows the opposite."

§4.6. [1] Leonardi v. A. Habermann Provision Co., 143 Ohio St. 623, 56 N.E.2d 232 (1944). Eisenbach v. Gimbel Bros., Inc., 281 N.Y. 474, 24 N.E. 2d 131 (1939), is not entirely on all fours, since the plaintiff was a restaurant keeper, not a consumer. Customary restaurant cookery may well be different from customary home cookery.

breach of warranty. Section 15 (3), which handles some of the contributory fault situations for warranty suits, hardly applies here. In *Eisenbach* v. *Gimbel Bros., Inc.*,[2] the New York Court of Appeals talked as if it were applying the doctrine of avoidable consequences, but in barring the action altogether (instead of giving nominal relief) it brought into food warranty suits a concept close to that of contributory negligence.

Whether the approach is "avoidable consequences" or "contributory negligence," it implies that the defendant has committed an actionable wrong for which he is at least nominally liable or would be liable but for the carelessness of the plaintiff. But why stigmatize an action that can have significant consequences for the plaintiff only if he disqualifies himself from recovering? The same substantive result is reached more directly by saying that the product is wholesome and the defendant has done no actionable wrong. Of course, if it is assumed that common cooking practice is *not* adequate, and the plaintiff has failed to come up even to that standard, a fault-of-the-plaintiff approach makes more sense.

§4.7. "Trichinous pork is unwholesome, but judgment for the defendant" — Want of defendant's fault. A more frequent approach taken in negligence cases excuses the defendant for want of common law fault. Examples are found in Michigan, New York, Pennsylvania, and Ontario.[1]

[2] 281 N.Y. 474, 24 N.E.2d 131 (1939). The plaintiff could not recover for breach of warranty against a wholesaler "for a loss that he could have averted by the exercise of due care."

§4.7. [1] Cheli v. Cudahy Bros. Co., 267 Mich. 690, 695, 255 N.W. 414, 415 (1934); Lucey v. Harstedt, 270 App. Div. 900, 61 N.Y.S.2d 157 (2d Dept. 1946); Dressler v. Merkel, Inc., 247 App. Div. 300, 284 N.Y. Supp. 697 (2d Dept. 1936); Yachetti v. John Duff & Sons Ltd., [1943] 1 D.L.R. 194, 197, [1942] O.R. 682, 685, [1942] O.W.M. 639, 640.

Although this theory goes directly to the question of the seller's obligation, its utility for protecting the defendant, like that of contributory negligence, is limited to negligence suits. It assumes that the presence of trichinae may well be a legal defect and leaves the way open for trichinae suits brought for breach of warranty. Here, there is a vital difference in practical effect, as well as in theory, between suing for negligence and suing for breach of warranty. The plaintiff's chances in warranty are good. But if the suit is in negligence, not even the doctrine of *res ipsa loquitur* will turn the trick, unless the defendant has failed to educate the court as to trichinae.[2]

§4.8. "Trichinous pork is unwholesome, but judgment for the defendant" — Want of plaintiff's reliance. Another possible approach might deny recovery on the ground that the consumer reasonably relies on his own cooking, not the defendant's, to remove the trichinae. Such an approach would be relevant only where the plaintiff sued for breach of a warranty of fitness.

§4.9. "Trichinous pork is unwholesome, but judgment for the defendant" — Other reasons why plaintiffs lose. In addition to the cases noted in Sections 4.6, 4.7, and 4.8 are those in which the plaintiff lost because he failed to notify the defendant in time,[1] because privity of contract was wanting,[2] because he failed to prove the sale in question,[3] or because of procedural considerations.[4]

[2] *E.g.*, Arena v. John P. Squire Co., 321 Mass. 423, 73 N.E.2d 836 (1947); Catani v. Swift & Co., 251 Pa. 52, 95 Atl. 931 (1914).

§4.9. [1] Hazelton v. First National Stores, 88 N.H. 409, 190 Atl. 280 (1937).

[2] *Id.* at 410, 190 Atl. at 281.

[3] Askam v. Platt, 85 Conn. 448, 83 Atl. 529 (1912); Occhipinti v. Buscemi, 267 App. Div. 874, 46 N.Y.S.2d 292 (2d Dept. 1944).

[4] Kneiss v. Armour & Co., 134 Ohio St. 432, 445, 17 N.E.2d 734, 739 (1938), holding that the suit against the packer, an out-of-state corpora-

§4.10. Violation of pure food law. The problem of what is fit to eat for the purposes of civil liability is further complicated where the suit is for negligence per se based on the breach of a pure food statute. Here the problem is not so much what is, broadly, a defect for the purposes of civil liability as it is whether or not the alleged defect comes within a specially defined class of statutory defects as to which criminal sanctions are applied and a civil plaintiff is relieved of showing actual negligence. The fact that trichinae are found to be outside the statutory class does not necessarily mean that they do not constitute a legal defect for warranty purposes. Accordingly, cases so holding [1] do not bear directly on the question except as they lean on general criteria of wholesomeness or indicate the court's views as to whether customary cooking is adequate.

§4.11. Trichinous pork as a basis of liability. Although the cases excusing the defendant from liability do not necessarily assume that the presence of trichinae involves no breach of the seller's duty to supply wholesome food, those that hold the seller liable necessarily assume that the presence of trichinae is such a breach. If the foregoing analysis is correct, these latter cases are sound only if customary consumer cooking practices are insufficient to intercept trichinae. Cases making this assumption (or permitting the

---

tion, was severable from that against the retailer and therefore should have been removed to the federal court.

§4.10. [1] Zorger v. Hillman's, 287 Ill. App. 357, 360, 4 N.E.2d 900, 901 (1936); Lucey v. Harstedt, 270 App. Div. 900, 61 N.Y.S.2d 157 (2d Dept. 1946); Blume v. Trunz Pork Stores, Inc., 269 App. Div. 1059, 59 N.Y.S.2d 217 (2d Dept. 1945); Dressler v. Merkel, Inc., 247 App. Div. 300, 303, 284 N.Y. Supp. 697, 702 (2d Dept. 1936); Feinstein v. Daniel Reeves, Inc., 14 F. Supp. 167, 168 (S.D.N.Y. 1936); Yachetti v. John Duff & Sons Ltd., [1943] 1 D.L.R. 194, 199, [1942] O.R. 682, 687, [1942] O.W.N. 639, 641. *Cf.* Cheli v. Cudahy Bros. Co., 267 Mich. 690, 694, 255 N.W. 414, 415 (1934).

jury to come to the same conclusion) are to be found in Massachusetts and New York. The Pennsylvania, Ohio, and Illinois courts also have found trichinae to constitute a defect, but they have not made specific findings on customary consumer cooking practices.

§4.12. Trichinous pork as a basis of liability — Massachusetts. The Massachusetts position was stated in *Holt* v. *Mann*,[1] where a retailer was held liable in warranty. "It could have been found that the ham was cooked as thoroughly as could be expected in a family, but without killing trichinae with which it was infected." In *Arena* v. *John P. Squire Co.*,[2] the manufacturer was held liable for negligence. With respect to contributory negligence, the court said that the plaintiff was new to this country and there was no evidence that she knew that cooking at 137° F. would kill live trichinae. "The jury could find that she cooked the pork as thoroughly as could be reasonably expected. . . ." The defendant's negligence, according to the court, was the failure to take the precaution of microscopic examination. The plaintiff's inability to reach the defendant in warranty (because of privity considerations) was thus compensated for by the defendant's failure properly to educate the court on the mysteries of trichinae. Inspection, it is generally conceded, is not only useless but in some respects unwise.[3]

§4.12. [1] 294 Mass. 21, 25, 200 N.E. 403, 405 (1936).

[2] 321 Mass. 423, 427, 73 N.E. 2d 836, 839 (1947).

[3] "While microscopic inspection would probably eliminate most of the heavily infested hog carcasses, many lightly infested carcasses would be overlooked, and the good that such inspection might accomplish would be largely offset by creating a false sense of security in the minds of persons who habitually eat raw or imperfectly cooked pork." The point has apparently been borne out by German experience. Leaflet No. 34, U.S. Dept. of Agric. 7 (rev. ed. May, 1946). See also the testimony of the chief of the Bureau of Animal Industry as reported in Ketterer v. Armour & Co., 247 Fed. 921, 930 (C.C.A. 2d, 1917); and Tavani v. Swift & Co., 262 Pa. 184, 186, 105 Atl. 55, 56 (1918).

§4.13. Trichinous pork as a basis of liability — New York. The New York warranty cases [1] are reasonably uniform in holding the retailer liable for breach of warranty (want of privity immunizes other sellers from direct responsibility). Liability was first imposed in 1918, in *Rinaldi* v. *Mohican Co.*[2] Eighteen years later, in *McSpedon* v. *Kunz*,[3] the Court of Appeals said:

> This requisite of thorough heating and the nature of trichinae may seem very simple things to us and to experts who are dealing with these matters daily, but there are many people in this country who know nothing about trichinosis or the danger lurking in meats or the requisite heating point to destroy parasites . . .

It added:

> . . . especially should this protection [that of the Uniform Sales Act] be afforded when there is a well-known means for the detection of trichinae in pork and a well-known method of killing the parasite before the pork is put upon the market.

The makeweight argument was of doubtful relevancy and wrong factually.

The New York position that trichinae are a legal defect sufficient to support a warranty action against the retailer has been reaffirmed in several later decisions.[4] The decisions that have consistently denied liability in negligence [5] are not necessarily out of line in result, because they can be

§4.13. [1] The New York cases are discussed in Note, 1 Intra. L. Rev. N.Y.U. 38 (1945).

[2] 225 N.Y. 70, 121 N.E. 471 (1918).

[3] 271 N.Y. 131, 135, 137, 2 N.E. 2d 513, 514, 515 (1936).

[4] Eisenbach v. Gimbel Bros., Inc., 281 N.Y. 474, 24 N.E.2d 131 (1939) (restaurant case); Greco v. S. S. Kresge Co., 277 N.Y. 26, 12 N.E.2d 557 (1938).

[5] Lucey v. Harstedt, 270 App. Div. 900, 61 N.Y.S.2d 157 (2d Dept. 1946); Blume v. Trunz Pork Stores, Inc., 269 App. Div. 1059, 59 N.Y.S. 2d 217 (2d Dept. 1945); Dressler v. Merkel, Inc., 247 App. Div. 300, 284 N.Y. Supp. 697 (2d Dept. 1936); Feinstein v. Daniel Reeves, Inc., 14 F. Supp. 167 (S.D.N.Y. 1936).

based on the lack of common law culpability and the probable inapplicability of the Agriculture and Markets Law, New York's pure food law. However, the Appellate Division has on several occasions founded the inapplicability of several of the provisions of that law on the theory that they exclude products whose defects are removed by ordinary, reasonably-to-be-expected cooking.[6] This assumes that ordinarily accepted cooking practices are successful in combating trichinae, a factual assumption expressly repudiated by the Court of Appeals.[7]

This dilemma could be resolved by taking one of the following approaches: (1) The Agriculture and Markets Law does not apply to trichinae, for reasons independent of normal consumer expectation; (2) the Agriculture and Markets Law does apply to trichinous pork; or (3) trichinous pork is not legally defective. Alternative (1) would support the *status quo* in New York. (Reasons independent of normal consumer expectation can be found in the existing cases.) Alternative (2) would allow the consumer to reach the manufacturer directly, where today he can reach him only indirectly through a chain of warranty actions.[8] Alternative (3) would turn the defendant loose in all cases not involving pork intended to be eaten without cooking by the consumer.

§4.14. Trichinous pork as a basis of liability — Pennsylvania. The situation in Pennsylvania with respect to trichinosis has been partially obscured by the court's apparent confusion of warranty and negligence and, as in Massachusetts, by the failure of the defendant's counsel adequately

[6] Blume v. Trunz Pork Stores, Inc., 269 App. Div. 1059, 59 N.Y.S.2d 217 (2d Dept. 1945); Dressler v. Merkel, Inc., 247 App. Div. 300, 303, 284 N.Y. Supp. 697, 702 (2d Dept. 1936).

[7] McSpedon v. Kunz, 271 N.Y. 131, 134–136, 2 N.E.2d 513, 514 (1936).

[8] McSpedon v. Kunz, 271 N.Y. 131, 2 N.E.2d 513 (1936).

to educate the court. In *Catani* v. *Swift & Co.*,[1] holding the manufacturer liable, the court talked as if it were dispensing with privity requirements in warranty suits against the manufacturer (suggesting that liability was for breach of warranty). At the same time it said that the defendant had a duty to inspect which was not discharged by federal inspection (suggesting that liability was for negligence). Four years later, in *Tavani* v. *Swift & Co.*,[2] the same defendant finally made it clear to the same court that inspection for trichinae is futile and that a failure to inspect is, therefore, no indication of carelessness. The defendant's victory in the later case leaves open the question whether the plaintiff could succeed in warranty. Taking the *Catani* opinion at its face value and the *Tavani* case's emphasis of the fact that the latter suit was for negligence, not breach of warranty, we may conclude that the presence of trichinae is a legal defect in Pennsylvania (and, incidentally, that privity of contract is no bar to a successful warranty suit against the manufacturer).

§4.15. Trichinous pork as a basis of liability — Ohio. The Ohio Supreme Court has taken a position somewhat similar to that taken in Pennsylvania. In a strong dictum in *Leonardi* v. *A. Habermann Provision Co.*,[1] it said:

> It it were known that fresh pork offered over the counter for sale was infected with trichinae it would require much fortitude to assert that it was wholesome, uninfected and marketable, even though notice was given to the purchaser that all portions of it must be sufficiently cooked to render it harmless.

This shows that, at least theoretically, the presence of trichinae is to be considered a defect in Ohio. This is true

§4.14. [1] 251 Pa. 52, 95 Atl. 931 (1914).
[2] 262 Pa. 184, 105 Atl. 55 (1918).

§4.15. [1] 143 Ohio St. 623, 632, 56 N.E.2d 232, 237 (1944).

both under the Ohio pure food statutes and at common law. Even so, the court upheld a judgment for the defendant on the ground that the verdict below was supportable under a proper charge relating to contributory negligence.[2] The decision drastically limits, if it does not wholly obliterate, the force of the dictum. Whether the dictum is wholly vitiated (at least in negligence cases) depends upon whether customary standards of cooking — the measure of contributory negligence — are considered to be an adequate protection against trichinae.

§4.16. Trichinous pork as a basis of liability — Illinois. The Illinois trichinosis cases, upon analysis, conflict. In *Wiedeman* v. *Keller*,[1] the Supreme Court, in remanding the case at the instance of the plaintiff, seems to have taken for granted, without expressly saying so, that trichinous pork is defective. Being preoccupied with correcting the views of the lower court on collateral points, it did not think it worth while even to mention the fact that the alleged defect was trichinae (this appears in the report of the lower court). In *Zorger* v. *Hillman's*,[2] an appellate court said that the Illinois pure food laws called only for pork that was fit when properly (adequately)[3] cooked. Since adequately cooked pork never contains live trichinae, this was the same as saying that the presence of trichinae is no threat to legal wholesomeness. In this respect the decision appears to be at variance with the tacit assumptions

[2] Similarly in Allen v. Marvin, 64 Ohio St. 608, 61 N.E. 1139, opinion in 46 Weekly L. Bull. 208 (1901).

§4.16. [1] 171 Ill. 93, 49 N.E. 210 (1898).

[2] 287 Ill. App. 357, 4 N.E.2d 900 (1936).

[3] That by "proper" the court meant "adequate" appears from the fact that it approved the trial court's instruction that the plaintiff could not win unless he showed that the meat sold by the defendant was unfit for human consumption after being heated to 137° F.

of *Wiedeman* v. *Keller*. The *Zorger* case was recently supported by *Nicketta* v. *National Tea Co.*[4]

§4.17. Trichinous pork as a basis of liability — The plaintiff's dilemma. So far as quality is concerned, the seller can owe a duty to the consumer in trichinosis cases only if customary cooking is inadequate cooking.[1] More than one court has fallen into this trap and one writer has made the amazing suggestion that "recovery should be allowed despite the impossibility of detection, such recovery to be limited only by a finding of the fact that the meat had not been properly cooked."[2] In other words, recovery should be allowed only where no basis for recovery exists![3]

If the foregoing analysis is correct the plaintiff, to be successful in a trichinosis case, must (1) be in a state where customary cooking is not necessarily adequate cooking, and (2) show that the meat was cooked at least as well as customarily required but not well enough to constitute adequate cooking.[4] If his cooking is poorer than this minimum,

[4] 338 Ill. App. 159, 87 N.E.2d 30 (1949).

§4.17. [1] The contributory negligence approach seems to imply that but for the plaintiff's fault he would have recovered, which in turn implies that the defendant was somehow at fault. But if the plaintiff had not been at fault and if he had cooked the meat effectively, there would have been no trichinosis and no basis for suit. Whether or not the contributory negligence approach is circuitous depends upon whether the standard of care to which the plaintiff is held is effective as against trichinae, that is, whether "had not been at fault" and "had cooked the meat effectively" are the same thing.

[2] Note, 16 Temp. L.Q. 80, 86 (1941).

[3] Unless, of course, by "properly" he meant only "in conformity with accepted, however ineffective, cooking practices." Cases using the word "properly" must be read carefully to see which meaning is intended.

[4] "The jury should have been authorized to give a verdict for the plaintiff only in case they found that the plaintiff was infected with trichinosis by eating the sausage after it was cooked in the usual or proper manner." Vaccarino v. Cozzubo, 181 Md. 614, 621, 31 A.2d 316, 319 (1943). The court assumes that the "usual or proper manner" does not necessarily exclude trichinae.

there is no showing that the meat was defective or he is barred on some theory of fault. If it is as good or better than adequate he has effectively proved, as the plaintiff did in *Zorger* v. *Hillman's*,[5] that he got his trichinosis elsewhere. This suggests that the soundest strategy for a plaintiff is to concentrate on showing (a) that he cooked the pork by a customary method and (b), by circumstantial evidence, that the trichinae came from the particular pork in question.

§4.18. The real issue. It is apparent from the foregoing sections that except for aberrations attributable to factual misinformation, the basic cleavage between the courts relates to whether customary consumer cooking is effective against trichinae.

Although most cases view trichinae theoretically as a legal defect, the net result of having to surmount the legal barriers of contributory negligence (or the doctrine of avoidable consequences), the impossibility of showing negligence without the help of a pure food statute, the privity restrictions, and the danger that proof of proper cooking will boomerang by shifting responsibility to another product and seller, together with the normal hazards of suit, have reduced the chances of recovery to a minimum. According to the reported cases, the consumer has apparently succeeded only seven or eight times. This raises the question, in states where the cumulative effect of these factors makes recovery virtually impossible, whether it would not reach the same practical result simply to hold that trichinous pork is not legally unwholesome.

A doctrinally clean result is reached by letting the legal question of wholesomeness turn on the court's factual finding

[5] 287 Ill. App. 357, 4 N.E.2d 900 (1936). So also in Nicketta v. National Tea Co., 338 Ill. App. 159, 87 N.E.2d 30 (1949); Wiehardt v. Krey Packing Co., 264 Ill. App. 504 (1932); and possibly in Prinsen v. Russos, 194 Wis. 142, 215 N.W. 905 (1927).

respecting normal consumer expectation as reflected in usual household cookery. Thus any court that now bars the plaintiff for failing to meet a customary level of cooking skill which is assumed to be adequate would do better to switch to the simpler and more direct theory that no legal defect exists.

§4.19. Pork to be eaten without cooking. Where the pork is to be eaten without cooking by the consumer, as in the case of salami, summer sausage, metwurst, pepperoni, lachshinken, Italian-style ham, capocollo, and similar products, the cases are with one exception uniform in holding that the presence of trichinae is a legal defect.[1] Here the nature of the transaction forecloses the possibility that live trichinae may be legitimately present at the time of sale.

In these cases the presence of trichinae traceable to the defendant's product is more likely to result in actual liability. Privity considerations are no less a threat to warranty actions, but contributory negligence is nonexistent and common law negligence is readily found if the local pure food law does not apply. Negligence of the manufacturer is readily discovered because the presence of trichinae after sale means that a process known to be entirely successful has been misapplied. The one exceptional case, *Ketterer* v. *Armour & Co.*,[2] though sometimes criticized, was sound when decided if the court was correct in assuming that in 1917 the most efficacious method known of curing lachshinken without destroying its character was no guarantee against tri-

§4.19. [1] Vaccarezza v. Sanguinetti, 71 Cal. App. 2d 687, 163 P.2d 470 (1945); Gindraux v. Maurice Mercantile Co., 4 Cal. 2d 206, 47 P.2d 708 (1935); Catalanello v. Cudahy Packing Co., 264 App. Div. 723, 34 N.Y.S. 2d 37 (2d Dept. 1942); Kurthe v. Krumme, 143 Ohio St. 638, 56 N.E.2d 227 (1944), *aff'g* 73 Ohio App. 524, 57 N.E.2d 77 (1943); Baum v. Murray, 23 Wash. 2d 890, 162 P.2d 801 (1945).

[2] 247 Fed. 921 (C.C.A. 2d, 1917).

chinae. Today, there are practicable methods for effectively curing all such products.

In any event, liability is contingent upon notice to the seller that the meat was to be eaten without cooking, either through the express statement of the purchaser or from the nature of the product itself. Wanting this, the plaintiff is certain to lose.[3]

In *Dressler* v. *Merkel, Inc.*,[4] the plaintiff, who was infected by trichinous metwurst, failed to recover for negligence against the packer who supplied the pork to the sausage-making retailer. The packer was held blameless in not foreseeing that the retailer might use the pork in a product to be eaten without further processing. Even if he had known its intended use, it is doubtful that the packer would have been responsible for the retailer's failure properly to cure the product.

If the *Dressler* suit had been for breach of warranty unfettered by privity considerations, a more difficult legal problem would have been raised. The pork eaten by the plaintiff was legally defective with respect to a suit against the manufacturing retailer but it was not the same product as that sold by the packer. In a few states, the latter's product, since it contemplated cooking by the consumer, would not be defective, and the packer would be excused. On the other hand, in the majority of states that find trichinae a defect, there would have been a difficult problem of legal causation. The real issue, of course, would be what the packer should reasonably expect of such a retailer.

The legal situation normally peculiar to trichinae likewise disappears where the plaintiff is a restaurant patron.

[3] *E.g.*, Yachetti v. John Duff & Sons Ltd., [1943] 1 D.L.R. 194, 202, [1942] O.R. 682, [1942] O.W.N. 639.

[4] 247 App. Div. 300, 284 N.Y. Supp. 697 (2d Dept. 1936).

Here, the defendant, not the plaintiff, does the cooking. Adequate cooking being apparently expected of restaurant keepers, trichinae are recognized as a defect.[5] Whether the defendant is to be held liable in a particular situation, however, depends on the legal vagaries applicable to restaurateurs generally.[6]

§4.20. Some policy considerations. Cases holding the defendant accountable for trichinous pork intended to be cooked by the consumer before eating raise difficult questions of public policy. Why impose absolute liability for defects which the defendant can neither discover nor prevent even if he could discover them? Imposing liability on innocent distributors has been justified as protecting the chain of liability to the packer or manufacturer.[1] But this assumes that the packer or manufacturer should be absolutely accountable.

From a policy standpoint, food manufacturers' liability has usually been justified as an incentive to guard against the sources of injury.[2] But with trichinae it is generally taken for granted that the packer is little more than an innocent bystander. Once trichinae have entered the hog, this assumption is almost unassailable.

There are several possible arguments for liability here. One is that liability might tend to encourage packers to extend their freezing facilities. In view of what is correctly known, this is unrealistic.[3] Another is that responsibility

[5] De Stefano v. Alpha Lunch Co., 308 Mass. 38, 30 N.E.2d 827, 828 (1941) (workmen's compensation case); Eisenbach v. Gimbel Bros., Inc., 281 N.Y. 474, 24 N.E.2d 131 (1939); Prinsen v. Russos, 194 Wis. 142, 215 N.W. 905 (1927).

[6] See Chapter III.

§4.20. [1] See Chapter I, Topic H, and Chapter II, Topic D.

[2] See Chapter II, Topic C.

[3] Freezing equipment is too expensive and too cumbersome for the general run of pork (especially carcasses and large cuts, which require lower temperatures or longer freezing periods).

would induce the manufacturer to put pressure on the farmer to improve the feeding conditions that encourage the infection of swine. Trichinae experts believe that trichinosis in swine (and therefore in humans) can be minimized by eliminating garbage feeding or by neutralizing the danger of uncooked pork scraps in garbage, either by cooking the garbage, or by eliminating meat from feed intended for hogs.[4] However, the possibility of such a procedure, even if practicable, does not in itself indicate that packers are in a position to bring effective pressure. The validity of this argument, therefore, turns on the resolution of difficult factual issues.

It has also been suggested that the desirability of "spreading the risk" (loss) is sufficient in itself to warrant liability.[5] This argument needs no elaboration at this place.[6]

§4.21. The duty to warn. In addition to the now conventional approaches to trichinosis, indicated in the preceding section, there may be another approach.

In the trial of a Canadian case,[1] it was suggested by the plaintiff's counsel that the seller should warn the purchaser that it is unsafe to eat fresh pork without cooking. The court brushed the suggestion aside on the ground that giving such a warning isn't customary, that the defendant had no opportunity to warn, and that the purchaser, having cooked the pork, didn't need the warning.

The court's first objection was beside the point. The second was questionable since posting suitable placards in

[4] Schwartz, "Trichinosis in Swine and Its Relationship to Public Health," Journal of the American Veterinary Medical Assn., Vol. XCII, (N.S. 45) 317, 332 (1938).
[5] Note, 16 Temp. L.Q. 80, 86 (1941).
[6] See Chapter I, Topic H, and Chapter II, Topic C.

§4.21. [1] Yachetti v. John Duff & Sons Ltd., [1943] 1 D.L.R. 194, 197, [1942] O.R. 682, 684, [1942] O.W.N. 639, 640.

butcher shops or enclosing printed slips with retail purchases, bolstered by institutional advertising by packers or trade associations, was not considered and shown to be impracticable.[2] The third objection confused cooking with effective cooking.

There is a well-established principle that a seller has a duty to warn in certain cases where he cannot remove, or has not removed, the defect itself.

In *Wellington* v. *Downer Kerosene Oil Co.*,[3] the Massachusetts court held that a seller of naphtha, which he knew was dangerous when used for illumination purposes but whose dangers he did not disclose to the buyer, was liable for injuries incurred in a subsequent explosion of the fluid. In *Gerkin* v. *Brown & Sehler Co.*,[4] the Michigan court held a wholesaler liable for injuries caused to the plaintiff's neck by a fur collar, on the ground that the defendant knew that a small percentage of people are allergic to the dye used and should have warned the plaintiff accordingly. In *White* v. *Steadman*,[5] the plaintiff and his wife had hired a landau. The horse was restive and when it shied both were injured. Of the owner and his horse, the Court of King's Bench said:

[2] The text of a poster developed by the Department of Agriculture reads as follows:

Pork is a Savory, Nourishing Food
Cooking is a Health Safeguard

COOK PORK and its PRODUCTS THOROUGHLY

U.S. DEPARTMENT OF AGRICULTURE

BUREAU OF ANIMAL INDUSTRY (SEAL) MEAT INSPECTION DIVISION

Pork is Rich in Protein, Fat, and Vitamin B.

[3] 104 Mass. 64, 79 (1870).

[4] 177 Mich. 45, 143 N.W. 48 (1913). The warning principle of this case was apparently accepted in Arnold v. May Department Stores Co., 85 S.W. 2d 748, 753 (Mo. 1935).

[5] [1913] 3 K.B. 340, 347. But *cf.* Levi v. Colgate-Palmolive Pty., Ltd., [1941] 41 S.R. (N.S.W.) 48, 58 W.N. 63, 65 (bath salts).

He is under a duty to warn not only the person who hires it, but any person who he knows or contemplates will use it. The duty is not dependent on and is not created by the contract. That which creates it is not the contract, but the supplying of a dangerous animal or chattel for the use of another person.

In *Maize* v. *Atlantic Refining Co.*,[6] the Pennsylvania court held that the manufacturer of cleaning fluid containing a high proportion of carbon tetrachloride had a duty to warn which was not discharged by providing, in small letters, "Do not inhale fumes. Use only in well ventilated place." In *Rosenbusch* v. *Ambrosia Milk Corp.*,[7] the infant plaintiff had been injured by the defendant's dried milk product, which had deteriorated because of inherent characteristics. A lower New York court held the defendant accountable in negligence. It said:

> . . . it will not be an unreasonable extension of principles of liability already established to hold that the manufacturer in such case is chargeable with negligence where it knows or should know that the product is liable to deteriorate either by time, climate, or temperature, or the manner in which it is kept, if it fails to affix to the package the date of manufacture and the time during which the ingredients may safely be used, or the manner in which they should be handled and preserved to prevent deterioration.

There are other cases to the same effect.[8]

In *Crist* v. *Art Metal Works*[9] and in *Henry* v. *Crook*,[10] the court felt that the plaintiff was legally entitled to a warning in view of the manufacturer's extravagant advertising claims. A hint that a warning may be appropriate in

[6] 352 Pa. 51, 55, 41 A.2d 850, 852 (1945).

[7] 181 App. Div. 97, 168 N.Y. Supp. 505 (1st Dept. 1917). See Cleary v. John M. Maris Co., 173 Misc. 954, 955, 19 N.Y.S.2d 38, 41 (1940).

[8] 86 A.L.R. 947 (1933).

[9] 230 App. Div. 114, 243 N.Y. Supp. 496 (1st Dept. 1930) ("absolutely harmless" toy gun).

[10] 202 App. Div. 19, 195 N.Y. Supp. 642 (3d Dept. 1922) ("harmless" sparklers).

trichinosis cases appears in *McSpedon* v. *Kunz.*[11] On the other hand, the court in *Leonardi* v. *A. Habermann Provision Co.*[12] suggests that a mere warning would not discharge the seller's obligation to provide a wholesome product.

Warning by the seller may be put in various legal settings.

Assuming that a seller's basic obligation is to avoid injury to the plaintiff where avoidance is reasonably possible, warning the unsuspecting plaintiff may be considered a specific legal duty where (as in the case of trichinae) that is the only practicable alternative.[13] The breach of this duty would therefore be ground for a civil suit, where the damages depended upon the injury suffered. The product may be considered legally defective until adequate warning is given.[14]

This approach seems preferable to those that appear to be accepted today by most courts that consider trichinae a legal defect. Since they do not expressly recognize a duty to warn against trichinae, and thus do not expressly recognize a warning as discharging the defendant's affirmative obligation, warning is presumably relegated to the following roles. A program of education by the industry can ultimately elevate the customary cooking of pork to the level of adequate cooking wherever customary cooking may not have already reached that level. The defendant would be in the clear as soon as the program sufficiently improved the

[11] 271 N.Y. 131, 135, 2 N.E.2d 513, 514 (1936). See also Note, 9 N.Y.U.L.Q. Rev. 360, 363 (1932).

[12] 143 Ohio St. 623, 632, 56 N.E.2d 232, 237 (1944).

[13] The full contours of the warning principle appear in Restatement, Torts §388 (1934).

[14] The existing warning cases apparently confine the duty to warn to cases where the defendant has actual knowledge or is negligently ignorant. Applied to trichinae, this would presumably mean knowledge of the general danger rather than knowledge that a particular piece of meat was so infected.

customary standards of cooking and the courts apprehended the fact. This would take trichinae out of the class of legally defective food, and put them in the same class as sand in spinach.

In the meantime, warning in specific sales presumably makes a difference in a few situations. Although it is undoubtedly a solid basis for a contributory negligence defense in many cases, such a defense is rarely needed in common law negligence cases because the defendant's own negligence can rarely be established and he already has a reliable defense. Even so, it is probably effective in any state where trichinae are held to be proscribed by statute and contributory negligence is an affirmative defense to negligence per se based on breach of statute.[15] In warranty actions the warning would presumably be effective under the doctrine of avoidable consequences.[16]

TOPIC C. *The Hypersensitive Plaintiff*

§4.22. The problem. Where the defendant injures an abnormally sensitive plaintiff, doubt may arise not only with respect to how much he should, if successful, recover, but with respect to whether he should recover at all.

There are two general kinds of cases here. The first covers diseases and other infirmities that make the plaintiff more susceptible than normal to illness, upset, or injury. The second covers the so-called allergy. The line between these two concepts is not easy to draw.

The basic question respecting both general kinds of hyper-

[15] On this subject generally, see Prosser, "Contributory Negligence as Defense to Violation of Statute," 32 Minn. L. Rev. 105 (1948).

[16] *E.g.*, Fredendall v. Abraham & Straus, Inc., 279 N.Y. 146, 18 N.E.2d 11 (1938) (failure to heed warning included with dry-cleaning fluid).

sensitivity is whether the defendant owes a duty to protect idiosyncratics. Is a product that harms such a person to be considered legally unwholesome?

Wanting sharp margins, the words "unwholesome" and "unfit" give no answer. Legally, the problem of individual hypersensitivity is too occasional and the problem of allergy too new to make it helpful to examine the general connotations of words.

The plaintiff's idiosyncrasy may appear in several legal contexts. The court may find that the plaintiff has failed to show that his injury is not simply a result of his predisposition, unrelated to the defendant's product. Here, whether or not the defendant's product is legally defective, the plaintiff inevitably loses for want of the necessary causal connection.[1] Second, it may find that part of the injury was caused by the predisposition and part by the defendant's product. Here the plaintiff has recovered for the apportioned harm.[2] Third, the court may find that the defendant's product caused the injury but that the injury was aggravated by, or aggravated, a pre-existing infirmity.[3] Here the plaintiff recovers for the whole injury.[4] Finally,

§4.22. [1] *E.g.*, Karr v. Inecto, Inc., 247 N.Y. 360, 160 N.E. 398 (1928) (hair dye; strictly speaking, not a consumer case, since the injury was to the operator who was applying the dye, not to the customer); Murphy v. Campbell Soup Co., 62 F.2d 564 (C.C.A. 1st, 1933) (illness probably resulted from psychoneurosis or other cause); Cannady v. Kroger Grocery and Baking Co., CCH Food Drug Cosmetic Law Serv. (W.D. Mo. 1942), ¶18,104 (1939) (death caused by hemorrhage from syphilis). "Cause" is used here in the sense of physical rather than "proximate" (legal) cause. For cases based on the latter concept see §4.26 *infra*, note 2.

[2] *E.g.*, Coca-Cola Bottling Co. of Southeast Arkansas v. Bell, 199 Ark. 386, 134 S.W.2d 549 (1939).

[3] The third situation differs from the second in this way: In the third case none of the injury would have occurred but for the defect in the plaintiff's product, whereas in the second the part of the injury allocated to the predisposition would have been incurred anyway.

[4] *E.g.*, Coca Cola Bottling Works, Inc. v. Catron, 186 Md. 156, 161, 46

the court may find that the defendant's product caused the plaintiff's injury but that the plaintiff would not have been injured had he been normal. Whether the plaintiff recovers in this last situation is the question to be considered in this topic.

§4.23. Abnormal susceptibility. It is clear that the plaintiff's sickness after eating the defendant's product does not, by itself, prove the plaintiff's case.[1] It does not prove that the defendant's product caused the upset and, even if it did, it would not, without more, indicate a legal defect. This raises the broad question of how unwholesomeness can be established where the only mark of defectiveness is the reactions of individual consumers.

The available evidence indicates that, in theory at least, the courts tend to hold the plaintiff to a general standard of susceptibility, so far as bodily reactions are to be the test of defectiveness. This is what is generally being done in the case of drugs, cosmetics, and apparel,[2] and in several Ohio food cases it has been held that a civil injury action succeeds only upon proof that the food in question was "deleterious to the health of normal persons generally." [3]

The distinction between the "normal" stomach and the

A.2d 303, 305 (1946); Grant v. Australian Knitting Mills, Ltd., [1936] A.C. 85, 92 (deleterious chemical in underwear). The court straddled this and the preceding doctrine in Arndt v. D. H. Holmes Co., 9 La. App. 36, 119 So. 91 (1928).

§4.23. [1] *E.g.*, Geisness v. Scow Bay Packing Co., Inc., 16 Wash. 2d 1, 132 P.2d 740 (1942). See Chapter II, Topic B, and Chapter III, Topic B.

[2] *E.g.*, Griffiths v. Peter Conway, Ltd., [1939] 1 All E.R. 685 (C.A.) (dermatitis from contact with coat). It has been held that a doctor administering chloroform is not bound to anticipate a special hypersensitivity arising out of an undisclosed accident. Bogle v. Winslow, 5 Phila. Rep. 136 (1863). See also cases cited *infra* §4.25, note 4, and §4.27, note 1.

[3] Great Atlantic & Pacific Tea Co. v. Hughes, 131 Ohio St. 501, 504,

plaintiff's peculiar physiology, however, loses force in some cases because of the leniency of the same courts in holding that a mere showing that the food in fact caused illness to the plaintiff, plus the assumption that the plaintiff is "normal," is a sufficient basis for inferring unwholesomeness.[4] Even so, the principle cannot be ignored.

Some of the "fright" cases are pertinent here. These are the decisions denying relief to consumers whose injuries resulted from mental or nervous upset, on the ground that their reactions were abnormal and thus did not tend to show that the defendant's products were defective or that the defendants had otherwise breached any duty to the plaintiffs.[5]

An unusual case is *Delta Nehi Bottling Co.* v. *Lucas.*[6] Here the plaintiff, while consuming a soft drink, discovered a paper clip covered with a greenish substance. An existing pyelitis condition made her more than normally susceptible to nausea. The nausea she suffered as a result "was attended with all the other concomitant and severer symptoms of the pyelitis." The court permitted recovery for breach of warranty and negligence, despite the fact that

---

3 N.E.2d 415, 416 (1936); Mills Restaurant Co. v. Clark, 45 Ohio App. 25, 185 N.E. 470 (1933). But *cf.* Delta Nehi Bottling Co. v. Lucas, 184 Miss. 693, 700, 185 So. 561, 562 (1939).

[4] Payne v. R. H. White Co., 314 Mass. 63, 65, 49 N.E.2d 425, 426 (1943); Cahill v. Inecto, Inc., 208 App. Div. 191, 203 N.Y. Supp. 1 (1st Dept. 1924); Great Atlantic & Pacific Tea Co. v. Hughes, 53 Ohio App. 255, 263, 4 N.E.2d 700, 703 (1935), *aff'd*, 131 Ohio St. 501, 3 N.E.2d 415 (1936).

[5] Legac v. Vietmeyer Bros., 7 N.J. Misc. 685, 147 Atl. 110 (1929) (bug in bread; "Physical suffering is not the probable or natural consequence of fright, in the case of a person of ordinary physical and mental vigor . . ."); Copeland v. F. W. Woolworth Co., 187 Misc. 456, 62 N.Y.S.2d 660 (1946) (nail contrasted with cockroaches).

[6] 184 Miss. 693, 700, 185 So. 561, 562 (1939). See also McCubbin v. Hastings, 27 La. Ann. 713 (1875) (pre-existing yellow fever caused death after decedent took enema prescription negligently filled by the defendant).

there was no evidence that the drink was chemically deleterious. It said:

> . . . while it may be said that such a likelihood as to a well and normal person is in the law only a remote possibility, yet, as already mentioned, the jury was justified in concluding from the testimony that as to a person suffering with pyelitis such a likelihood was more than a remote possibility, but was a real and substantial likelihood of appreciable weight and moment.

The case is significant, not so much as a "fright" case, as one in which the court measured the defectiveness of the product by the reactions of a limited class of idiosyncratics, persons suffering from a particular disease. In this respect it is unique. An important feature of the case, however, is the fact that the presence of an ascertainable foreign substance provided an objective mark of unwholesomeness, thus lessening the fraud potential.

§4.24. Allergies other than food allergies. The problem of legal defect is seen most vividly in the case of allergies.[1] The drug industry is familiar, for example, with claims for skin eruption caused by skin tonics harmless to all but a very few. The apparel industry has had similar experience with the dyes in fur collars. The problem has arisen also for cosmetics,[2] and mechanical devices such as nipple guards [3] and eyeglass frames.[4] It has arisen in fields of personal professional services involving the administering of X-rays or anesthetics.[5]

§4.24. [1] For a general discussion of allergies, see Barasch, "Allergies and the Law," 10 Brooklyn L. Rev. 363 (1941); Cull, "Allergy and the Law," 12 Ins. Counsel J. 45 (1945).

[2] *E.g.*, Reynolds v. Sun Ray Drug Co., 135 N.J.L. 475, 52 A.2d 666 (1947).

[3] Cleary v. John M. Maris Co., 173 Misc. 954, 19 N.Y.S.2d 38 (1940).

[4] Walstrom Optical Co. v. Miller, 59 S.W.2d 895 (Tex. Civ. App. 1933).

[5] *E.g.*, Bogle v. Winslow, 5 Phila. Rep. 136 (1863) (administering of chloroform); Hamilton v. Harris, 204 S.W. 450 (Tex. Civ. App. 1918),

The allergy situation closely parallels the third situation described in Section 4.22. It differs in that the condition is normal to the person and there is no other test of the alleged defectiveness of the product than the reactions of its users. So far no case squarely involving a food allergy has appeared in the law reports.[6] But with the increased understanding of food allergies, and particularly with the constant resort to new chemicals in the processing of food products, [7] we may sooner or later anticipate legal experience with the same problems in the food industry.

Most of the possible legal approaches to the hypersensitive plaintiff are to be found in a canvass of existing authority. So far as allergies are concerned, these consist wholly of nonfood cases.

§4.25. Allergies other than food allergies — Liability in warranty. Where suit is for breach of warranty, the weight of authority appears, on superficial examination, to deny recovery.[1] But although appearances here may be

223 S.W. 533 (Tex. Civ. App. 1920) (treatment by X-ray). For additional cases involving X-rays or anesthetics, see Barasch, "Allergies and the Law," 10 Brooklyn L. Rev. 363, at 364 nn.17 and 18 (1941).

[6] In MacLehan v. Loft Candy Stores, 172 So. 367 (La. App. 1937), the plaintiff, who was allergic to certain proteins, was allowed to recover for illness following the eating of mince pie. The court said that the plaintiff's reactions were too violent to be explained on an allergy basis. The inference seems to be that had the reactions been somewhat less the plaintiff might not have recovered. In Swengel v. F. & E. Wholesale Grocery Co., 147 Kan. 555, 564, 77 P.2d 930, 935 (1938), the defendant failed in his attempt to show that the plaintiff's injury resulted from allergy.

[7] *E.g.*, surface active agents, antioxidants, preservatives, synthetic sweetening agents, synthetic rubbers, resins, and plasticizers. Lehman and others, "Procedures for the Appraisal of the Toxicity of Chemicals in Foods," 4 Food Drug Cosmetic L.Q. 412, 419 (1949).

§4.25. [1] Relief was denied in Zager v. F. W. Woolworth Co., 30 Cal. App. 2d 324, 86 P.2d 389 (1939) (freckle cream); Cicarelli v. Lipshetz, 8 Conn. Supp. 526 (1940) (lipstick); Stanton v. Sears, Roebuck & Co., 312 Ill. App. 496, 38 N.E.2d 801 (1942) (rayon dress); Ross v. Porteous,

deceiving, even the view that favors recovery apparently agrees on one point: The plaintiff is certain to lose if he shows no more than his personal idiosyncrasy.

Although it is no assurance of success, a *sine qua non* of recovery appears to be the fact that the troublesome ingredient is known to be an irritant or deleterious substance.[2] If this means knowledge of the particular seller, the cases are out of key with the notion of warranty, a responsibility imposed without regard to the seller's knowledge that the defect exists. It is probably doctrinally consistent, on the other hand, to consider general knowledge of consumer reactions in determining whether or not the presence of the ingredient should, on policy, be considered a legal defect.[3] Insofar as the distinction turns on the general knowledge of the *industry* it assumes that absolute liability is less desirable here than elsewhere in the field of food products liability. Insofar as it turns on the general knowledge of *scientists* it imposes an absolute liability that offers an incentive to keep abreast of scientific knowledge. To go still further and elim-

---

Mitchell & Braun Co., 136 Me. 118, 3 A.2d 650 (1939) (dress shield); Longo v. Touraine Stores, Inc., 319 Mass. 727, 66 N.E.2d 792 (1946) (gloves); Graham v. Jordan Marsh Co., 319 Mass. 690, 693, 67 N.E.2d 404, 405 (1946) (cold cream); Payne v. R. H. White Co., 314 Mass. 63, 66, 49 N.E.2d 425, 426 (1943) (dress); Bradt v. Hollaway, 242 Mass. 446, 136 N.E. 254 (1922) (fur neckpiece); Barrett v. S. S. Kresge Co., 144 Pa. Super. 516, 19 A.2d 502 (1941) (cotton dress). See also Flynn v. Bedell Co. of Mass., 242 Mass. 450, 453, 136 N.E. 252, 253 (1922). Relief was granted in Bianchi v. Denholm & McKay Co., 302 Mass. 469, 19 N.E.2d 697 (1939) (face powder); Reynolds v. Sun Ray Drug Co., 135 N.J.L. 475, 52 A.2d 666 (1947) (lipstick); Zirpola v. Adam Hat Stores, Inc., 122 N.J.L. 21, 4 A.2d 73 (1939) (hat). *Cf.* Smith v. Denholm & McKay Co., 288 Mass. 234, 242, 192 N.E. 631, 634 (1934) (depilatory).

[2] See cases cited *supra* note 1, and *infra* note 4 and §4.27, note 1.

[3] It is probably appropriate, for example, to distinguish between, at the one extreme, a plaintiff who is a member of a substantial, well-recognized group of chronic idiosyncratics and, at the other extreme, one whose hypersensitivity is a relatively special, unknown, and perhaps temporary physical condition.

inate knowledge altogether as a condition of liability would probably impose an undue burden on industry in a field so full of uncertainty and confusion. No case has gone so far.

By "irritant" or "deleterious substance," these cases usually refer to ingredients that are known to be capable, in sufficient quantities, of irritating even normal persons.[4] But why the law, in defining what is legally defective, should distinguish in principle between an ingredient that is unsafe for idiosyncratics because of the quantity used, and an ingredient that is unsafe for idiosyncratics because of its physical structure, has not been explained. Surmise suggests that the fear of fraud leads courts to withhold recovery unless the case falls within a class for which some objective, determinable factor serves as a *sine qua non* of injury. The "foreign object" cases form one such category [5] except in states where the appearance of a mental link in the causal chain limits that category to "impact" cases. The "known irritant" cases apparently form another.

The fear of fraud is understandable. However, if each seller is held to what is generally known by the industry or by science, it would seem that a sufficiently objective test is occasionally provided even in the allergy cases.

In *Bianchi* v. *Denholm & McKay Co.*,[6] the Massachusetts Supreme Judicial Court appears to have adopted a result consistent with this view. Here the plaintiff was allowed to

[4] Smith v. Denholm & McKay Co., 288 Mass. 234, 192 N.E. 631 (1934) (thalium acetate); Zirpola v. Adam Hat Stores, Inc., 122 N.J.L. 21, 4 A.2d 73 (1939) (aniline dye). See Flynn v. Bedell Co. of Mass., 242 Mass. 450, 454, 136 N.E. 252, 253 (1922). In Reynolds v. Sun Ray Drug Co., 135 N.J.L. 475, 52 A.2d 666 (1947), the nature of the offending ingredient and the reactions of persons generally to it were not discussed. The Massachusetts view appears now to be otherwise. Bianchi v. Denholm & McKay Co., 302 Mass. 469, 19 N.E.2d 697 (1939).

[5] And see Delta Nehi Bottling Co. v. Lucas, 184 Miss. 693, 185 So. 561 (1939).

[6] 302 Mass. 469, 473, 19 N.E.2d 697, 699 (1939).

recover for a rash caused by two aniline dyes included in the defendant's face powder. She was found to be "one of a class of persons not defined as to numbers or percentage, the only qualifications being that the members of the class are 'allergic' and not 'average.'" The court said:

> We do not think that a seller of face powder containing a known irritant to "some" persons' skins can be heard to say that he is not liable for a breach of an implied warranty of fitness where injury results from a use of the powder by one such as is described by the evidence in the case at bar.[7]

The Maine Supreme Judicial Court[8] and a lower Connecticut court,[9] holding otherwise, conditioned recovery upon the presence of a "deleterious" or "harmful" ingredient (i.e., one injurious to people generally). The persuasiveness of these decisions is lessened by the fact that for authority they relied solely on two Massachusetts decisions,[10] in neither of which did the plaintiff show more than his personal idiosyncrasy and both of which were accordingly distinguished, by the court that decided them, in the *Bianchi* case. That the Maine and Connecticut courts were aware of the possible significance of this distinction does not appear from their opinions.

[7] The significance of this case was for a time clouded by the broad language used in later Massachusetts cases. Longo v. Touraine Stores, Inc., 319 Mass. 727, 66 N.E.2d 792 (1946) (gloves); Graham v. Jordan Marsh Co., 319 Mass. 690, 693, 67 N.E.2d 404, 405 (1946) (cold cream); Payne v. R. H. White Co., 314 Mass. 63, 65, 49 N.E.2d 425, 426 (1943) (dress). None of these cases, however, appear to have involved an ingredient known to cause an allergy shared by a class of persons. That this is a sound basis for distinguishing these cases is borne out by Taylor v. Newcomb Baking Co., 317 Mass. 609, 611, 59 N.E.2d 293, 294 (1945).

[8] Ross v. Porteous, Mitchell & Braun Co., 136 Me. 118, 3 A.2d 650 (1939) (dress shields).

[9] Cicarelli v. Lipshetz, 8 Conn. Supp. 526 (1940) (lipstick).

[10] Bradt v. Hollaway, 242 Mass. 446, 136 N.E. 254 (1922) (fur neckpiece); Flynn v. Bedell Co. of Mass., 242 Mass. 450, 136 N.E. 252 (1922) (fur collar; dictum only).

In *Zirpola* v. *Adam Hat Stores, Inc.*,[11] the New Jersey Court of Errors and Appeals upheld recovery by the purchaser of a hat containing an aniline dye. There was expert testimony "that four or five per cent of all persons coming in contact with this dye would react to and be injured by it to an appreciable extent, but that all persons are somewhat sensitive to the poison." The court said:

> The mere fact that only a small proportion of those who use a certain article would suffer injuries by reason of such use does not absolve the vendor from liability . . .

Whether a different result would have been reached had there been no evidence that all persons are "somewhat sensitive" cannot be determined from the opinion. (The court's later opinion in *Reynolds* v. *Sun Ray Drug Co.*,[12] in which the plaintiff was also successful, is silent both as to the offending ingredient and its effect on persons generally.)

§4.26. Allergies other than food allergies — Liability in negligence. Where the suit is for negligence, the problems of proof that beset the plaintiff in other products liability negligence cases, both as to negligence and causation, exist to a lesser degree because he is dealing with something ordinarily common to the product and intentionally introduced by the defendant, rather than one affecting a single unit or batch and unintentionally caused by the momentary lapse of an anonymous employee. Even so, the plaintiff usually loses. Some courts refuse relief because the plaintiff's injury was unforeseeable.[1] Some hold that the

[11] 122 N.J.L. 21, 23, 4 A.2d 73, 75 (1939).
[12] 135 N.J.L. 475, 52 A.2d 666 (1947).

§4.26. [1] In Briggs v. National Industries, Inc., 92 Cal. App. 542, 207 P.2d 110 (1949), the plaintiff's injury was attributed to a 6.28 per cent concentration of thioglycollate in the cold wave solution made by the defendant and applied by a beauty shop operator. A physician testified that the ingredient was a direct irritant only if used in concentrations

plaintiff's condition, not the defendant's product, was the legal cause.[2] At least one has held that the plaintiff assumes the risk of his hypersensitivity.[3] A New South Wales

---

greater than 7 per cent or 8 per cent. Wanting evidence that anyone other than the plaintiff had ever been injured, the court found that the defendant had no reason to anticipate the danger. There was also some indication that the operator had not properly applied the neutralizer.

In Singer v. Oken, 193 Misc. 1058, 87 N.Y.S.2d 686 (1949), the plaintiff developed a facial infection from a 1 per cent concentration of phenol in the calomine lotion prepared by the defendant pharmacist. Finding that the defendant had no reason to anticipate the plaintiff's injury, the court held for the defendant.

In Walstrom Optical Co. v. Miller, 59 S.W.2d 895 (Tex. Civ. App. 1933), the plaintiff was injured by the dye used in the defendant's eyeglass frames. The dye was one commonly used for many years. The plaintiff had a "rare" hypersensitivity and there was no evidence that others shared it. The court denied recovery for want of negligence and proximate causation.

According to Barasch, "Allergies and the Law," 10 Brooklyn L. Rev. 363, 370 n. 59, folio 403 of the appeal record in Kinkead v. Lysol, Inc., 250 App. Div. 832 (memo) (N.Y. 1937) shows that the court ruled as follows: "If she used it (Lysol) diluted as prescribed, it did her harm only because of the allergy and I am holding that *that is something the manufacturer does not have to anticipate within the law of negligence.*" Also: ". . . for all that appears, the plaintiff's was the first instance of injury that was ever known to arise . . ." (*Id.* at 373). See Arnold v. May Department Stores Co., 85 S.W.2d 748 (Mo. 1935).

[2] Walstrom Optical Co. v. Miller, 59 S.W.2d 895 (Tex. Civ. App. 1933) (injury from dye in eyeglass frames). In Crean v. Inecto, Inc., 99 N.Y.L.J. 2283 (May 11, 1938), the plaintiff lost in her suit for damages for injuries following use of the defendant's hair dye. The court said the injury resulted from the allergy, not the dye. The case stands more properly on the failure to show negligence. The incidence of allergy was one in 8000. The product included a warning and suggested test. The plaintiff had twice tested herself a year before, without positive results. Hamilton v. Harris, 204 S.W. 450, 451 (Tex. Civ. App. 1918), 223 S.W. 533 (Tex. Civ. App. 1920) (X-rays; "A physician is not required to take precaution against a peculiar temperament or abnormal idiosyncrasy of which he had no knowledge and for detecting which there is no means"). See Grant v. Australian Knitting Mills, Ltd., [1936] A.C. 85, 92.

[3] Antowill v. Friedmann, 197 App. Div. 230, 232, 188 N.Y. Supp. 777, 778 (2d Dept. 1921). "There are a few people, probably not more than one out of every 200 to 300, who are supersensitive to X-ray treatment, and apparently that disposition of the patient cannot be known in ad-

case has simply said that in the absence of "special circumstances" a seller owes no duty to abnormal buyers.[4]

Whether or not the approach of unforeseeability makes sense would seem to depend upon the nature of the plaintiff's weakness and how reasonable it is to anticipate it.

The Michigan Supreme Court has found an obligation where injury to a substantial group of idiosyncratics is reasonably predictable. In *Gerkin* v. *Brown & Sehler Co.*,[5] the court held the defendant liable for dermatitis contracted from dyed fur. It said:

> When the fact is once established and demonstrated by experience that a certain commodity apparently harmless contains concealed dangers, and when distributed to the public through the channels of trade and used for the purposes for which it was made and sold is sure to cause suffering to, and injure the health of, some innocent purchaser, even though the percentage of those injured be not large, a duty arises to and a responsibility rests upon the manufacturer and dealer with knowledge to the extent, at least, of warning the ignorant consumer . . .

The Supreme Judicial Court of Massachusetts has taken a similar position. In *Taylor* v. *Newcomb Baking Co.*,[6] the plaintiff, a hypersensitive dishwasher, suffered a rash caused by trisodium phosphate in the soap furnished by his employer, the defendant restaurateur. The court upheld a judgment for the plaintiff on the basis of expert testimony that "quite a percentage" of people are hypersensitive to soap powder and this fact was known to the trade, though

---

vance of the test of actual treatment and its results. Such cases are so rare that evidently physician and patient have to take that risk — the one in administering, and the other in receiving, the treatment." But *cf.* Valmas Drug Co. v. Smoots, 269 Fed. 356, 360 (C.C.A. 6th, 1920).

[4] Levi v. Colgate-Palmolive Pty., Ltd., [1941] 41 S.R. (N.S.W.) 48, 58 W.N. 63, 65 (bath salts).

[5] 177 Mich. 45, 143 N.W. 48 (1913).

[6] 317 Mass. 609, 611, 59 N.E.2d 293, 294 (1945).

not necessarily to persons in the plaintiff's position. The court, citing the *Bianchi* case, said:

> It is not necessary that the majority of possible employees be susceptible. It is enough if a sufficient number are susceptible so that a jury could reasonably say that the defendant ought to have known and recognized the danger of injury and ought to have guarded against it.[7]

Several New York cases have said that the defendant is liable if the product is "inherently dangerous and poisonous," [8] but that no product falls into such a category if it is not harmful to the normal person.[9] This effectively locks the door while seeming momentarily to open it. The causation and assumption-of-risk approaches, as justifications, simply beg the question.

At least one court has added a further hurdle by withholding relief unless the defendant knew of the particular plaintiff's idiosyncrasy.[10] The rationale of this position is uncertain. For weaknesses personal to the plaintiff it makes sense, but for chronic group weaknesses in the field of allergy it seems to confuse negligence with the implied warranty of fitness for a particular purpose. The law of negligence is full of instances where the defendant owes a duty of care to a class of unidentified membership. The requirement possibly assumes that consumers are as fully aware of their individual peculiarities as sellers are of general allergy statistics.

[7] This language is quoted with approval in Carter v. Yardley & Co., 319 Mass. 92, 64 N.E.2d 693 (1946).

[8] Drake v. Herrman, 261 N.Y. 414, 185 N.E. 685 (1933) (hair dye); Karr v. Inecto, Inc., 247 N.Y. 360, 160 N.E. 398 (1928) (hair dye); Cleary v. John M. Maris Co., 173 Misc. 954, 955, 19 N.Y.S.2d 38, 42 (1940) (lead nipple shields). See Arnold v. May Department Stores Co., 85 S.W.2d 748 (Mo. 1935) (hair dye).

[9] Cleary v. John M. Maris Co., *supra* note 8, at 956, 958, 19 N.Y.S.2d at 42, 43; Drake v. Herrman, *supra* note 8.

[10] Arnold v. May Department Stores Co., 85 S.W.2d 748 (Mo. 1935) (hair dye).

§4.27. Allergies other than food allergies — Reconciliation of authorities. Examination shows that while formidable in comparative numbers and probably soundly decided on their facts, the cases that seem to oppose the *Gerkin*, *Taylor*, and *Bianchi* cases in the sweeping language of "allergy" and "idiosyncrasy" are not wholly persuasive in that respect. In most instances the plaintiff failed to show that his predisposition was other than personal or, if it was more than that, that it was sufficiently widespread to be known to the kind of seller represented by the defendant.[1] In some instances this was the necessary result of failing to identify the offending ingredient. What the same courts would do if faced with a clean-cut allergy that was (1) severe, (2) shared by a substantial proportion of people, (3) known to exist, and (4) traced to an ingredient in the defendant's product, cannot be taken for granted. The X-ray and anesthetic cases do not involve sales of goods and, even if that feature is ignored, they do not adequately deal with the feasibility of a warning. At least it is fallacious to argue that the consumer has assumed the risk, even an irreducible one, until he has been warned or otherwise put on notice.[2]

§4.28. Allergies other than food allergies — Some policy considerations. Apart from the fear of pretended

§4.27. [1] *E.g.*, Gould v. Slater Woolen Co., 147 Mass. 315, 17 N.E. 531 (1888) (injury from handling cloth dyed with common mordant; first injury of its kind known); Karr v. Inecto, Inc., 247 N.Y. 360, 160 N.E. 398 (1928) (hair dye; strictly speaking, not a consumer case, since the injury was to operator applying dye to customer's hair); Willson v. Faxon, Williams & Faxon, 138 App. Div. 359, 364, 122 N.Y. Supp. 778, 781 (4th Dept. 1910), *rev'd* on other grounds, 208 N.Y. 108, 101 N.E. 799 (1913) (calomel in cathartic; "A preparation is not deleterious to human health in the ordinary acceptance of that term simply because one person in a multitude of those using it happens to meet with ill effects from taking it").

[2] Valmas Drug Co. v. Smoots, 269 Fed. 356, 360 (C.C.A. 6th, 1920).

illness and malingering, it is suspected that underlying the general reluctance of courts to award recovery to hypersensitive plaintiffs is some such feeling as this: The seller has done nothing reprehensible in selling a product which the normal person finds acceptable, especially when no reasonable way appears by which the offending ingredient can be eliminated. To hold him liable would let the tail wag the dog; it is unfair to expect the seller to please the abnormal few at the expense of the normal many. Besides, the fact that many allergies are personal matters makes it reasonable to condition recovery upon the consumer's giving notice of his condition.

On this line of analysis several comments can be made. First of all, the seller's obligation to the consumer is not necessarily one of removing the offending condition. An appropriate *warning* by the seller requires no choice between pleasing the normal consumer and safeguarding a small minority. Though specifically repudiated in several cases, the possibility of giving appropriate warning to allergic consumers has not been adequately considered by the courts.[1]

Secondly, although hypersensitivity is frequently personal to the consumer, and therefore unknown and unpredictable by the seller, there are instances where (1) the seller knows in advance that an ingredient in the product can reasonably be expected to cause harm to a substantial number of consumers, (2) he alone has information which if given to the consumer would substantially reduce the incidence of harm, and (3) giving that information to the consumer is practicable.

§4.28. [1] For a discussion of the warning cases, see §4.21 *supra*. The warning cases involving hypersensitivity are Gerkin v. Brown & Sehler Co., 177 Mich. 45, 143 N.W. 48 (1913), and Cleary v. John M. Maris Co., 173 Misc. 954, 19 N.Y.S.2d 38 (1940). See also Arnold v. May Department Stores Co., 85 S.W.2d 748, 753 (Mo. 1935). But *cf.* Levi v. Colgate-Palmolive Pty., Ltd., [1941] 41 S.R. (N.S.W.) 48, 58 W.N 63, 65.

The seller is not ordinarily in a position to tell the consumer that he is allergic but the seller can sometimes tell him that some people are allergic to the product and suggest caution and perhaps a means of personally testing it.

Generally, the consumer's opportunity of knowing the presence of an ingredient is much less than that of knowing whether he is sensitive to it. His need to find it out from the seller is correspondingly greater. On the seller's side, the practical burden of warning the consumer of its presence is substantively less since all that it ordinarily entails is adding an appropriate phrase to the label.

In both cases, the duty to warn comes within accepted principles of liability. It can be handled as a tort matter within the field of negligence: The defendant has voluntarily set in motion a force that can reasonably be expected to cause substantial harm to a significant class of persons unless the defendant gives notice of facts that are peculiarly within his knowledge.

In a warranty suit liability for failure to warn can appropriately be imposed on the theory that the goods are legally unwholesome unless adequate warning is given. Under this approach, manufacturer and ignorant distributor alike would be liable. The arguments supporting the liability of innocent distributors have already been outlined.[2]

If the foregoing analysis is sound, policy considerations and, to a substantial extent, existing authority [3] suggest that factors harmful to idiosyncratics may appropriately be held legal defects if the particular consumer makes known his

[2] See Chapter I, Topic H, and Chapter II, Topic D.

[3] Taylor v. Newcomb Baking Co., 317 Mass. 609, 611, 59 N.E.2d 293, 294 (1945); Bianchi v. Denholm & McKay Co., 302 Mass. 469, 19 N.E.2d 697 (1939); Gerkin v. Brown & Sehler Co., 177 Mich. 45, 143 N.W. 48 (1913); Delta Nehi Bottling Co. v. Lucas, 184 Miss. 693, 185 So. 561 (1939); Reynolds v. Sun Ray Drug Co., 135 N.J.L. 475, 52 A.2d 666 (1947); Zirpola v. Adam Hat Stores, 122 N.J.L. 21, 4 A.2d 73 (1939).

hypersensitivity and relies on the seller to provide something compatible with it, or if all the following conditions are met: (1) the plaintiff is one of a significant group of idiosyncratics who unless warned will be ignorant of the danger; (2) the existence of the group and the nature of the idiosyncracy are known to scientists, if not to the industry itself; (3) the manufacturer fails to avail himself of a reasonable opportunity either to switch to another ingredient or formula or to give an appropriate warning; and (4) the degree of harm threatened is substantial.

Assuming that these are proper criteria, qualifying examples can be drawn from the fields of drugs, cosmetics, and apparel.[4] The remaining questions relate to what food allergies, if any, can qualify.

§4.29. Food allergies. Anyone writing about food allergies from the standpoint of products liability is embarrassed by the almost complete lack of reported cases[1] and by the sparse and conflicting nature of the available medical data. Wanting a sure footing, he leans heavily on legal speculation and factual surmise.

The lack of reported food allergy cases is explainable at least in part by the fact that unlike those resulting from other allergents, food allergy reactions are in general easily confused with reactions to other organic disturbances. Whether increased skill in diagnosing allergies and tracing

[4] *E.g.*, Taylor v. Newcomb Baking Co., 317 Mass. 609, 611, 59 N.E.2d 293, 294 (1945) (dermatitis from soap); Bianchi v. Denholm & McKay Co., 302 Mass. 469, 19 N.E.2d 697 (1939) (rash from dye in face powder); Gerkin v. Brown & Sehler Co., 177 Mich. 45, 143 N.W. 48 (1913) (dermatitis from dyed fur).

§4.29. [1] MacLehan v. Loft Candy Stores, 172 So. 367 (La. App. 1937), is the nearest thing to a food allergy holding in the reports. See also Swengal v. F. & E. Wholesale Grocery Co., 147 Kan. 555, 77 P.2d 930 (1938). Both cases are briefly summarized in §4.24 *supra*, note 6.

their immediate causes may ultimately change this situation cannot be accurately predicted.

Almost every food is an allergent to someone, but with greatly varying degrees of incidence and seriousness. Unguided by statute, the common law can hardly afford to do more, if it is to act at all, than take account of allergents that have a high incidence and create substantial harm. Unfortunately, the inadequacy and conflicting nature of the available data on food allergies make it highly questionable whether a reliable list of allergents meeting both tests could be compiled at this time. Pending the development of such a list, the way is open for particular courts to receive evidence and make determinations respecting specific allergents and their relative significance.

But even if a specific food allergent is found to be both widespread and serious, responsibility should not be imposed on the producer unless the court also finds that consumers-in-general of the product lack knowledge of the allergy problem which it is practicable for producers-in-general of the product to give them, and, without it, lack the reasonable opportunity to avoid the injury. The situation here is uncertain and changing.

Beside these considerations are the difficulties in spelling out the specific nature of the defendant's obligation. If the offending ingredient is an optional ingredient, is the producer to be required to remove it? If he has a duty to warn, what should he say? Should he have an option to remove or warn?

Replacement, even of a "nonessential" ingredient will be a highly dubious alternative, especially when it may merely mean trading the more potent allergent for the less. Warning the consumer means telling the consumer something specific. That some people are allergic to the product? That the consumer had better test it [2] (in accordance, perhaps, with a suggested method)? That the product contains a certain ingredient?

In the resolution of these questions, important differences appear between, at the one extreme, a simple, standardized, unprocessed allergent, such as cabbage,[3] as produced by a farmer, and, at the other extreme, a complicated, unstandardized, processed product, such as health bread, as produced by a manufacturer. These differences involve the relative sophistication of consumer and producer, the consumer's opportunity of determining from the product itself what kind of food he is getting, the feasibility of giving warning, and the content of a helpful and practicable warning.

It is questionable whether a general problem that is at the same time so full of variables and in so great a state of change can be dealt with adequately other than by statute and, on the basis of present knowledge, even by statute. In the meantime, the consumer is fortunate in getting valuable protection from the general labeling requirements of the pure food laws, particularly the Federal Food, Drug, and Cosmetic Act.[4] Fabricated products for which standards of identity have not been established must show their ingredients on the label.[5] So also for standardized fabricated

[2] Section 601 of the Federal Food, Drug, and Cosmetic Act, 52 Stat. 1054 (1938), 21 U.S.C. §361 (1946), provides that coal-tar hair dye does not adulterate a cosmetic (other than eyelash or eyebrow dyes) if the following label is used, together with appropriate directions:

> Caution — This product contains ingredients which may cause skin irritation on certain individuals and a preliminary test according to accompanying directions should first be made. This product must not be used for dyeing the eyelashes or eyebrows; to do so may cause blindness.

[3] Other well-known allergents include milk, eggs, cheese, shellfish, strawberries, and cantaloupes.

[4] 52 Stat. 1040 (1938), 21 U.S.C. §§301–392 (1946).

[5] Federal Food, Drug, and Cosmetic Act §403(i), 52 Stat. 1048 (1938), 21 U.S.C. §343(i) (1946).

products with respect to optional ingredients.[6] These labeling requirements, however, have been developed without special regard to the allergy problem.

With respect to products for which standards of identity are established, the consumer is protected so long as he is familiar with what the standard of identity entails. This gap is not large, because except when the category is new the consumer has the same general opportunity of predicting his reaction to a standardized product such as mayonnaise as he has with respect to a standardized product such as fresh strawberries. Unprocessed food products, of course, identify themselves.

On the civil liability side, legal machinery is available. What is wanting is a clean-cut factual understanding of the existing patterns of hypersensitivity to food. Until the facts are known, there can be no worth-while appraisal either of specific legal techniques or general over-all policy.

From what is presently known, it is doubtful that any burden should be imposed on the defendant, even in cases meeting the conditions suggested above, beyond the direct or indirect disclosure of allergent ingredients.

[6] *Id.* §403(g), 52 Stat. 1047 (1938), 21 U.S.C. §343(g) (1946).

CHAPTER V

Adequacy of the Civil Action in Food Cases

C H A P T E R V

Adequacy of the Civil Action in Food Cases

Topic A. *Introduction*

§5.1. Standards for evaluating the civil action. So far as the civil action for damages is concerned, the consumer interest at stake is wholesomeness, much more than price. This means food that is not only not violently injurious but has the affirmative qualities necessary to sustain a high level of well-being. In this context, consumer needs are paramount.

The individual consumer sues because he wants a sum of money. But although compensation for his hurt is the immediate inducement, there are also means, in such a proceeding, to achieve broader objectives outside the litigants' immediate view. It was suggested earlier [1] that when it can be directed the cumulative effect of individual actions can be made, in many cases, as significant a force in gaining legitimate social objectives as direct governmental regulation. And in some respects it may be the more desirable alternative.

Where the defendant could reasonably have avoided the plaintiff's injury and the plaintiff could not, holding the defendant liable not only indemnifies the plaintiff but places a financial pressure on the defendant (besides serving as a warning to others) to avoid a recurrence. Another result of

§5.1. [1] Page 14.

liability, it has been frequently suggested, may be to distribute inevitable losses among those who benefit generally from the consumption of the defendant's product.

These are not isolated compartments. Compensation, prevention, and the fair distribution of their inevitable costs are factors that tend to appear in all personal injury actions brought against suppliers. But they must be kept doctrinally separate in the evaluation of substantive legal rules.

The compensation factor in a given remedy is measured by how far it provides in practice an adequate recompense for injuries incurred.

The prevention factor is measured by how far it provides in practice adequate protection against individual injury and, beyond that, the assurance of appropriate general standards of quality.

The distribution factor is measured by the way it spreads in practice the costs of compensation and prevention among those who benefit from the consumption of the product.

Having already examined the broad doctrinal contours of food products liability, let us now consider how well the consumer's civil action is doing and can do these three jobs in cases involving the sale of food.

TOPIC B. *Compensation*

§5.2. The law of compensation (damages). Where the individual consumer succeeds in an action for breach of warranty, he is entitled to recover not only the value of his money bargain but foreseeably consequential damages as well.[1] In food cases, the former is negligible. The rule of

§5.2. [1] *E.g.*, Challis v. Hartloff, 136 Kan. 823, 828, 18 P.2d 199, 202 (1933); Doyle v. Fuerst & Kramer, 129 La. 838, 841, 56 So. 906, 907

including the latter is the rule normally applied in contract: The defendant is liable for all damages which as of the time of contracting it is reasonable to foresee as occurring in the event of breach.[2] The difference here is that only the consequential damage has practical significance.

The negligence rule is theoretically different in that the defendant in such cases is responsible for all damages that are foreseeable as of the time of the wrongful act,[3] which for a contract would be the time of breach, not the time of contracting. In consumer food cases, however, sale and breach are simultaneous, and the courts use a rule of damages in tort no different in practical effect from that used in warranty.[4] This result seems assured under the wording of the Uniform Sales Act.[5]

Accordingly, consumers have been successful in collecting for trichinosis; botulism; lead poisoning; tularemia; throat infection; tyrotoxicon poisoning; undulant fever; indigestion; stomach inflammation and ulcers; diarrhea; nausea, vomiting, and cramps; hernia; hemorrhoids; fainting spells; lacerations of the tongue, gums, mouth, and intestinal tract; broken teeth or dental plate; loss of teeth; mouth burns; depleted vitality; loss of weight; impairment of general health; miscarriage; fever; pain, suffering, and nervous shock; mental anguish and "humiliation"; aggravation of existing disease; hospital expenses, X-rays, and medical

---

(1911); Wadleigh v. Howson, 88 N.H. 365, 367, 189 Atl. 865, 867 (1937); Ryan v. Progressive Grocery Stores, 255 N.Y. 388, 395, 175 N.E. 105, 107 (1931); West v. Katsafanas, 107 Pa. Super. 118, 123, 162 Atl. 685, 687 (1932).

[2] Restatement, Contracts §§329, 330 (1932).

[3] Restatement, Torts §917 (1939).

[4] Exceptions growing out of the wording of particular death statutes are discussed *infra*.

[5] Section 69(6).

treatment; loss of work; and loss of capacity to work. Punitive damages are not normally allowed.[6]

Where the person injured is not the purchaser but a member of his family, the purchaser may recover for medical and other outlays which he is legally obliged to provide.[7] Injury to the purchaser's wife or child gives rise to recovery for loss of services and, with respect to the wife, for loss of consortium insofar as this common law right has not been abridged by statute or otherwise.[8] The problem here is not peculiar to food.

§5.3. The law of compensation (damages) — The "fright" cases. In some jurisdictions recovery is limited in cases involving mental and nervous distress. There are two main questions here: (1) whether the plaintiff can recover for physical harm resulting from the mental and nervous distress, and (2) whether the plaintiff can recover for the mental and nervous distress itself. Again, the problem is not peculiar to food.

Where some of the food is eaten and sickness or injury

[6] Crews v. Sikeston Coca-Cola Bottling Co., 225 S.W.2d 812 (Springfield Ct. of App., Mo. 1949).

[7] Stave v. Giant Food Arcade, 125 N.J.L. 512, 16 A.2d 460 (1940); McAllister v. Stevens & Sanford, Inc., 147 Misc. 317, 265 N.Y. Supp. 142 (1933); Minkus v. Coca Cola Bottling Company of California, 44 F. Supp. 10 (N.D. Cal. 1942).

[8] Moreno v. France Milling Co., Inc., 261 App. Div. 991, 26 N.Y.S.2d 400 (2d Dept. 1941) (negligence); Kennedy v. F. W. Woolworth Co., 205 App. Div. 648, 649, 200 N.Y. Supp. 121, 122 (1st Dept. 1923) (warranty); Corsaro v. Great Atlantic & Pacific Tea Co., CCH Food Drug Cosmetic Law Serv. ¶18,238 (W.D. Pa. 1942) (negligence); Jackson v. Watson & Sons, [1909] 2 K.B. 193, 100 L.T. (N.S.) 799, 3 B.R.C. 182 (warranty). See Gimenez v. Great Atlantic & Pacific Tea Co., 264 N.Y. 390, 393–394, 191 N.E. 27, 28 (1934), where, the wife being the buyer, the husband, who sued for breach of warranty, lost for want of privity. The court inferred that had the suit been for negligence, loss of services would have been a proper element of damages. *Contra:* Gearing v. Berkson, 223 Mass. 257, 111 N.E. 785 (1916) (warranty). See Melick, The Sale of Food and Drink c. XI (1936).

results from mental and nervous shock rather than from any chemical or physical threat to physical well-being, the overwhelming weight of authority allows recovery for the physical harm.[1] In only a few of the reported cases examined did

§5.3. [1] Relief was allowed in Coca-Cola Bottling Co. of Arkansas v. Langston, 198 Ark. 59, 127 S.W.2d 263 (1939) (glass in Coca-Cola); Medeiros v. Coca-Cola Bottling Co. of Turlock, Ltd., 57 Cal. App. 2d 707, 135 P.2d 676 (1943) (cleaning brush in Coca-Cola); White v. Coca Cola Bottling Co., 16 So.2d 579 (La. App. 1943) (mucuous substance and fermentation in Coca-Cola); Laborde v. Louisiana Coca-Cola Bottling Co., Ltd., 15 So.2d 389 (La. App. 1943) (cockroach in Coca-Cola); Biedenharn Candy Co. v. Moore, 184 Miss. 721, 186 So. 628 (1939) (mouse in Coca-Cola); Delta Nehi Bottling Co. v. Lucas, 184 Miss. 693, 185 So. 561 (1939) (paper clip in RC Cola); Beyer v. Coca-Cola Bottling Co. of St. Louis, 75 S.W.2d 642 (Mo. App. 1934) (mouse in Coca-Cola); Kenney v. Wong Len, 81 N.H. 427, 128 Atl. 343 (1925) (mouse in chicken pie); Carroll v. New York Pie Baking Co., 215 App. Div. 240, 213 N.Y. Supp. 553 (2d Dept. 1926) (cockroaches in pie); Barrington v. Hotel Astor, 184 App. Div. 317, 171 N.Y. Supp. 840 (1st Dept. 1918) (mouse in kidney sauté); Wolfe v. Great Atlantic & Pacific Tea Co., 143 Ohio St. 643, 56 N.E.2d 230 (1944) (worms in canned peaches); Corsaro v. Great Atlantic & Pacific Tea Co., CCH Food Drug Cosmetic Law Serv. ¶18,238 (W.D. Pa. 1942) (glass in bottle of vanilla).

See Hattiesburg Coca Cola Bottling Co. v. Cawley, 2 So.2d 143 (Miss. 1941) (roach in Coca-Cola); Coca-Cola Bottling Co. of Fort Worth v. Burgess, 195 S.W.2d 379 (Tex. Civ. App. 1946) (mouse in Coca-Cola); Coca Cola Bottling Co. of Fort Worth v. Smith, 97 S.W.2d 761 (Tex. Civ. App. 1936) (cockroach in Coca-Cola).

Relief was denied in Levine v. Wilson & Co., 16 Conn. Supp. 404 (C.P. 1950) (fly in bacon); Wheeler v. Balestri, 304 Mass. 257, 23 N.E.2d 132 (1939) (cockroach in bread); Legac v. Vietmeyer Bros., Inc., 7 N.J. Misc. 685, 147 Atl. 110 (1929) (bug in bread); Koplin v. Louis K. Liggett Co., 322 Pa. 333, 185 Atl. 744 (1936) (centipede in soup); Young v. Great Atlantic & Pacific Tea Co., 15 F. Supp. 1018 (W.D. Pa. 1936) (mouse in preserves). See Martin v. Waycross Coca-Cola Bottling Co., 18 Ga. App. 226, 228, 89 S.E. 495, 496 (1916). And see Sapiente v. Waltuch, 127 Conn. 224, 227, 15 A.2d 417, 418 (1940); Alma Canning Co. v. Rorie, 216 Ark. 444, 226 S.W.2d 64 (1948).

In Copeland v. F. W. Woolworth Co., 187 Misc. 456, 62 N.Y.S.2d 660 (1946), the plaintiff claimed that she became sick upon discovering a nail in food which she said smelled and tasted bad. The court, holding for the defendant, distinguished the Carroll case, *supra*, on the basis of the difference between mashed cockroaches and nails. It is not clear whether the court refused to believe the plaintiff or it felt that the plaintiff's reaction was abnormal.

the plaintiff come into direct physical contact with the offending condition. In none of them, on the other hand, did he discover the condition before beginning to eat. It is difficult therefore to evaluate the cases in terms of any requirement of "impact." If "impact" means direct contact with the offending condition (the most plausible interpretation of the requirement), few food cases are requiring it. If "impact" means simply contact with the food, whether or not the parts touched present any organic threat to the plaintiff, the requirement is almost invariably met in practice and becomes, in any event, a meaningless technicality incapable of intercepting fraud.

The authorities just referred to include only those which have expressly dealt with the problem. Equally important are the many cases that ignore the presence of a mental link in the causal chain.[2] Whenever the plaintiff's condition is directly related to the *discovery* of the offending condition, it may be taken for granted that psychological factors have played the preponderate part. Cases that allow recovery without proof that the food eaten was organically deleterious [3] necessarily align themselves with the majority rule. These cases accurately appraise normal human reactions and they are not properly to be minimized by the use of trick witnesses whose demonstrations of bug-eating and even glass-eating are designed only to show that the defect in question presented no immediate organic danger.[4]

[2] *E.g.*, Jackson Coca-Cola Bottling Co. v. Chapman, 106 Miss. 864, 64 So. 791 (1914) (mouse in Coca-Cola).

[3] *E.g.*, Duley v. Coca-Cola Bottling Co. of St. Louis, CCH Food Drug Cosmetic Law Rep. ¶22,223 (St. Louis Ct. of App. 1950).

[4] In Coca-Cola Bottling Co. of Arkansas v. Langston, 198 Ark. 59, 62, 63, 127 S.W.2d 263, 264, 265 (1939), the court said: "It may be that the doctor could have taken into his mouth a teaspoonful of the glass and swallowed the same without any kind of damage . . . but even if that had been done, it would have been no more convincing of the rights of the

As for the mental and nervous distress itself, the courts have universally allowed it as a legitimate damage item where some of the food is eaten and the distress is caused by or accompanied by illness or physical injury.[5] No case has been found where none of the food had been eaten and no physical injury accompanied the plaintiff's mental distress. Again it is difficult to say how significant these factors may be. It may be assumed that cases denying recovery for the physical consequences of mental and nervous distress would, a fortiori, deny recovery for the mental and nervous distress itself. This conclusion is bolstered by frequent statements

---

parties involved in this litigation than it would have been had a professional glass eater appeared before the court and put on his show . . . ordinary people must be the objects of solicitude, rather than the exceptions that might be pointed to as glass eaters, or those who might not have any squeamishness about swallowing flies, bugs, or spiders. . . ." But *cf.* Coca-Cola Bottling Co. v. Wood, 197 Ark. 489, 123 S.W.2d 514 (1939); Coca-Cola Bottling Company v. Breckenridge, 114 S.W.2d 7 (Ark. 1938); Guiher and Morris, "Handling Food Products Liability Cases," 1 Food Drug Cosmetic L.Q. 109, 128 (1946); Moss, "Food Products Liability," [1950] Ins. L.J. 418.

[5] Coca-Cola Bottling Co. of Arkansas v. McNeece, 191 Ark. 609, 87 S.W.2d 38 (1935) (fly in Coca-Cola); Dryden v. Continental Baking Co., 11 Cal. 2d 33, 77 P.2d 833 (1938) (glass in bread); Martin v. Waycross Coca-Cola Bottling Co., 18 Ga. App. 226, 89 S.E. 495 (1916) (putrid mouse in Coca-Cola); Day v. Rains, CCH Food Drug Cosmetic Law Rep. ¶22,175 (Ky. App. 1949) (razor blade in Pepsi Cola); Coca Cola Bottling Works, Inc. v. Tate, 193 Miss. 883, 11 So.2d 695 (1943) (glass in Coca-Cola); Kelley v. John R. Daily Co., 56 Mont. 63, 181 Pac. 326 (1919) (impure pigs' feet); Kenney v. Wong Len, 81 N.H. 427, 128 Atl. 343 (1925) (mouse in food); Ward Baking Co. v. Trizzino, 27 Ohio App. 475, 161 N.E. 557 (1920) (needle in cake); Menaker v. Supplee-Wills-Jones Milk Co., 125 Pa. Super. 76, 189 Atl. 714 (1937) (mouse in ice-cream cone); Stein v. Woodlawn Farm Dairy Co., 50 Lack. Jur. 1 (Pa. C.P. 1949) (glass in milk); Hayes v. S. H. Kress and Co., CCH Food Drug Cosmetic Law Rep. ¶85,102 (W.D.S.C. 1947) (burs in beef stew). In Watson v. Augusta Brewing Co., 124 Ga. 121, 125, 52 S.E. 152, 153 (1905), the court allowed recovery for apprehension up to the time the glass was removed from the plaintiff's stomach. "He may not continue for an indefinite period to vex his soul with dread on account of having been 'cut on the inside' . . ."

in the decisions treating mental or nervous distress and the results of mental or nervous distress as phases of the same problem. As for the cases that have granted relief, it is believed that relatively few would have come to a different conclusion had discovery come before rather than after the plaintiff began to eat.

To speculate on what a court would do with a food case involving bare mental or nervous distress is academic. It would be hard to imagine a situation where such an injury was serious enough to justify the expenses of suit. No such case has been discovered in the reports.[6] Cases in which a buyer has sought recovery for distress brought on by physical injury to a member of his family are hardly comparable, although at least one has denied recovery for want of an accompanying physical injury.[7]

The rational basis, if any, for denying recovery in cases of mental and nervous distress is the fear of fraud. But although mental and nervous upset, and even nausea, are easily simulated, they are all that can be readily faked without fear of exposure. If nothing else is shown and courts are vigilant in keeping damages commensurate with proved

[6] Almost in point is Kelly v. Wegman's Food Markets, Inc., 262 App. Div. 687, 31 N.Y.S.2d 976 (4th Dept. 1941), where the plaintiff suffered mental distress as a result of grasping a mouse when removing some of the defendant's tea from a cannister. Judgment was for the defendant. The case is unique in that the plaintiff suffered her distress when preparing rather than eating the food.

[7] In Minkus v. Coca Cola Bottling Co. of California, 44 F. Supp. 10 (N.D. Cal. 1942), the court held that the parents of a child injured by a decomposed mouse in a bottle of Coca-Cola could not recover for nervous distress caused by the child's peril. In Frank v. Justine Caterers, Inc., 271 App. Div. 980, 68 N.Y.S.2d 198 (2d Dept. 1947), a New York court held that a caterer was not liable for mental anguish resulting from the poisoning of his guests. On fright generally, see McCormick, Damages 315–322 (1935); Melick, The Sale of Food and Drink 297–301 (1936); McNiece, "Psychic Injury and Tort Liability in New York," 24 St. John's L. Rev. 1, 59–60 (1949).

injuries,[8] plaintiffs will not be found suing for simple mental distress or nausea (at least they will not collect large judgments) unless more substantial physical harm occurs as a result of that distress. If physical harm makes suit worth while, the courts will have a fraud problem no larger than in any other food case. Where physical injury occurs first and mental distress is simply a further consequence, the courts are willing to see a few extra dollars thrown in the pot to pay for the latter, even though the opportunities for fraud are greater than where simple mental distress has resulted. The courts apparently assume that the fact that the plaintiff received a substantial injury assures his general veracity, whereas every claim adjuster knows that the defendant's most persistent fraud problem is that of claim *exaggeration*. Courts must always be vigilant when allowing recovery for fakable injuries and it should make no difference whether the fakable part comes first, last, or alone.

To deny relief would be particularly onerous in the first situation mentioned, where the physical injuries suffered may have been substantial. It seems likely that the course of decision will tend to conform to the thought expressed in a Mississippi case,[9] where the court said, "Whether this physical ailment was preceded by and resulted from emotional distress . . . is of no consequence . . ."

§5.4. The law of compensation (damages) — Death. Where the injured person dies, there are additional complications. Death may affect the situation either by creating a basis for claiming additional damages or by abating an existing cause of action.

Death creates no rights on behalf of the decedent or his

[8] As in Stein v. Woodlawn Farm Dairy Co., 50 Lack. Jur. 1 (Pa. C.P. 1949).

[9] Biedenharn Candy Co. v. Moore, 184 Miss. 721, 727, 186 So. 628, 630 (1939).

estate. The only question is whether his right to collect for injuries sustained while he still lived survives so as to be enforceable by his estate. The answer is that it does not unless there is an applicable survival act.[1] This is a matter of local statutory construction and it lies outside the immediate scope of inquiry.

Nor does death create rights in any member of the decedent's family (even one who was the purchaser or who is otherwise free of privity limitations), in the absence of an applicable Lord Campbell's Act.[2] Such enactments usually apply only to "wrongful acts." This concept includes negligence,[3] and some cases say that it also includes breach of warranty.[4] The wording of the particular statute, of course, prevails. Here, again, there is no problem peculiar to food.

§5.4. [1] See Burkhardt v. Armour & Co., 115 Conn. 249, 161 Atl. 385 (1932). In Bernstein v. Queens County Jockey Club, 222 App. Div. 191, 225 N.Y. Supp. 449 (2d Dept. 1927), a cause of action for breach of warranty against a restaurant keeper was held to abate on the defendant's death.

[2] Burkhardt v. Armour & Co., 115 Conn. 249, 161 Atl. 385 (1932); Hasson Grocery Co. v. Cook, 196 Miss. 452, 17 So.2d 791 (1944); Wadleigh v. Howson, 88 N.H. 365, 189 Atl. 865 (1937); Howson v. Foster Beef Co., 87 N.H. 200, 177 Atl. 656 (1935). In Jackson v. Watson & Sons, [1909] 2 K.B. 193, 100 L.T. (N.S.) 799, 3 B.R.C. 182, the Court of King's Bench held that while his wife's death from eating the defendant's canned salmon did not generate any cause of action in itself, the purchaser's loss of consortium could be included as an item of damages, inasmuch as the breach of the warranty to the purchaser (who was also injured) generated a cause of action independently of the wife's death.

[3] *E.g.*, Salmon v. Libby, McNeill & Libby, 219 Ill. 421, 76 N.E. 573 (1905) (construing the Kansas statute).

[4] Greco v. S. S. Kresge Co., 277 N.Y. 26, 12 N.E.2d 557 (1938) ("wrongful act, neglect or default"); Doherty v. S. S. Kresge Co., 227 Wis. 661, 278 N.W. 437 (1938) ("wrongful act"). *Cf.* Burkhardt v. Armour & Co., 115 Conn. 249, 161 Atl. 385 (1932) ("caused by the negligence of the defendant or by his wilful, malicious or felonious act"); Hasson Grocery Co. v. Cook, 196 Miss. 452, 17 So.2d 791 (1944) ("any real wrongful or negligent act"); Howson v. Foster Beef Co., 87 N.H. 200, 177 Atl. 656 (1935) ("tort for physical injuries").

§5.5. The facts of compensation. With the reservations discussed in the preceding sections, it seems fair to conclude that, in legal theory at least, the civil action provides adequate compensation. It remains to be seen how fully this is reflected in actual returns.

It is impossible to say even approximately how many persons are injured or made sick by defective food during a given period, even if it were possible to define "injury" satisfactorily. Some kinds of injuries, such as arsenic poisoning or amoebic dysentery, are rarely reported because they show up at such a time or in such a way that they are either not recognized as food injuries or not traceable to their sources. Others are never reported because they are slight, the victims are apathetic or not "claim-conscious," or the seller is believed to be financially irresponsible. Another (and partly offsetting) distortion is that created by fraudulent or unfounded claims. These are discussed more fully in Section 5.14 *infra*.

Here we are principally concerned with the consumer's opportunities for success once his injury has been discovered and he decides to make a claim against a particular seller. A scientific study would perhaps use as a base the total number of claims made in the country during a typical year and follow their statistical fortunes to ultimate success or failure. Such a study is not feasible on the basis of information now available. Little has been done to collect data that would be useful here. In addition to getting the impressions of a number of claims experts, it has been necessary to resort to a crude sampling of the experience of a number of concerns representative of the larger types of food enterprises. Some of the smaller enterprises were approached but little is known of their experience beyond the fact that unless they carry products liability insurance, claims are a small worry to them. What have been collected are a few fragments that seem to verify certain curbstone judgments. They hardly represent a scientific sampling, but the support which these figures give to the opinions of reliable firsthand observers makes them significant. Thus with fingers crossed and a skeptical eye, we can proceed to consider the following data.

In evaluating claim data, it is important to keep in mind the difference between the claim for money and the bare complaint. Both point out the alleged defect, but only the former asks for money compensation and is thus directly relevant to the law of food products liability. Generally, the two must be kept separate when appraising the compensatory aspects of civil liability, but considered jointly when appraising the preventive aspects of civil liability discussed in the next section.

A practical evaluation of the civil remedy in its compensatory aspects considers (1) what kinds of injury it reaches and (2) how fully it reaches them.

The first fact that emerges is the great preponderance of "foreign substance" claims [1] over those based on illness alone. The records of the "National Restaurant Company," for instance, show that during a recent representative two-year period they had 394 foreign substance claims as against 67 for mere illness. The "Service Restaurants Company" had 55 as against 3, in an eighteen-month period; the "M Packing Company," 289 and 113, in a one-year period; the "X Dairy," 133 and 14, in a similar period; the "R.M. Grocery Company," 124 and 16, in a six-year period; the "Good Grocery Wholesalers, Inc.," 26 and 3, in a three-month period.

§5.5. [1] Claims based on the presence of a readily ascertainable but unexpected object. See Chapter IV, Topic A.

Several things may be indicated. One is that there is a greater inherent risk to the consumer from the intrusion of foreign bodies than from contamination or other deficiency. Although this may generally be so, there is good reason to believe, from the comparative difficulties of proof as shown by the reported cases, and from discussions with claims experts, that the true situation is obscured by the fact that illness alone, unidentified by a tangible mark with a specific source, has much less opportunity of becoming the subject of a claim. This is because it is difficult to trace the fault and the product at fault, and to find a defendant to sue. It is particularly true of a cumulative poison such as arsenate of lead.

If this appraisal is sound, there is a serious gap in the consumer's ability actually to recover for injuries where a cause of action theoretically exists. The extent of this gap cannot be determined until it is possible to measure inherent risks. At present we know little more than that there are many more foreign substance claims than illness claims and that this probably does not accurately reflect comparative inherent risks. Actually, knowing the inherent risks would probably make little difference, so far as compensating the injured consumer is concerned, because there is little that can be done to lessen the difficulties of proof. Tighter pure food laws might help to prevent the kinds of elusive defect missed by the civil action but they could not compensate those anonymous consumers who were injured despite the precautions taken.

Even where the consumer gets to the point of making a claim for money, his chances of making it stick are substantially less where he has no tangible clew to the seller's responsibility. This is borne out by the figures collected and by the statements of insurance company claim department officials. Thus, an analysis of National Restaurant Company claims shows that of 394 foreign substance claims, 337 were settled for an average of $41.70 a claim (median not available), an 86 per cent record of success for the consumer; of 67 illness claims, 45 (67%) were settled for an average of $33.09 (median not available). In the case of the X Dairy, 70 (53%) of 133 foreign substance claims brought an average of $23.68 and a median of $15.00, while 5 (36%) of the 14 illness claims were settled for an average of $14.60 and a median of $10.00.

These figures also show that if the consumer gets to the claim stage he has an excellent chance of receiving at least partial compensation for his injury. Similarly, claimants against the M Packing Company received compensation in 236 of 402 cases. The claim experience of the X Dairy over a six-year period shows a comparable result. Only 21 per cent received money from the R.M. Grocery Company, but the figures appear to be diluted with mere complaints (*i.e.*, not involving claims for money). Of the reported litigated cases studied, 63 per cent were decided in the plaintiff's favor, while the recoveries in which the awarded damages are reported averaged $1282.29, with a median recovery of $600. (At best these figures are representative only of reported appealed claims, which are presumably larger than unappealed or unlitigated claims.)

In the appraisal of claim data, mere complaints should be excluded from the sample when the problem is to measure the chances of receiving compensation, because they do not seek the payment of money; but they should be included when the problem is to measure inherent risk. In either case, settlement data should be evaluated in the light of the particular company's (or insurer's) settlement policy. The settlement data of sellers whose adjustment policy reflects their estimated chances of winning in court tend to understate inherent risks. At the other extreme, the settlement data of sellers, such as the X Dairy, whose adjustment policy calls for a small settlement whenever the claim is believed to have been made in good faith, tend to overstate the inherent risk and dilute the average received for claims justified by the actual facts.

How adequately these recoveries and settlements fulfill the plaintiff's legitimate claims for compensation it is impossible to know. Pending an adequate study, it may be legitimate to say that a reading of the reported cases, studies of claim files, and discussions with officials of large claim departments give the impression that on the whole claimants who succeed in getting paid by large food companies or companies carrying products liability insurance are generously compensated. The situation with respect to small uninsured food sellers remains obscure. As for the legitimate but unsuccessful claimants, there is little to be done beyond the correction of those defects in the legal rights of the food consumer which we considered at some length in earlier chapters.

Topic C. *Prevention*

§5.6. Claims and complaints — An operating problem for the X Dairy. How fully does the threat of civil liability deter the flow of unwholesome food products? How much pressure does the unpleasant notoriety attaching to claims and complaints exert on the manufacturer, dealer, or restaurant keeper to improve his product, his handling of it, or his housekeeping standards? [1]

§5.6. [1] General housekeeping problems are discussed in Duffy, "Better Housekeeping in Food Plants," 5 Food Drug Cosmetic L.J. 546 (1950).

Some inkling of the potential here is found in *Southwest Ice and Dairy Products Co.* v. *Faulkenberry.*[2] The defendant dairy supplied the plaintiff retailer with a bottle of milk containing a dead mouse. One of the latter's customers discovered the mouse while in the presence of other customers. The devastating effect of the incident is reflected in the judgment for $300 which the court awarded the plaintiff for the resulting loss of business.

Each class of food product has its peculiar risks. Both claims and complaints tend to bunch around these risks and call attention to the sore spots. For large milk companies, the experience of the X Dairy in a recent year is probably typical. In its metropolitan business, the X Dairy received 1724 complaints of various kinds, of which about 700 represented claims for money. Two hundred of the 1724 were individually examined. Of these, 69 were for glass, 17 for dirt, 10 for solder pellets (in canned milk), 12 for unclassified foreign substances, 5 for cockroaches, 4 for wire or tin, 3 for wood, 2 for soap, 2 for kerosene, and one each for tacks, lead soldiers, rubber darts, matchsticks, wax, cereal flakes, rust, snails, straw, bottle caps, pieces of meat, potash, hairpins, and tinfoil. There were also 14 illness cases whose precise causes other than peculiar odor or taste were unidentified, 35 hand laceration claims caused by defective bottles or bottles to which broken glass adhered, 2 sour milk complaints, 2 defective caps, 2 defective hood wires, and one bottle explosion.

The principal risk, plainly, is glass. The manufacture of the bottles is carefully checked as well as their handling both in the plant and by milkmen. The other main problem is housekeeping, since the claims and complaints relate almost entirely to foreign substances.

[2] — Okla. —, 220 P.2d 257 (1950).

The X Dairy says that the pressure from claims is substantial, even though the outlay in actual settlements is not large. Of the approximately 700 claims mentioned above, 395 were settled for an average of $24.58 (median not available). Total: $9710.85. Successful claims are serious claim-breeders. There is the ever present threat of claim epidemics, resulting not only in a depletion of claim reserves but a substantial loss of business. The pressure of claims is evident also in the experience of the M Packing Company during a recent one-year period. The total outlay for the period was $33,841, a figure well worth paring even though the company had only one claim for each two million dollars of sales, or $.0005 for each dollar of sales.

§5.7. Claim distribution and claim-consciousness. An analysis of 38,000 claims (food and other products), made by a products liability insurance expert who wishes his name withheld, reached the startling conclusion that 67½ per cent of all claims came from the New York metropolitan area, 12½ per cent from the Boston area, and 20 per cent from the remainder of the country.[1]

These figures suggest that claim distribution is strongly affected by claim-consciousness, a phenomenon that is shown equally by other figures that were obtained. Thus the "ABC Grocery Chain" reports for a recent year the

§5.7. [1] Partial corroboration is found in the premium rates quoted by the Product Liability Manual (National Bureau of Casualty Underwriters, Oct. 16, 1950). The prevailing $.50 rate for bakeries gives way to a $.70 rate in New York and a $1.15 rate in Massachusetts; $.40 for confectioners becomes $.70 in New York; $.18 for cracker and cookie manufacturers becomes $.30 in New York; $.25 for ice-cream manufacturers becomes $.50 in New York.

A more recent estimate puts the New York State figure, for the canning industry alone, at 30 to 40 per cent. 6 Business Lawyer, A.B.A. 191 (1951).

following amounts paid out in claims (the figures are approximate):

Metropolitan New York area	$14,000
Boston	8,000
Chicago	1,500
Pittsburgh	1,360
Detroit, Grand Rapids, Indianapolis, Louisville, and Toledo, combined	430
Vermont, New Hampshire, and Maine, combined	56
Los Angeles	0

The "LMN Bakeries" found great unevenness even within the New York City area. According to their experience, Bayonne to Englewood, New Jersey, is claim-conscious, while across the Hudson in Westchester, claims average about two a year; beyond the Meadows, about one a year; in Nassau County, New York, none at all. Next to New York City, Boston is for them the most claim-conscious spot in the United States. Compare the experience of this chain in Philadelphia, where with the same line of goods in 50 stores nine years of operation produced a grand total of one claim.[2]

From the erratic and patchwork nature of claim distribution the basic fact is evident: Despite the fact that claims tend to bunch around inherent risks, there is a marked disparity, quantitatively, between the distribution of claims and the distribution of inherent risks. This is caused by the fact that in areas where people are claim-minded there is not only a greater likelihood that legitimate claims will be pressed but a greater likelihood that fraudulent claims will be made and that otherwise legitimate claims will be fraudu-

[2] That claim-consciousness is largely a city phenomenon is suggested by the experience of the ABC stores: $14,000 for the New York City area as against $500 for the rest of New York and $56 for Vermont, New Hampshire, and Maine combined.

lently exaggerated. This means that in those broad areas and social groups in which people are not "claim-wise" there is a fertile field the food companies greatly prefer to leave uncultivated. If all areas and groups were to pull abreast of present leaders, the number of even legitimate claims would increase enormously. Most large food companies, therefore, continue to sit on a small keg of gunpowder. The phenomenon of claim-consciousness is shown also by the sharp dip in claims during World War II and by the following upswing moderated by conditions of relatively high prosperity. Harder times would presumably accelerate the increase. Thus there is claim-bunching in time as well as by locality.

A scientific analysis of plaintiffs needs making. Meanwhile, the following hypothesis is offered. Large claimants with serious injuries are presumably drawn from all financial and social classes in rough proportion to the inherent risk involved in the particular product. (We defer for the moment the problem of fraudulent claims.) Similarly, persons making only complaints we should expect to find coming from all localities and social strata in general proportion to the occurrence of defects. For example, the milk complaints examined came frequently from regular customers of good credit standing, who wanted only to have the defect corrected. One of these, incidentally, came from a large railroad, which had a glass-in-cream complaint. Drastic steps were taken to prevent a recurrence. In the same way, and in direct proportion to the business done with the customer, the company is generally solicitous of complaints unaccompanied by requests for money. Thus, even the bare complaint is a strong component of consumer pressure.

In the largest class of claims, where injury is slight or

moderate but compensation is sought, particular plaintiff characteristics begin to make a difference. It is here that claim-mindedness seems to play an extravagant role. Claimants tend to come disproportionately from the poorer classes or otherwise outside the circle of "nice" people who are reluctant to press legal claims. Included are those who are quick to seize any technical pretext for picking up easy money. The out-and-out fraudulent claim is not so prevalent as the valid claim in which the severity of injury is exaggerated in order to exact a generous settlement from a company plainly able to afford it. It is this class which the food companies probably fear the most, because in the aggregate they represent the larger loss. Accordingly, there is a strong inducement to minimize all factors that may serve as an excuse for making claims.

The growth of significant claim-consciousness seems to have begun at the end of World War I. Again, the story of the X Dairy seems typical. Until that time claims were negligible in the milk business. As a large, reputable concern, the X Dairy prided itself on its up-to-date plant, stocked with the best and most sanitary equipment. In 1919 a streetcar motorman got judgment against the company for $450 for injuries caused by the alleged presence of a tack in a bottle of milk. Whether this precipitated the X Dairy's particular snowball is not known, but it marked the beginning of a public claim-consciousness which grew steadily until the early thirties, when it generally leveled off. To the question, "What was done to stem the tide?" the head of the claim department replied that the company replaced its "best" machinery with "better" and drastically tightened its housekeeping standards.

§5.8. Claim pressure and preventive measures. There is little reason to doubt the effectiveness of claim pressure in inducing the large food companies to take all feasible precautions to minimize consumer injury. Money settlements are well worth shaving and the loss of existing or potential business is to be avoided if possible. Not only is each complainant a potential customer for competing products, but he is a potential claim-breeder or business-dampener as to all persons within gossiping distance. Word-of-mouth notoriety is far more devastating in its cumulative effect than the fleeting shadow of a single publicized judgment awarded an unknown plaintiff.

Claims men were approached in a number of representative large food concerns and casualty companies. The same story was told: a rising claim-consciousness since World War I, resulting in the adoption of all known feasible precautions in an attempt to make food products as claim-proof as possible. The defects which this mass of claims has unearthed, and the steps taken to deal with them, are legion. They have had amazing and often unsuspected results in protecting the consumer.

A large national packing house, for example, reports that trichinosis claims led them to put in a 20-day freezing process for pork to be eaten without cooking. Soap and cockroaches have tightened housekeeping methods. Metal in sausage has brought greater care in the inspection and use of shovels for handling sausage filler. Glass in sausage has resulted in rules forbidding workers to include milk bottles with their lunch boxes or to wear wrist watches with glass faces. Thermometers have to be of shatter-proof glass. "Sausage in oil" was originally distributed in 50-pound tins to retailers who sold them in bulk from the open can, but delay in sale under unsanitary conditions tolerated by many retailers sometimes permitted contamination resulting in bona fide but misdirected illness claims against the packer.

The spoiled sausage risk has been appreciably reduced by packing the product in smaller, 10-pound tins. (This shows the occasional necessity of protecting the product even after it passes into other hands.) Stones in pork and beans were partially discouraged by a water tank in which only beans were supposed to float. Porous stones have been finally conquered by a centrifugal device that discards the heavier object.

Probably the best-known example of the precautions developed by manufacturers in an attempt to minimize claims and complaints is the system developed by the Coca-Cola Company as a defense to what is probably the heaviest barrage of claims ever directed toward a single product. Briefly, this system [1] depends on fully automatic machines for washing, rinsing, disinfecting, filling, and capping, supplemented by inspectors who examine the bottles, before and after filling, against the glare of bright lights. In addition, housekeeping methods have been developed for keeping machinery and premises clean.

Machines are equipped with devices for minimizing the risks of contamination and the intrusion of foreign objects. With the bottles inverted throughout, the washing process begins with a preliminary rinse at a moderate temperature, continues in a special chamber with several baths of hot caustic soda solution of graduated temperatures and concentrations, and ends with several rinses, again at moderate temperatures. Water pressure and air pressure, assisted by rotating brushes, are applied. Both the syrup and the water to be mixed with it are carefully filtered, and the latter is

§5.8. [1] Described in Patargias v. Coca-Cola Bottling Co. of Chicago, 332 Ill. App. 117, 74 N.E.2d 162 (1947); Coca Cola Bottling Works, Inc., of Columbus v. Petty, 190 Miss. 631, 200 So. 128 (1941); Coca-Cola Bottling Co. v. Rowland, 16 Tenn. App. 184, 66 S.W.2d 272 (1933); Jordan v. Coca Cola Bottling Co. of Utah, — Utah —, 218 P.2d 660, 661–662 (1950).

subjected to a process for killing germs. Filters and brushes are inspected daily. Tops of bottles are shielded during the filling process. Capping follows immediately, with filled bottles moving only about four feet before they are capped. That even this system is not infallible, however, is reflected in the reported cases.[2]

One of the classifications most susceptible to claims is bakery goods.[3] Foreign substances predominate here as elsewhere, but also involved are such complaint breeders as "rope in bread" (a form of bread mold) and staphylococcus in custard filling. The latter is a tasteless bacterial contamination that propagates readily in cooling cornstarch. The famous Westchester County éclair claim epidemic of the mid-thirties, caused by staphylococcus, resulted in 250 claims against a large baking company. This company, while protesting against "mere finger-pointing," was nevertheless induced to fortify itself against recurrence. The only safe precaution, it discovered, was to discontinue custard-filled products. Because bakery goods are generally more susceptible to contamination and the intrusion of foreign objects, this company was also moved to adopt various devices to assure scrupulous cleanliness in all departments. One scheme has been to conduct a perpetual cleanliness contest in which weekly prizes are awarded to winning departments by foremen who rotate as inspectors and who are themselves subject to reward in proportion to the number of rule infractions they bring to light.[4]

Restaurants have their share of injury preventives in-

[2] *E.g.*, see Laborde v. Louisiana Coca-Cola Bottling Co., Ltd., 15 So.2d 389 (La. App. 1943). Of the 98,709,851 bottles of Coca-Cola manufactured by the defendant in 1942, 17,225 contained foreign substances, according to this case.

[3] The rates quoted by the Product Liability Manual for bakery goods are among the highest charged.

[4] Llewellyn suggests that such a "Hitler procedure" as the prizes for the foremen may boomerang moralewise.

duced by complaints and claims. In this class a national restaurant chain was studied. This company reported that because of the éclair epidemic against the bakery just referred to, it adopted as one precaution the policy of cutting its Boston cream pie from the menu after the 15th of May. By carefully selecting its pork and by adequate cooking, it kept its trichinosis risk down to a single claim in its entire history. Even this claim it believes was probably mistaken because it was made respecting a day on which there was no pork on the menu. The success of this enormous enterprise in protecting itself from trichinosis claims shows how adequately a restaurant can protect itself and the consumer from this kind of risk.

Claims against this company also uncovered a glass menace. Despite all precautions, glass chips kept appearing in many kinds of food. Patrons made claims. When it was discovered that waitresses were occasionally dropping glass ice-cream dishes on the cement kitchen floors and that disposing of food in the immediate vicinity did not take care of fragments spattered even ten feet away, glass dessert dishes were replaced with metal. Bugs, dirt, and pebbles in spinach were discouraged as complaint-producers by the adoption of a seven-washings routine.

One further risk unearthed by claims is worth mentioning: the disgruntled employee. Iron filings in canned tomatoes have had such a genesis, and New York City bakery owners still recall the arsenic epidemic of 1922, traced to a vindictive pastry cook in a bakery at 25th Street and Broadway; 100 people were affected, 12 died. The immediate measures induced in this case need not be outlined.

§5.9. Claim pressure on insured sellers. Also significant is the experience of companies that have sought and obtained products public liability insurance. Before obtaining coverage they are normally required to submit samples of products to be chemically analyzed, together with advertising claims and lists of ingredients. Inspectors are sent into plants to make a careful checkup of operating conditions and housekeeping methods. If the significant deficiencies are not corrected, the application is rejected.[1]

One writer[2] doubts that purchasers of products liability insurance will be under any substantial inducement to minimize injury risks until sufficient experience is available that premiums can be geared to risks instead of volume of business.

This line of thought suggests several comments. First, it is not wholly true that the present method of basing premiums on the insured's volume of business[3] fails to reflect the nature and extent of the particular risk. Premium rates for particular food classifications reflect at least the risk differences between the classifications. As between individual sellers, risk differences are partially reflected. In several classifications uniform rates are not quoted and the particular seller must submit his risk for a rating tailored to his individual experience. More important, even uniform premium rates are subject to individual revision in some cases. For instance, individual risks that develop a sufficiently large total premium may be submitted for a rating based on the experience of the insured, entitling him in appropriate cases to a lower premium. Conversely, bad claims experience may subject the insured to an adverse

§5.9. [1] According to a leading products liability insurance expert, "the line of suckers has never run out," and a company seeking products liability insurance can, if it perseveres, sooner or later find a casualty insurer to insure its product. What is said in the text, then, would seem inapplicable in such cases. But the general statement holds.

[2] Comment, 9 Duke B.A.J. 23, 25 (1941).

[3] Usually gross sales; sometimes units produced or receipts.

experience rating or even cancellation. Accordingly, current methods of figuring premiums offer a real incentive, at least to many of the larger sellers.

Second, even after premiums are fixed or adjusted, most companies police their larger risks with a view to discovering and removing conditions that may be the source of claims. They conduct periodic inspections and sometimes provide technical assistance. By education and persuasion, this too encourages care by the seller. Again, this is truer of the larger risks than it is of the smaller.

In general it seems fair to assume that purchasers of products liability insurance are under a substantial inducement to minimize injury risks not significantly different from that affecting companies not carrying insurance. If anything, the inducement may even be more extensive among companies that are insured, particularly for small sellers among whom there would otherwise be little pooling of claims and prevention experience.

Many of the factors at work where insurance is taken out affect the larger food companies that are "self-insurers." These are concerns whose breadth of experience and volume of business mean a predictable claim risk and who handle their own claim problems through a centralized claim department financed out of a reserve for claims. As in the claim department of an insurance company, claim work becomes a routine of settlement or suit, and close cooperation with the engineering department. Claims are frequently tabulated by locality and kind, so that if, for example, the X Dairy finds that half a dozen glass claims have come in during the past week from its Eastham plant, steps are taken to locate and remove the source of the trouble.[4]

[4] Claims sometimes unearth illusory defects. A leading soup company reports that a large number of "worm" complaints directed toward its canned chicken soup induced them to remove all veins from the chicken meat used.

§5.10. Effectiveness of claim pressure. Although private action by the consumer serves its preventive function well as to those defects which in practice it catches and as to those concerns which it actually reaches, there are serious gaps in its effectiveness as a shield to the consumer from unwholesome food. Some of these gaps are correctable but many can probably be filled only by direct governmental action.

§5.11. Effectiveness of claim pressure — "Foreign substance" claims and "illness" (latent defect) claims. To be the subject of a claim the food defect must be traced to its source. As already seen, the overwhelming majority of food claims are those involving readily ascertainable foreign substances. Illness claims, on the other hand, can arise only when symptoms are manifest soon after exposure to the defect. Trichinosis claims can occasionally be made because noticeable reactions occur within thirty-six to seventy-two hours and the source is necessarily pork. But what of the frequent case where persons are merely affected by "food poisoning" or "ptomaine"? Unless suspicious food remnants have been preserved for analysis or the food was eaten under circumstances permitting the use of persuasive deductions, the source of the sickness will probably remain a mystery. Occasionally an arsenic case comes to light but if the dose is not large enough to cause a quick and severe reaction, the reaction may never be recognized for what it is. Beyond this the civil action does not go. It does not adequately reach food defects that make themselves felt after long delay or only cumulatively. Much less does it deter the flow of goods whose substandard qualities or over-refinements are detectable only by the dietician or chemist. In other words the pressure of civil claims helps to protect the consumer only from the more violent and dramatic personal injuries. It does not assure him a fully wholesome product, nor even one that is acceptable under minimum standards of wholesomeness.

§5.12. Effectiveness of claim pressure — Large sellers and small sellers. Even in discouraging the violent, dramatic personal injury, the civil remedy has deficiencies.

How much claim work is taken by lawyers on a contingent fee is not known. Whatever the basis of payment, plaintiffs and their lawyers are discriminating in choosing defendants. Money claims go where money is known to be available and although the small independant grocer, for example, is usually thrown in as a makeweight, the rich (or presumably rich) wholesaler or manufacturer is the real game. The sausage-in-oil cases are as good an example as any.[1] Claimants prefer names such as Armour and Swift to the Excelsior Meat Market, even though the latter is absolutely liable in warranty. Even a casual perusal of the reported cases shows that the great majority of defendants come from the ranks of the large, well-known, and financially impressive producers, distributors, and restaurant keepers.

Even in the aggregate, the small sellers are a less shot-at target than the Big Names. This means that the pressure of claims is not only proportionately less, but it is spread over a wider base, over individual companies among which there is very little pooling of experience. Except where products liability insurance is secured, there are no claim departments to tabulate claims or inform one branch plant or store of what is happening at another. Although trade journals give general advice on risks and risk prevention, vicarious experience offers a less effective warning than direct contact

§5.12. [1] *E.g.*, Swift & Co. v. Mabry, 203 Ark. 818, 159 S.W.2d 61 (1942); Floyd v. Swift & Co., 59 Ga. App. 383, 200 S.E. 531 (1938); Johnson & Swift & Co., Inc., 186 Miss. 803, 191 So. 423 (1939); Cudahy Packing Co. v. Baskin, 170 Miss. 834, 155 So. 217 (1934).

with the problem. Independent storekeepers and small manufacturers [2] pay less attention to preventing serious claims because for an individual seller they are a wholly unusual occurrence. Small merchants know almost nothing of the degree of products liability risks.

Not only is there much less pressure from claims on the small food merchant to provide a claim-proof product but there is a correspondingly greater temptation to pass on to the consumer unwholesome or substandard products even known to be so. An extreme example is the driver-peddler who is compelled by his bakery to "purchase" the goods he delivers from door to door and to estimate his daily requirements without benefit of return allowances. This has meant that high-guessing drivers have commonly succumbed to passing off stale carry-overs as fresh goods. Fortunately, this arrangement has been generally discouraged, possibly because of repercussions against the bakery. But the petty temptations of the shoestring merchant remain.

§5.13. Sharpening preventive pressures. Apart from its inherent limitations, the question remains whether the civil action is allowed to work as effectively as it can. In earlier chapters various legal discrepancies resulting in unfairness to the consumer were pointed out. It is now suggested that the aggregate effect of correcting these matters would substantially improve the effectiveness of the limited preventive weapons of the consumer.

To hold the defendant to a standard of "due care" is to encourage only his keeping abreast of existing technology. To hold him absolutely accountable is to put pressure on him to better those standards. This is borne out by the experience of the X Dairy. On the firing line of ordinary

[2] Unless their customers are large wholesalers or retail chains who are themselves claim targets.

claim settlement many food companies feel impelled to make a settlement whenever the claimant's injury is properly laid at their door. The virtual absolute liability which thus exists for small claims induced the X Dairy to replace the "best" with better. When suit is brought, legal defenses are used as they are available. Yet even the courts are tending to impose liability in all cases in which the injury can be traced to the defendant.

It is urged, therefore, that without unduly increasing the burden now resting on food sellers, absolute liability without privity limitations should be squarely adopted. The step is not a big one but it will sharpen the consumer's action and do away with the confusing intrusion of issues that are not actually being tried.

An argument sometimes made against holding the food seller to an absolute standard of wholesomeness is that compelling prompt compliance might put him out of business. However true this may be, it does not follow that imposing absolute liability means necessary disaster, because it encourages rather than compels compliance. No one expects the defendant to take unreasonable precautions, and at the point where it is no longer profitable to make technological improvements, it is to be expected that preventive measures will cease and the risk of practically unavoidable injuries be assumed instead. At least the absolute responsibility that now exists for retailers does not appear to have affected that class of seller unduly.

§5.14. The problem of fraud. A more persuasive objection to absolute liability is the contention that it subjects the food seller to an undue risk of fraud, one that cannot be met merely by taking all technological precautions or even by meeting the legal standards of wholesomeness in full.

What proportion of claims is wholly fraudulent it is impossible to know. It is known, of course, that there is widespread exaggeration of real injuries. But this practice is no argument against absolute liability because it is a type of fraud that attaches with equal facility to all kinds of liability for personal injury, including that based on fault. Nor are we concerned with claims which, though made in good faith, are actually unfounded.

Even so, there is a fraud problem in food and other casualty cases that cannot be ignored. A large number of claims are fraudulent in the sense that they are brought either for wholly pretended injuries or for real injuries for which the defendant is in no way responsible. Only speculation can measure the full proportions of this problem, but they are suggested in a recent bulletin issued by the National Canners Association. This says:

> Thirty years' experience . . . demonstrated that a large proportion of the claims are either grossly exaggerated or fraudulent. . . . Claims of this character have increased to such an extent in some cities that the local courts have found it necessary, with the cooperation of the local bar association, to call for an investigation into the activities of certain attorneys.[1]

The serious threat of fraud is also attested by the existence of the Index System of the Claims Bureau of the Association of Casualty and Surety Companies, a service that catalogues and furnishes information on all kinds of casualty claimants. Subscribers, including (as of October 1, 1950) about 202 insurance companies and 132 self-insurers, report the names, addresses, doctors, and lawyers of accident claimants. From the information pooled the Claims Bureau is frequently able to intercept the fraudulent claim repeater.

But whatever the magnitude of the fraud problem, it is not increased in any legitimate sense by imposing absolute

§5.14. [1] Consumers' Claims Against Food Canners 5, 6 (National Canners Assn. Pamphlet, Sept. 1945).

liability. To dispense with culpability is to dispense with something that is rarely provable in practice and is not specifically fakable; it is no easier to simulate a breach of warranty case than one based on "negligence." This, of course, does not solve the problem of fraud but it shows that the ever present opportunity for fraud has no force as an argument against absolute liability.

As for meeting the general fraud problem, consideration should be given to the possibility of improving the available procedural safeguards. It has been suggested, for example, that allowing an adequate pre-trial examination of the plaintiff by the defendant would materially reduce fraud in food products liability cases.[2]

In the meantime, an individual defendant not covered by products liability insurance and whose claim bill justifies spending the $100 yearly minimum can buy the services of the Claims Bureau and for that price feel fairly sure that about 625 of his more doubtful claimants are not fraudulent repeaters or "claim artists." Claims services are also provided by some of the trade associations.[3]

Food companies have generally found it wise not to make nuisance value settlements, for nothing is so conducive to breeding claims as the rumor that a certain soft-drink bottling company is good for an easy $50.[4] At the same time

[2] Wolfram, "Fraud in Food Cases," 5 Food Drug Cosmetic L.J. 559, 566 (1950).

[3] The National Canners Association also provides for the employment of legal counsel to defend unfounded or unjust suits against individual members or their distributors. It has even set up a trust fund to cover the payment, in certain cases, of individual losses exceeding $1000.

[4] "Settlement of claims on any basis other than their merit simply breeds more claims, creates more expense, and jeopardizes the reputation of the products of the individual canner and the industry as a whole." Consumers' Claims Against Food Canners 5 (National Canners Assn. Pamphlet, Sept. 1945). See also Levinson, "The Foreign Substance Racket," 244 Northwestern Miller 34 (December 5, 1950).

settlements are readily made with customers in good standing whose claims appear to be made in good faith (one eye is usually fixed on the value of the customer's patronage). By a cautious settlement policy that is fair but not generous, food claim targets can do much to reduce the fraud risk to a point where it is not unduly burdensome. In cases that reach trial, defendants will be adequately shielded from fraud and fraudulent exaggeration if the courts are vigilant in limiting damages to proved injuries persuasively related to the defendant.

Claim departments are justifiably peevish about the claim situation, because the average small claimant is not a wholly admirable human, and there are just enough "claim artists" at large to make them feel that food liability ought to be given the same sort of dressing down that the breach of promise suit has received at some hands. At the same time, there is the larger interest of the innocent consumer to be considered; and since it is his needs that give meaning in the first instance to the operation of the food business, he should not be compelled to accept without redress the individually devastating effects of risks that can be better borne or distributed by those who profit from the enterprises to which they attach.

§5.15. Products liability insurance. With the small enterpriser, whether retailer or producer, the problems of absolute responsibility are more perplexing. Where the defendant is a chain store, or even a large independent, it is very well to say that a constant and moderate claim pressure is a useful inducement. But with the corner grocer or shoestring manufacturer the pressure of claims will not only be sporadic but entail the risk that a single blow may put the victim out of business. Since it is the purpose of food laws to encourage standards of absolute wholesomeness rather than compel them at all costs, how is the small merchant adequately to be protected?

This brings up the question of the practical availability of products liability insurance.[1] There are two problems here. Many small sellers are either unaware of the risk or that this kind of coverage is available. As for the others, there may be some question whether they can afford the premium expense.

Fortunately, the latter problem has greatly lessened in the past ten years. Premium rates were originally high because an underwriting practice that concentrated on the livelier risks resulted in an adverse selection of business. Now that more of this insurance is in effect, a broader and more favorable experience has lowered loss ratios sufficiently to permit substantial reductions in premium rates. On the average, rates for bodily injury have been about halved since 1939 and minimum premiums have dropped in most cases from $75 to $35 or less; the minimum for some food stores has dropped from $75 to as low as $15 or less. The result has been to make this kind of protection much more widely available. Even so, some doubt remains as to how many small sellers can even now afford protection.

There have been various devices for providing cheap insurance for the small dealer and manufacturer. One of these is the deductible policy, under which the insured pays all losses up to $25, $50, $75, $100, or more; the insurer, all losses in excess of the named limit, to the extent of the excess (that is, the more serious risks). There are corresponding reductions in premium rates. However, such a policy is not

§5.15. [1] For an excellent account of products liability insurance, see Houtz, "The Insurance Response to a Shifting Caveat," Rep. Proc. of Sec. of Ins. Law, A.B.A. 296 (Chicago Meeting, Sept. 1944); Cahill, "Product Public Liability Insurance," Proceedings, Casualty Actuarial Soc., Vol. XXI, Pt. I, No. 43, p. 26 (1934).

wholly attractive to either insurer or insured. The hitch is in getting together on a mutually satisfactory settlement policy. The insurer usually prefers to handle all claims in order to keep as many as possible within the deductible amount. This means that he is tempted to settle all claims that can be settled primarily at the insured's expense and that the insured's premium will have to help pay for a claim service the larger part of which he would rather handle himself. For his part, the insured tends to be uncooperative in the settlement of larger claims.

Ironically, those who are in the best position to buy insurance need it least. Large risks tend to level off and big companies taking out products liability insurance are in effect only purchasing the services of a claim department. Although large companies are entitled to lower rates in appropriate cases, based on their own experience, the costs of this claim service are found by many to be greater than that necessary to finance their own claim departments. Hence the large number of "self-insurers."

There is an intermediate group of risks for whom the pressure of claims and the possibility of a large judgment present a threat more serious than it is desirable to permit. These are the firms that can afford insurance and for whom insurance will remove the risk of the extraordinary and possibly crippling judgment. For their needs, products liability insurance would seem to be best adapted.[2]

According to the Product Liability Manual,[3] coverage against bodily injury liability is for claims arising out of ". . . the handling or use of or the existence of any condition in goods or products manufactured, sold, handled or dis-

[2] "Medium size risks [are the] best listeners." Casualty Insurer 2 (December, 1931).

[3] Page 1 (National Bureau of Casualty Underwriters, Oct. 16, 1950).

tributed by the insured if the accident occurs after the insured has relinquished possession thereof to others and away from premises owned, rented or controlled by the insured . . ." In the case of restaurants, the policy includes food consumption accidents on the premises. Sellers' responsibility to buyers under hold-harmless agreements, however, is excepted (this responsibility may be covered by specially written contractual liability insurance).[4]

Coverage is limited to accidents arising during the policy term, which is normally one year (three years is the maximum), and to sales reported to the insurer as the exposure basis on which premiums are determined.[5] Because food products are normally consumed soon after sale, insurers accept all claims incurred during the policy period, regardless of the date of actual sale. Policies are written usually on a "5-and-10" maximum basis with an aggregate limit of $25,000, although higher limits are sometimes written upon the basis of factors shown in increased limits tables. Products liability insurance would seem to furnish adequate protection to at least the intermediate risk.

Our serious concern rests with the small enterpriser who is either ignorant of the protection available or feels that he cannot afford the cost. But the dangers here are more apparent than real. With the substantial reduction in rates (which are geared to the insured's volume of business) and

[4] As an alternative, a seller may provide for his hold-harmless agreements, as well as his products liability generally, by buying a comprehensive policy covering all risks. Here his protection against claims from defective products is only one phase of a broader protection. For this kind of coverage he pays at the outset a deposit premium based on the relevant factors then known. This is later replaced by adjusted premiums based on his known "exposure," that is, his experience since the issuance of the policy.

[5] For food, premium rates are quoted per thousand dollars of sales, except in a few instances where the basis of exposure is number of units produced.

minimum insurance premiums, this category has been substantially narrowed and is now highly marginal. More important, it is the Big Name in the chain of distribution that attracts and absorbs the pressure of claims, even though the little fellow is thrown in as makeweight. Moreover, large food concerns customarily stand behind their products, so far as their distributors are concerned, except possibly in the case of job lots or where the fault is clearly the distributor's. Occasionally the large manufacturer includes his distributors as an additional risk when taking out insurance. Actually, therefore, the small seller has little to fear where his products are sponsored by large reputable houses. His own financial insignificance is his best protection.

Where the manufacturer is equally shaky or the fault is clearly the small distributor's, it is true that the exaction of liability may mean a crushing blow to the paying defendant. And yet there is no reason to believe a denial of recovery would be any less crushing to an individual plaintiff, whether the ultimate loss is solely financial or includes a permanently disabling physical injury. It is believed, therefore, that the claim risk of a marginal food seller, which is more theoretical than real, is insufficient reason for not maintaining the rule of absolute liability of the retailer and fully extending it to the wholesaler and the manufacturer.

TOPIC D. *Spreading the Risk or Loss* *

§5.16. Who bears the costs of compensation and prevention? How well does the consumer's civil action spread the risk or loss among the persons who benefit from the sale and consumption of the commodity?

The answer depends not only on how the costs of compen-

* For the meaning and significance of this subject, see §§1.28 and 2.20.

sation and prevention are ultimately being borne but on the specific criteria chosen.

If the object is to spread the risk or loss among the consumers of particular products and brands, it is doubtful that this is now being achieved or is even capable of being achieved. The food industry is for the most part still highly competitive and prices are as fully a function of competitive selling conditions as they are of costs. This means that even for a manufacturer an increase in costs does not necessarily mean a compensatory price increase.[1] Moreover, it would be a rare seller who allocated his claim losses to particular products and, when raising prices on a specific item, either selected the item or measured the increase with the problem of claim risks in mind, except as preventive measures already taken might be reflected in the direct cost of the item. The manufacturer, more likely than not, makes a number of different products and he normally treats the products liability problem on a company-wide, rather than departmentalized or product-by-product, basis. Accordingly, if the manufacturer raises his prices, consumers of product A may in many cases pay higher prices because of defects in product B.

Another factor is worth noting. A price increase by a retailer is automatically felt by consumers, whereas a price increase by a manufacturer or intermediate distributor may not be. Although it is true that a price increase at the manufacturing or an intermediate level is usually

§5.16. [1] Misgivings have been felt by at least one writer over the problem of the manufacturer's passing on small fractional increases to the consumer, particularly for 5-cent or 10-cent items. Note, 92 U. of Pa. L. Rev. 306, 316 (1944). Apparently this writer was unfamiliar with the commonly used device of the "hidden price increase": maintaining the price but changing the composition of the product or the size of the unit. This was one of the commonest forms of violating price ceilings during World War II.

passed on intact [2] because the distributive food trades attempt to operate on relatively standardized markups over delivered cost, in a particular case competitive conditions may require partial or total absorption of the increase. Thus "spreading the risk" may mean spreading the risk between distributors at several levels of distribution and possibly between individual consumers, depending upon what competitive conditions at particular places and times make feasible.

This does not mean that the idea of spreading the costs of compensation or prevention must be discarded. It merely means that in view of the existing pricing and marketing practices the most that can be hoped for is that a given segment of the food industry may be able to protect itself against the undue encroachment of compensation and prevention costs by shifting the aggregate burden to the aggregate of persons consuming the products represented by the segment. The metaphysics of accounting provide no adequate way of going farther and attempting to deal with particular commodities, particular kinds of loss, and particular groups of consumers. In the long run, fortunately, reciprocity between products and the law of averages probably cancel out individual unevennesses and reach about the same total result that would be reached if costs could be nicely spread product by product, with individual price increases passed along intact.

For present purposes the important question is whether the great bulk of sellers in the food industry can feel the full impact of civil responsibility and still operate with normal or reasonable profitability. Insofar as the typical seller can absorb the costs of compensation and prevention (as by

[2] The fact that fractions must be rounded at least to the full cent does not detract from the main point of the statement. And see note 1 *supra*.

narrowing profit margins or making offsetting savings), the consumers of the various products involved have been adequately protected with no undue burden on the sellers. Insofar as he cannot absorb these costs without unduly threatening reasonable profitability, it is appropriate that those ultimately benefiting should foot the bill. The most that it is reasonable to expect of risk- or loss-spreading is that the aggregate burden be shifted without placing a disproportionate burden on any particular consumer group. Unfairness is best avoided by spreading particular cost factors as widely as possible.

How much in the aggregate is being passed on to consumers it is impossible to say. It seems fair to assume that, insofar as the food market is competitively free, prices tend to reach levels that reflect the cost of unavoidable risks — that is, risks that even the most careful must assume. The cost of individually avoidable risks, on the other hand, tends to rest with particular defendants, or at least meet downstream resistance, because the attempt to pass them on involves raising prices above the competitive levels of sellers who have successfully avoided these risks. Unfortunately these things cannot be adequately measured.

The objective of spreading the unavoidable costs of prevention and compensation is best fulfilled when claim pressure is concentrated on those sellers in particular chains of manufacture and distribution who exercise the widest control over the character and prices of the particular product. The answer to the question asked at the beginning of this section must be deferred, therefore, until we can examine more fully upon whom claim pressure is now falling and upon whom it should fall to do the most good. Because the problem of risk- and loss-spreading is the same as that of focusing preventive pressures, it will be reserved for the next section.

TOPIC E. *Focusing Civil Responsibility*

§5.17. Who should carry the load? It is frequently assumed that for improperly fabricated goods the manufacturer is the proper person to bear the full brunt of civil responsibility. The reasons appear to be three: (1) the manufacturer made the goods and ought, therefore, to stand behind them; (2) he is in the best position to control their quality; and (3) he is the appropriate person to generate the basic price increase which, with increases by subsequent sellers, results in spreading the risk or loss.[1]

In the background are these standardized economic assumptions: (1) The consumer is a small, unorganized, and unsophisticated buyer. (2) The retailer and intermediate distributors are relatively small enterprisers with no substantial knowledge or control of the product and, with relatively small dollar volume, they play an incidental or subordinate economic role.[2] (3) The relatively rich and powerful manufacturer produces a single product in large

§5.17. [1] The manufacturer is not necessarily the only person who can do this. Any distributor who handles the product can, to the extent that he can raise prices, take the initiative in spreading the compensatory burden of injuries actually incurred, within the distributive pyramid of which he is the apex. The only difference is that if he does not have the exclusive handling of the product at that level of distribution, the burden will be spread over a smaller consumer base. Thus, even the small independent retailer can spread liability losses, to all or classes of his customers, by raising his prices on the product involved, on groups of products, or on all his products. As for the costs of prevention, there is no occasion for a distributor to initiate a price increase except to cover the cost of his own preventive measures, if any.

[2] The economic condescension shown distributors in general is well typified here: Note, 18 Corn. L.Q. 445, 451 (1933) ("The retailer is frequently but a conduit. . . ."); Note, 42 Harv. L. Rev. 414, 417 (1929) ("The interjection of middlemen into the chain of distribution is commonly a matter of the mere mechanics of marketing, yet under the law it has frequently been allowed to affect substantive rights."); Note, 22 Wash. U.L.Q. 406, 407, 416 (1937) ("mere conduits," "mere agent of the manufacturer"). What about the "mere mechanics of manufacturing"?

volume and is the source of all defects.[3] With such a picture in mind, one can argue plausibly that the manufacturer is always the key person to prevent defects and spread the cost of compensating and protecting the consumer.

The first assumption appears generally valid. The second and third are grossly oversimplified.

A more realistic economic picture was drawn in an able comment appearing in the Columbia Law Review.[4] This study emphasized the diversity in kinds of marketing channels and for the purposes of legal analysis delineated several type-situations in the field of standardized noninspectable goods: (1) the large manufacturer-jobber-small-retailer combination, where a rule imposing liability on the first was advocated; (2) the manufacturer-chain-store (or voluntary group) combination, where the liability of the chain store was urged; and (3) the intermediate combination of small manufacturers and dealers between which a large wholesaler, marketing under his own brand, acts as intermediary. In the last instance, the wholesaler was marked for liability.

Such a classification is useful to illustrate the diversity in production-distribution channels and the necessity of resting liability on a rule that takes due account of actual marketing conditions. But as an adequate account of food distribution (which it does not pretend to be), it too is greatly oversimplified. Even if logically proliferated, any such classification would be useless as a practical yardstick. The permutations and combinations of producer, middleman,[5] and retail merchant in their relative financial posi-

[3] One writer states categorically, "The manufacturer gets well paid for his product." Russell, "Manufacturer's Liability to the Ultimate Consumer," 21 Ky. L. Rev. 388, 404 (1933).

[4] Comment, 37 Col. L. Rev. 77 (1937).

[5] The term is used collectively to refer to all distributors operating be-

tions and opportunities to control the quality and prices of particular products are practically unlimited. At the same time, their common boundaries have little to identify them.

This difficulty suggests that a simpler badge of liability is needed, one that reaches the main objective of directing preventive pressure where it will be most effective, without resorting to criteria that involve a myriad of arbitrary distinctions and gradations. Instead of the puzzle of specific marketing patterns, a simpler one might be found in a test such as the original sponsorship of the product, as manifest in the control of the label, if any, without regard to whether the seller's role as mere distributor is made clear on the label.[6]

This test presumes that the man who sells a product as his own is usually in the best position to (a) control its quality, even though another manufactures it, and (b) spread the costs of compensation and prevention. Both jobs, of course, must be done in the same gesture and, therefore, through the same defendant.

Under this approach, sellers marketing private brands of vicarious manufacture would carry the principal burden of liability. If a distributor did not in fact occupy the predominant position, liability might induce him to abandon the brand. (This is probably not too high a price to exact of those who wish to lend their names to the products of others.)

Even this approach has serious limitations. Many food products are unbranded and thus unsponsored. Even with

---

tween the producer and the retailer. For some food products the list is surprisingly long. Fresh vegetables, for example, after leaving the farmer and before reaching the retail grocer, may pass through the hands of (a) a country shipper, (b) a carlot distributor, (c) a carlot receiver, and (d) a secondary jobber.

[6] See Llewellyn, Cases and Materials on the Law of Sales 341 (1930).

respect to branded products, focusing direct responsibility by affirmative legal action is difficult. For one thing, although it may be possible to indicate where ultimate liability ought to go, there is difficulty in stopping it there. The hold-harmless arrangement, for example, is widely exacted of suppliers by private branders, large wholesalers, and retail chains. By this device the burden of a judgment against a large retailer or wholesaler is almost automatically shifted to the manufacturer, who may be small and financially vulnerable. Ironically, indemnity is most easily exacted of those upon whom it may be least desirable to place the social burdens of prevention and compensation.

Hold-harmless arrangements are brought about in several ways. One is the agreement whereby the seller undertakes to make good any liability incurred by the buyer because of defects in the product.[7] In other cases there is no formal agreement and the seller is merely induced to buy products liability insurance including the buyer as an additional interest. Sometimes this is given as a gratuity or talking point by the manufacturer. More often it is demanded by the buyer as a condition of doing business.

Where the manufacturer can afford insurance,[8] the only hardship is the premium. Where the insurance burden is too onerous, a manufacturer who has assumed the obliga-

[7] This is the form exacted by the X Dairy:

> We hereby agree to hold you harmless from any claim, demand or suit by any purchaser from you of the products mentioned herein who has been damaged or injured in any way by the use or consumption thereof as supplied to you by us, and defend you in actions or proceedings brought by federal or state authorities, provided that we are given immediate written notice of such claim, demand or suit.

[8] This will be contractual liability or comprehensive insurance if there is a hold-harmless *agreement*, because liability under such an agreement is now excepted from products liability insurance coverage. See §5.15, especially note 4.

tion himself must risk the chance that the hold-harmless agreement will expose him to serious financial injury.

Nor would doing away with hold-harmless arrangements protect the small manufacturer against a possibly staggering liability. The manufacturer who supplies the large branding wholesaler or retailer, even if free from legal liability, would have no assurance that he would not lose his best, if not only, customer if his product fell below par. The only significant effect of the hold-harmless arrangement, therefore, is to grease the shifting of the ultimate burden.

So far as the consumer is concerned, it makes little difference who ultimately pays the bill so long as he is compensated and the product is improved. The social issue is whether the law should permit the easy crippling of an enterprise whose defective product is made under the economic dictation of another. Confining the immediate pressure to the latter will as adequately compensate the consumer and protect him against recurrence. Not confining it may mean life or death to the insecure manufacturer.

Notwithstanding these considerations, it is believed that the simplest, fairest, and most workable approach is the following: If all sellers in the chain of manufacture and distribution are made absolutely accountable to the consumer for the quality of the goods leaving their hands, the way is paved for reaching the person who is in the best position to correct the defect. The problem is not so much that of using affirmative legal machinery to focus ultimate legal responsibility on any particular seller or kind of seller, as it is the negative one of removing existing impediments. Effective claim concentration ultimately depends not on affirmative legal direction but on the financial attractiveness of particular defendants. Where plaintiffs may recover directly against any seller to whom or through whom defective goods can be traced, claims tend naturally to gravitate to the closest available Big Name in the chain of manufacture and distribution, whether he is the retailer, intermediate distributor, or manufacturer. The most attractive defendant, from the compensation viewpoint, is very likely either to control the quality and price of the product or to be in a position to collect, by suit or by peaceful negotiation, from earlier handlers who do. Thus, if legal doctrine and practical considerations of distance permit, liability will be passed back at least as far as the predominant seller in the chain, provided, of course, that the defect itself is traceable that far. This facilitates compensation and probably prevention and risk- or loss-spreading as well.

Whether the predominant seller seeks to pass responsibility to earlier sellers has no bearing on the compensatory aspects of the consumer's action. Responsibility facilitates prevention if it reaches back to the source of the defect or to a seller capable of intercepting it. (The bargaining position of the predominant seller may make it unnecessary for him to use legal action to accomplish this end.) As for spreading the risk or loss, this too is facilitated by bringing the key seller closer to the consumer.

If the predominant seller is the manufacturer, no special problem arises. If he is a branding wholesaler he is in a position not essentially different from the manufacturer himself. He effectively controls the quality of the product as well as its price, and the economic pressure he brings to bear on the actual manufacturer is at least as strong as that exerted by the manufacturing defendant on his own operating departments. Nor is the pressure likely to be inordinate unless the seller has alternative sources of supply. The probability that the predominant seller will put his supplier out of business does not appear to be significantly greater than the probability that a manufacturer will fire a number of his own employees or stop making a particular product.

TOPIC F. *Conclusions*

§5.18. Final appraisal and suggestions for improving the law. The consumer's civil action in food cases seems to be doing a generally adequate job in providing compensation for injuries from the causes it actually reaches. Unfortunately it fails to reach many defects that result in delayed or diffuse and cumulative injuries. It is further circumscribed by a number of artificial legal limitations, such as the privity requirement.

In its preventive aspects, the consumer's civil action is similarly circumscribed. It is also limited by the fact that the preventive force of the civil action operates successfully only where it is consolidated into something more than a sporadic and contingent threat. It has only moderate value, then, against products not involving Names, Money, or Insurance.

The same limitations do not apply to spreading the costs of prevention and compensation, except in the sense that they tend (a) to obviate the occasion for such spreading, by suppressing the costs themselves, or (b) to cause losses to be borne at a later stage of distribution and thus to be spread over a smaller consumer base. Where these limitations do not operate, risk- and loss-spreading appear to be crude but generally adequate, in a way that is not always visible even to the accounting eye. (Appraisal, therefore, is necessarily tentative.)

Some of the defects in the consumer's action are curable. These can be remedied by frankly adopting absolute liability at all levels of production and distribution, abolishing privity requirements, doing away with the "no sale" doctrine in restaurant cases and the sealed container exception in retailer cases, and eliminating such groundless releases from responsibility as the doctrine that a mental link is insufficient to sustain the legal chain of causation. Permitting the consumer to sue any seller to whom or through whom the defect is traceable, with immediate rights over in all, will facilitate the placing of the ultimate burden of liability on those who are best able to control the manufacture of the article and the price at which it is to be retailed.

There is also the problem of how existing legal defects can best be removed. Except possibly for the privity problem (particularly in Sales Act states), there seems to be no insuperable barrier to making the suggested changes by common law decision. Where precedent is too strongly entrenched or where the Uniform Sales Act is believed to require privity of contract, the result must be reached by statute.

With respect to the privity requirement the question arises at the outset whether it should be removed for all commodities, some commodities, or food alone. So far as this discussion is concerned the question must be left open. What other commodities, if any, should be similarly treated must be determined from additional studies.

Where legislation is necessary, it is probably preferable, pending a general overhauling of the warranty provisions of the Uniform Sales Act, to create a special statutory obligation applicable to food, rather than to tinker with the complexities of the general warranties now found there. Such an enactment might read as follows:

> If a food dealer sells goods intended for use or consumption as human food, there is an implied warranty that the goods are wholesome. This warranty runs to (a) the buyer, (b) every

later buyer who buys the goods, or goods of which they are a part, for use or consumption as human food, and (c) members of the household and guests of every buyer who buys the goods, or goods of which they are a part, for consumption as human food. As used in this section, the term "wholesome" means fit to eat after the goods are subjected to normal handling or processing.

Statutes dealing specially with food have heretofore appeared in California, Montana, and Pennsylvania.[1] Such an enactment solves not only the privity and fault problems but eliminates the danger that particular courts will become confused by the mysteries of reliance or of sales by description in transactions whose individual essence is impossible to recapture. It forestalls such aberrations as the sealed container or buyer's selection doctrines. If necessary, the no-sale difficulty in restaurant cases can be dealt with in a special provision defining "sale" to include transactions by restaurant keepers. In Sales Act states the special food obligation can be included as a new clause (7) under Section 15.

The proposed Uniform Commercial Code—Sales[2] would remove many of these difficulties. Section 2–318, for example, would remove privity limitations in all sales by retailers, though not by other sellers.[3] The merchantability warranty (Section 2–314) would be raised wherever the seller was a merchant with respect to the goods and would apply expressly to restaurant transactions. This would make it

§5.18. [1] Cal. Civ. Code (1929) §1775 (Mar. 21, 1872; repealed by the Uniform Sales Act, 1931); Mont. Rev. Codes Ann. (1947) §74–321; Act of May 4, 1889, Pa. P.L. No. 87, §1 (repealed July 14, 1917, by P.L. No. 840, §1500, following enactment of the Uniform Sales Act, 1916).

[2] Uniform Commercial Code (1951). See Appendix C.

[3] Section 2–719 of the 1950 proposed draft would, in effect, have removed privity limitations in many sales by wholesalers and manufacturers, by letting a buyer (including a consumer) sue any person subject to impleader under Section 2–718 of that draft. Both sections were omitted from the final proposed draft (1951).

unnecessary, in food products liability cases, either to determine whether the particular sale was "by description" or to look to the implied warranty of fitness, except in unusual circumstances such as individual hypersensitivity. The implied warranty of fitness (Section 2–315) would depend upon the seller's having "reason to know any particular purpose for which the goods are required and that the buyer is relying on the seller's skill or judgment to furnish suitable goods . . ." (No exception would be recognized for a sale made under a patent or trade name.) Thus the existence of the warranty in a particular instance could be ascertained from the general relationship of the parties, where necessary, without the pretense of determining particular words and mental attitudes. Whether these provisions would also be acceptable as across-the-board warranty principles is beyond the scope of this inquiry.

An indirect and much less satisfactory method would be to extend the local pure food laws to cover all food transactions to which absolute responsibility is intended to apply. This would work, at least in part, in all states except those, such as New Hampshire, which do not recognize the doctrine of "negligence per se." One basic difficulty is that pure food laws generally relieve sellers of criminal responsibility for unwholesomeness where they have received appropriate guarantees from their suppliers. The same difficulty would attend any attempt to engraft on the Federal Food, Drug, and Cosmetic Act a provision analogous to Section 16 (b) of the Fair Labor Standards Act,[4] providing that an employer violating the minimum wage or maximum hours restrictions of that law is liable to the affected employee, in any court of competent jurisdiction, for (a) the prescribed

[4] 52 Stat. 1069 (1938), as amended 61 Stat. 87 (1947), 29 U.S.C. §216(b) (1946).

compensation and (b) an equal amount as liquidated damages.

The practical problem of reaching the out-of-state manufacturer or wholesaler might be materially reduced by developing a uniform statute along the lines of the "Unauthorized Insurers Process Acts," now in effect in about eighteen states.[5] These laws provide that if a foreign insurer not authorized to do business in the state effects, by mail or otherwise, certain acts within the state, any insured or beneficiary may serve process on the state superintendent with the same legal effect as personal service on the insurer. Although the ensuing judgment is not always physically collectable within the state, the fact that suit on it in the insurer's home state is not subject to a defense on the merits furnishes a real inducement to the foreign insurer to come into the state, defend on the merits, and make itself vulnerable to the collection of a judgment by putting up the security required by these laws as a condition of taking part in the suit.

Questions with respect to the survival of actions, rights accruing on death, "fright" doctrines, or the reduction of fraud [6] raise problems that are not peculiar to food or even sales law as a whole and are to be treated, if at all, without special regard to the problems under discussion.

Statutory changes, however, cannot cure defects that

[5] Cal. Ins. Code (1949) §§ 1610–1620; Conn. Pub. Acts (1949) 154; Fla. Stat. (1949) §§ 625.28–625.33; Ga. Laws (1950) No. 759 (H.1041); Ill. Rev. Stat. (1949) tit. 73, § 735; Ia. Code Ann. (1949) c. 507A; Kan. G.S. (1949) §§40–2001 to 40–2006; Ky. Ins. Code (1950) §304.583; La. Ins. Code (1948) §1253; Me. R.S. (1949) c. 56, §§13–A to 13–D; Md. Ann. Code (1949) art. 48A, §§273–278; Mich. Stat. Ann. (1949) §§24.567 (101)–24.567(106); Neb. Rev. Stat. (1943) §§44–137.01 to 44–137.10; N.H. Rev. Laws (1949) c. 325–A; N.Y. Ins. Law (1949) §59–A; N.C. Gen. Stat. (1945) §58–164(e); Pa. Stat. Ann. (Purdon, 1949) tit. 40, §§1005.1–1005.6; Tex. Civ. Stat. (Vernon, 1949) art. 5068e, §§1, 6, 7.

[6] See §5.14 *supra*, note 2.

inhere in the civil action. Thus the failure of the civil action to compensate for delayed, cumulative, or otherwise untraceable defects cannot be cured at all. The preventive job cannot be completed without the supplementary aid of direct governmental regulation in the form of adequate pure food laws and laws setting standards for labeling, packaging, and advertising. In this connection, let it be said that civil and criminal sanctions operate more effectively where they supplement, and not merely duplicate, each other. With respect to the kinds of defects now reached by claims, health departments will do their communities a greater service by concentrating more of their attention on the smaller food sellers, than by watching only those larger enterprises which the individual consumers themselves are keeping well in line. Even where it is appropriate to emphasize direct governmental surveillance, the pressure of unfettered civil responsibility is frequently a valuable instrument of government in buttressing hard-to-enforce criminal sanctions.

Appendices

APPENDIX A

English Sale of Goods Act, 1893[1]

(56 & 57 Victoria, c. 71; 1A Uniform Laws Annotated (1950), Appendix)

13. Where there is a contract for the sale of goods by description, there is an implied condition that the goods shall correspond with the description; and if the sale be by sample, as well as by description, it is not sufficient that the bulk of the goods corresponds with the sample if the goods do not also correspond with the description.

14. Subject to the provisions of this Act and of any statute in that behalf, there is no implied warranty or condition as to the quality or fitness for any particular purpose of goods supplied under a contract of sale, except as follows:

(1) Where the buyer, expressly or by implication, makes known to the seller the particular purpose for which the goods are required, so as to show that the buyer relies on the seller's skill or judgment, and the goods are of a description which it is in the course of the seller's business to supply (whether he be the manufacturer or not), there is an implied condition that the goods shall be reasonably fit for such purpose, provided that in the case of a contract for the sale of a specified article under its patent or other trade name, there is no implied condition as to its fitness for any particular purpose;

(2) Where goods are bought by description from a seller who deals in goods of that description (whether he be the manufacturer or not), there is an implied condition that the goods shall be of merchantable quality; provided that if the buyer has examined the goods, there shall be no implied condition as regards defects which such examination ought to have revealed;

(3) An implied warranty or condition as to quality or fitness for a particular purpose may be annexed by the usage of trade;

[1] Reprinted by special permission of the publishers of Uniform Laws Annotated.

(4) An express warranty or condition does not negative a warranty or condition implied by this Act unless inconsistent therewith.

15. — (1) A contract of sale is a contract for sale by sample where there is a term in the contract, express or implied, to that effect.

(2) In the case of a contract for sale by sample —

(a) There is an implied condition that the bulk shall correspond with the sample in quality;

(b) There is an implied condition that the buyer shall have a reasonable opportunity of comparing the bulk with the sample;

(c) There is an implied condition that the goods shall be free from any defect, rendering them unmerchantable, which would not be apparent on reasonable examination of the sample.

APPENDIX B

Uniform Sales Act [1]

(1 Uniform Laws Annotated (1950) §§12, 14, 15, and 16; 1A Uniform Laws Annotated (1950) §69)

§12. *Definition of express warranty.* — Any affirmation of fact or any promise by the seller relating to the goods is an express warranty if the natural tendency of such affirmation or promise is to induce the buyer to purchase the goods, and if the buyer purchases the goods relying thereon. No affirmation of the value of the goods, nor any statement purporting to be a statement of the seller's opinion only shall be construed as a warranty.

§14. *Implied warranty in sale by description.* — Where there is a contract to sell or a sale of goods by description, there is an implied warranty that the goods shall correspond with the description and if the contract or sale be by sample, as well as by description, it is not sufficient that the bulk of the goods corresponds with the sample if the goods do not also correspond with the description.

§15. *Implied warranties of quality.* — Subject to the provisions of this act and of any statute in that behalf, there is no implied warranty or condition as to the quality or fitness for any particular purpose of goods supplied under a contract to sell or a sale, except as follows:

(1) Where the buyer, expressly or by implication, makes known

[1] In force in Alabama (1931), Alaska (1914), Arizona (1907), Arkansas (1941), California (1931), Colorado (1942), Connecticut (1907), Delaware (1933), District of Columbia (1937), Hawaii (1929), Idaho (1920), Illinois (1915), Indiana (1929), Iowa (1919), Kentucky (1928), Maine (1923), Maryland (1910), Massachusetts (1909), Michigan (1913), Minnesota (1917), Nebraska (1921), Nevada (1915), New Hampshire (1923), New Jersey (1907), New York (1911), North Dakota (1917), Ohio (1909), Oregon (1919), Pennsylvania (1916), Rhode Island (1908), South Dakota (1921), Tennessee (1919), Utah (1917), Vermont (1921), Washington (1926), Wisconsin (1912), Wyoming (1917). Reprinted by special permission of the publishers of Uniform Laws Annotated.

to the seller the particular purpose for which the goods are required, and it appears that the buyer relies on the seller's skill or judgment (whether he be the grower or manufacturer or not), there is an implied warranty that the goods shall be reasonably fit for such purpose.

(2) Where the goods are bought by description from a seller who deals in goods of that description (whether he be the grower or manufacturer or not), there is an implied warranty that the goods shall be of merchantable quality.

(3) If the buyer has examined the goods, there is no implied warranty as regards defects which such examination ought to have revealed.

(4) In the case of a contract to sell or a sale of a specified article under its patent or other trade name, there is no implied warranty as to its fitness for any particular purpose.

(5) An implied warranty or condition as to the quality or fitness for a particular purpose may be annexed by the usage of trade.

(6) An express warranty or condition does not negative a warranty or condition implied under this act unless inconsistent therewith.

§16. *Implied warranties in sale by sample.* — In the case of a contract to sell or a sale by sample:

(a) There is an implied warranty that the bulk shall correspond with the sample in quality.

(b) There is an implied warranty that the buyer shall have a reasonable opportunity of comparing the bulk with the sample, except so far as otherwise provided in section 47(3).

(c) If the seller is a dealer in goods of that kind, there is an implied warranty that the goods shall be free from any defect rendering them unmerchantable which would not be apparent on reasonable examination of the sample.

§69. *Remedies for breach of warranty.* — (1) Where there is a breach of warranty by the seller, the buyer may, at his election . . .

(b) Accept or keep the goods and maintain an action against the seller for damages for the breach of warranty; . . .

(6) The measure of damages for breach of warranty is the loss directly and naturally resulting, in the ordinary course of events, from the breach of warranty.

APPENDIX C

Uniform Commercial Code Proposed Final Draft, 1951 [1]

Article 2: Uniform Commercial Code — Sales
Section 2–313. *Express Warranties by Affirmation, Promise, Description, Sample.*

(1) Express warranties by the seller are created as follows:

(a) Any affirmation of fact or promise made by the seller to the buyer which relates to the goods and becomes a basis of the bargain creates an express warranty that the goods shall conform to the affirmation or promise.

(b) Any description of the goods which is made a basis of the bargain creates an express warranty that the goods shall conform to the description.

(c) Any sample or model which is made a basis of the bargain creates an express warranty that the whole of the goods shall conform to the sample or model.

(2) It is not necessary to the creation of an express warranty that the seller use formal words such as "warrant" or "guarantee" or that he have a specific intention to make a warranty, but an affirmation merely of the value of the goods or a statement purporting to be merely the seller's opinion or commendation of the goods does not create a warranty.

Section 2–314. *Implied Warranty: Merchantability; Usage of Trade.*

(1) Unless excluded or modified (Section 2–316), a warranty that the goods shall be merchantable is implied in a contract for their sale if the seller is a merchant with respect to goods of that kind or though not a merchant states generally that they are

[1] As approved May 18, 1951. Copyright 1951, by The American Law Institute and National Conference of Commissioners on Uniform State Laws. Printed by permission.

guaranteed. The serving for value of food or drink to be consumed either on the premises or elsewhere is a sale.

(2) Goods to be merchantable must at least be such as

(a) pass without objection in the trade under the contract description; and

(b) are of fair average quality in the trade and within the description; and

(c) are fit for the ordinary purposes for which such goods are used; and

(d) run, within the variations permitted by the agreement of even kind, quality and quantity within each unit and among all units involved; and

(e) are adequately contained, packaged, and labeled as the agreement may require; and

(f) conform to the promises or affirmations of fact made on the container or label, if any.

Section 2–315. *Implied Warranty: Fitness for Particular Purpose.*

Where the seller at the time of contracting has reason to know any particular purpose for which the goods are required and that the buyer is relying on the seller's skill or judgment to select or furnish suitable goods, there is unless excluded or modified under the next section an implied warranty that the goods shall be fit for such purpose.

Section 2–316. *Exclusion or Modification of Warranties.*

(1) If the agreement creates an express warranty, words disclaiming it are inoperative.

(2) Exclusion or modification of the implied warranty of merchantability or of fitness for a particular purpose must be in specific language and if the inclusion of such language creates an ambiguity in the contract as a whole it shall be resolved against the seller; except that

(a) all implied warranties are excluded by expressions like "as is," "as they stand," "with all faults" or other language which in common understanding calls the buyer's attention to the exclusion of warranties and makes plain that there is no implied warranty; and

(b) when the buyer has examined the goods or the sample

or model as fully as he desired or has refused to examine the goods there is no implied warranty with regard to defects which an examination ought in the circumstances to have revealed to him; and

(c) an implied warranty can also be excluded or modified by course of dealing or course of performance or usage of trade.

(3) Remedies for breach of warranty can be limited in accordance with the provisions of this Article on liquidation or limitation of damages and on contractual modification of remedy (Sections 2–718 and 2–719).

Section 2–317. *Cumulation and Conflict of Warranties Express or Implied.*

Warranties whether express or implied shall be construed as consistent with each other and as cumulative, but if such construction is unreasonable the intention of the parties shall determine which warranty is dominant. In ascertaining that intention the following rules apply:

(a) Exact or technical specifications displace an inconsistent sample or model or general language of description.
(b) A sample from an existing bulk displaces inconsistent general language of description.
(c) Express warranties displace inconsistent implied warranties other than an implied warranty of fitness for a particular purpose.

Section 2–318. *Third Party Beneficiaries of Warranties Express or Implied.*

A seller's warranty whether express or implied extends to any natural person who is in the family or household of his buyer or who is a guest in his home if it is reasonable to expect that such person may use, consume or be affected by the goods and who is injured in person by breach of the warranty. A seller may not exclude or limit the operation of this section.

APPENDIX D

Select List of Authorities Relating to Liability for Defective Products Other than Food

Like the text of this book, the following list centers on the problem of personal injury to the consumer. Concentrating on the more recent authorities, it for the most part excludes general sales law that has no special significance in this field. Texts, articles, and notes that cover food in addition to other products are included even though they have already been cited.

TREATISES

ARTHUR, WILLIAM REED. *The Law of Drugs and Druggists*, Chs. 5, "Prescriptions"; 6, "Degree of Care and Skill"; 7, "Labels"; 8, "Poisons"; 9, "Patents and Proprietary Medicines"; 11, "Specific Problems of Retail Druggists"; 12, "Negligence as a Foundation of Civil Liabilities"; 13, "Contributory Negligence"; 18, "Manufacturers and Wholesalers of Drugs"; 20, "Miscellaneous Transactions" (3d ed. 1947).

COOLEY, THOMAS M. *Torts*, Sec. 498 (4th ed. 1932).

CORPUS JURIS SECUNDUM, Vol. 60, "Motor Vehicles," Secs. 165–167; Vol. 65, "Negligence," Sec. 100.

HARPER, FOWLER VINCENT. *Torts*, Sec. 106 (1933).

MELICK, HARRY C. W. *The Sale of Food and Drink*, Ch. VII, "Defective Containers" (1936).

PROSSER, WILLIAM L. *Torts*, Secs. 82–83 (1941).

RESTATEMENT, TORTS, Secs. 388–408 (1934).

WILLISTON, SAMUEL. *Sales*, Ch. IX, "Implied Warranties of Quality" (3d ed. 1948).

Digests and Services

American Digest System. "Druggists," Key Nos. 7–10; "Negligence," Key No. 27; "Sales," Key Nos. 255, 274.

Food Drug Cosmetic Law Reporter. Commerce Clearing House.

American Law Reports (*Annotations*)

Applicability of "res ipsa loquitur" to explosion of gases or chemicals, 56 A.L.R. 593; 39 A.L.R. 1006; 8 A.L.R. 500.

Duty of seller of explosives to guard against improper condition of containers, 55 A.L.R. 194.

Express or implied warranty of quality, condition, or fitness of automobile or truck sold by retail dealer, 43 A.L.R. 648; 34 A.L.R. 535.

Intervening purchaser's knowledge of defects in or danger of article, or failure to inspect therefor, as affecting liability of manufacturer or dealer for personal injury or property damage to subsequent purchaser or other third person, 164 A.L.R. 371.

Liability for injuries by breaking or bursting of container in which goods are sold, 4 A.L.R. 1094.

Liability of druggist for injury in consequence of mistake, 44 A.L.R. 1482; 31 A.L.R. 1336.

Liability of manufacturer or packer of defective article for injury to person or property of ultimate consumer who purchased from middleman, 142 A.L.R. 1490; 140 A.L.R. 191; 111 A.L.R. 1239; 105 A.L.R. 1502; 88 A.L.R. 527; 63 A.L.R. 340; 39 A.L.R. 992; 17 A.L.R. 672.

Liability of seller of article not inherently dangerous for personal injuries to the buyer, due to the defective or dangerous condition of the article, 168 A.L.R. 1054, 74 A.L.R. 343; 13 A.L.R. 1176.

Liability of seller of article not inherently dangerous to third persons for injury or death through the dangerous condition of the article, 60 A.L.R. 371; 42 A.L.R. 1243.

Liability of seller of defective or unsafe automobile for injury or damage caused thereby, 122 A.L.R. 997; 99 A.L.R. 240.

Manufacturer's liability for negligence causing injury to persons or property, of ultimate consumer, 164 A.L.R. 569.

Seller's advertisements as affecting rights of parties to sale of personal property, 158 A.L.R. 1413; 28 A.L.R. 991.

Seller's or manufacturer's liability for injuries as affected by peculiar or unusual susceptibility of buyer or use to injury from dye or other ingredient in the article sold, 121 A.L.R. 464.

Articles

BAILEY, JACK B. "The Res Ipsa Loquitur Doctrine and the Bottled Beverage," [1949] *Insurance Law Journal* 331.

BARASCH, CLARENCE S. "Allergies and the Law," 10 *Brooklyn Law Review* 363 (1941).

BELLI, MELVIN M. "Res Ipsa Loquitur and the 'Exploding Bottle,' " 19 *State Bar Journal of California* 353 (1944).

BOHLEN, FRANCIS H. "Liability of Manufacturers to Persons Other than Their Immediate Vendees," 45 *Law Quarterly Review* 343 (1929).

CARPENTER, CHARLES F. "The Doctrine of Res Ipsa Loquitur," 1 *University of Chicago Law Review* 519 (1934).

CLARK, JOHN KIRKLAND. "Let the Maker Beware," 19 *St. John's Law Review* 85 (1945).

CORBETT, J. H., and J. H. JAMIESON. "Implied Conditions as to Merchantable Quality," 4 *Alberta Law Quarterly* 89 (1941).

COTTON, ALBERT H. "A Note on the Civil Remedies of Injured Consumers," 1 *Law Contemporary Problems* 67 (1933).

CULL, FRANCIS X. "Allergy and the Law," 12 *Insurance Counsel Journal* 45 (1945).

ELDRIDGE, LAURENCE H. "Vendors' Tort Liability," 89 *University of Pennsylvania Law Review* 306 (1941).

FEEZER, LESTER W. "Manufacturer's Liability for Injuries Caused by His Products: Defective Automobiles," 37 *Michigan Law Review* 1 (1938).

———. "Tort Liability of Manufacturers," 10 *Minnesota Law Review* 1 (1925); 19 *Minnesota Law Review* 752 (1935).

HOUTZ, MARY COATE. "The Insurance Response to a Shifting Caveat," *Report of Proceedings of Section of Insurance Law* 296 (Chicago Meeting, American Bar Association, Sept. 1944).

JEANBLANC, LINDSEY R. "Manufacturers' Liability to Persons Other than Their Immediate Vendees," 24 *Virginia Law Review* 134 (1937).

LEGG, S. V. "The Modern Extensions of the Rule in M'Alister v. Stevenson," 4 *Alberta Law Quarterly* 119 (1941).

LEWIS, MAHLON E. "Theories of Action in Products Liability Litigation," [1947] *Insurance Law Journal* 30.

LLEWELLYN, KARL N. "On Warranty of Quality, and Society," 36 *Columbia Law Review* 699 (1936); 37 *Columbia Law Review* 341 (1937).

MINTENER, BRADSHAW. "Food Products Liability Law," 1 *Food Drug Cosmetic Law Quarterly* 96 (1946); 2 *Food Drug Cosmetic Law Quarterly* 62 (1947).

———. "Product Liability," 3 *Food Drug Cosmetic Law Quarterly* 76 (1948).

———. "Progress of Product Liability Law in 1948," 4 *Food Drug Cosmetic Law Quarterly* 110 (1949).

———. "Product Liability Law," 5 *Food Drug Cosmetic Law Journal* 168 (1950).

———. "Report on 1950 Developments in Product Liability Law," 6 *Food Drug Cosmetic Law Journal* 225 (1951).

PEAIRS, C. A., JR. "The God in the Machine — A Study in Precedent," 29 *Boston University Law Review* 37 (1949).

PHELPS, RALPH G. "Extent of Manufacturer's Duty of Care to Persons Other than the Immediate Purchaser," 2 *John Marshall Law Quarterly* 387 (1937).

PILCHER, N., and O. H. BEALE. "Grant v. Australian Knitting Mills — Liability of Manufacturers and Retailers," 9 *Australian Law Journal* 288 (1935).

PROSSER, WILLIAM L. "The Implied Warranty of Merchantable Quality," 27 *Minnesota Law Review* 117 (1943).

———. "The Procedural Effect of Res Ipsa Loquitur," 20 *Minnesota Law Review* 241 (1936).

RONEY, EDWARD. "Liability for Defects in Manufacture of Machines Intrinsically Dangerous," 10 *Bi-Monthly Law Review* 70 (1926).

RUSSELL, A. J. "Manufacturers' Liability to the Ultimate Consumer," 21 *Kentucky Law Review* 388 (1933).

SCHNEIDER, JOSEPH. "The Presumptive Rule of Negligence or

When Do the Facts Speak," 13 *Boston University Law Review* 50 (1933).

SEEFELD, GEORGE H. "Tort Liability of Manufacturers to Users of Their Goods," 25 *Marquette Law Review* 173 (1941).

SIZER, BURNET. "Recourse of a Remote Purchaser," [1947] *Insurance Law Journal* 483.

SPRUILL, JAMES A., Jr. "Privity of Contract as a Requisite for Recovery on Warranty," 19 *North Carolina Law Review* 551 (1941).

THOMPSON, KENNETH R. "Negligence and the Liability of Aircraft Manufacturers," [1945] *Insurance Law Journal* 6.

UNDERHAY, F. C. "Manufacturers' Liability, Recent Developments of Donoghue v. Stevenson," 14 *Canadian Bar Review* 283 (1936).

———. "Tort Liability of Manufacturers," 10 *Canadian Bar Review* 615 (1932).

WICKHAM, ARTHUR. "Products Liability in Wisconsin," 29 *Marquette Law Review* 20 (1945).

WILLIAMSON, A. S. "M'Alister v. Stevenson — and After," 4 *Alberta Law Quarterly* 123 (1941).

NOTES AND COMMENTS

Case of the Exploding Bottle, 28 *Boston University Law Review* 490 (1948).

Developments in the Law — Warranties, 45 *Harvard Law Review* 1415 (1932).

Effect of Advertising on the Manufacturer's Liability, 22 *Washington University Law Quarterly* 406 (1937).

Liability of a Manufacturer to a Sub-vendee, 18 *Cornell Law Quarterly* 445 (1933).

Liability of a Supplier of Goods to One Other than His Immediate Vendee, 21 *Minnesota Law Review* 315 (1937).

Liability of Manufacturer or Vendee to an Allergic Consumer, 49 *Michigan Law Review* 253 (1950).

Liability of Manufacturer or Vendor to Persons Other than Immediate Vendees in Missouri, [1950] *Washington University Law Quarterly* 85.

Liability of Manufacturer to Remote Vendee for Breach of War-

ranty — "Privity of Warranty," 29 *Boston University Law Review* 107 (1949).
Liability of Manufacturer to Sub-purchaser for Breach of Express Warranty — Negligence — Deceit, 25 *Minnesota Law Review* 83 (1940).
Liability of Manufacturer to Ultimate Consumer, 61 *American Law Review* 770 (1927).
Liability of Manufacturer to Ultimate Consumer, 99 *Century Law Journal* 201 (1926).
Liability of the Manufacturer to the Ultimate Consumer Under Modern Merchandising Practices, 9 *Montana Law Review* 101 (1948).
Manufacturer's Advertisement as Express Warranty to Consumer, 7 *Washington Law Review* 351 (1932).
Manufacturers' and Vendors' Liability Without Fault to Persons Other than Their Immediate Vendees, 33 *Columbia Law Review* 868 (1933).
Manufacturer's Liability for a Defective Article, 71 *Solicitors' Journal* 941 (1927).
Manufacturer's Liability in Aircraft Accidents, 16 *Journal Air Law and Commerce* 240 (1949).
Manufacturers' Liability in Tort, 46 *Yale Law Journal* 709 (1937).
Manufacturers' Liability — McPherson v. Buick Comes of Age, 4 *University of Chicago Law Review* 461 (1937).
Manufacturer's Liability to the Ultimate Consumer, 14 *Temple University Law Quarterly* 116 (1939).
Marketing Structure and Judicial Protection of the Consumer, 37 *Columbia Law Review* 77 (1937).
Necessity for Privity of Contract in Warranties by Representation, 42 *Harvard Law Review* 414 (1929).
Privity Rule and Implied Warranties, 1 *Intramural Law Review*, New York University 25 (1945).
Pure Food and Drugs — Protection and Civil Remedies Afforded the Consumer, 11 *New York University Law Quarterly Review* 615 (1934).
Reasonable Care as Between Manufacturer and Consumer, 185 *Law Times* 123 (1938).
Res Ipsa Loquitur and Exploding Bottles, 22 *St. John's Law Review* 128 (1947).

Rule in Donoghue v. Stevenson — Possibility of Intermediate Examination, 15 *Australian Law Journal* 8 (1941).

Tort Liability of Manufacturers and Contractors: Some Recent Developments, 40 *Harvard Law Review* 886 (1927).

Trends in the Non-promissory Liability of the Chattel Vendor, 96 *University of Pennsylvania Law Review* 863 (1948).

Case Notes

Allergic condition of buyer as defense to breach of implied warranty of fitness, 19 *Boston University Law Review* 501 (1939) [face powder].

Application of implied warranty of merchantability to the containers of food products, 36 *Illinois Bar Journal* 564 (1948).

Application of res ipsa loquitur doctrine in bottle explosion cases [Georgia and Louisiana], 3 *Washington and Lee Law Review* 343 (1942).

Automobiles — liability of manufacturer — nature of liability, 19 *Washington Law Review* 38 (1944).

Bottler's liability to ultimate consumers for injury caused by defective products, 4 *Louisiana Law Review* 606 (1942) [bottle explosion].

Consumer's action against retailer and manufacturer, 79 *Solicitors' Journal* 952 (1935) [underwear].

Dangerous chattel — proceeding against retailer instead of manufacturer, 7 *Canadian Bar Review* 198 (1929) [ginger-beer bottle].

Distributor of dangerous goods, 189 *Law Times* 358 (1940) [hair dye].

Doctrine of Donoghue v. Stevenson — application to distributors of goods manufactured by another, 18 *Canadian Bar Review* (1940).

Duty of manufacturer — defective stool chair, 17 *Texas Law Review* 100 (1938).

Implied warranties of fitness — skin disease caused by deleterious substance in a dress, 4 *University of Pittsburgh Law Review* 319 (1938).

Implied warranty — liability of bottler for explosion of defective container, 23 *Texas Law Review* 87 (1944).

Implied warranty of fitness, 4 *Georgia Bar Journal* 58 (1941) [hot-water bag].

Liability in trespass on the case for personal injuries resulting from negligent misrepresentations, 86 *University of Pennsylvania Law Review* 107 (1937) [washing machine].

Liability of a manufacturer for misrepresentations to subpurchaser, 13 *Indiana Law Journal* 508 (1938) [automobile windshield].

Liability of cigarette manufacturer, 27 *Georgetown Law Journal* 1147 (1939).

Liability of distributor of reconditioned car, 18 *Canadian Bar Review* 58 (1940).

Liability of distributors of manufactured goods, 74 *Irish Law Times* 339 (1940).

Liability of manufacturer, 16 *Texas Law Review* 591 (1938) [cigar].

Liability of manufacturer to a remote vendee, 26 *Boston University Law Review* 411 (1946) [perfume].

Liability of manufacturer to sub-vendee, 10 *Georgia Bar Journal* 228 (1947) [sofa bed].

Liability of manufacturer to sub-vendee for breach of warranty, 14 *Tulane Law Review* 470 (1940) [automobile].

Liability of manufacturer to sub-vendee for misrepresentation, 24 *Virginia Law Review* 80 (1937) [automobile].

Liability of manufacturer to third parties for defective product, 14 *New York University Law Quarterly Review* 542 (1937) [coffee urn].

Liability of manufacturer to ultimate consumer for breach of express warranty, 3 *University of Detroit Law Journal* 105 (1940) [automobile top].

Liability of manufacturer to ultimate user, 19 *Tennessee Law Review* 800 (1947) [automobile hood latch].

Liability of manufacturer to ultimate user, 20 *Tennessee Law Review* 193 (1948) [hearing aid].

Liability of manufacturers and vendors, 5 *Ohio State Law Journal* 119 (1938) [hair dye].

Liability of manufacturers and vendors of chattels, 9 *Notre Dame Lawyer* 358 (1941) [truck door handle].

Liability of supplier of chattels manufactured by third person, 4 *Missouri Law Review* 85 (1939) [automobile].

Liability of supplier of chattels manufactured by third person, 4 *Missouri Law Review* 91 (1939) [bed].

Liability of vendor to vendee in the sale of articles potentially dangerous, 7 *Fordham Law Review* 456 (1938) [washing machine].

Manufacturer's liability for injury from inherently dangerous article, 19 *St. John's Law Review* 63 (1944) [dress].

Manufacturer's liability — intervening negligence, 13 *U. of Chicago Law Review* 518 (1946) [automobile hood latch].

Negligence — vendor-vendee — sales — implied warranty, 22 *Temple Law Quarterly* 236 (1948) [stove polish].

Reliance on sales talk, 15 *Temple University Law Quarterly* 310 (1941) [mascara].

Res ipsa loquitur as applied to bursting bottles, 21 *Tennessee Law Review* 334 (1950).

Res ipsa loquitur in exploding-bottle cases, 1 *University of Florida Law Review* 470 (1948).

Res ipsa loquitur — liability of bottler of beverage for injuries resulting from breaking of bottle, 17 *Southern California Law Review* 330 (1944).

Res ipsa loquitur — necessity of control of instrumentality by defendant, 31 *California Law Review* 608 (1943) [bottle explosion].

Res ipsa loquitur not applicable to breaking of beverage bottle in hands of purchaser, 42 *Michigan Law Review* 536 (1943).

Responsibility of manufacturers for injuries from defective products, 33 *California Law Review* 637 (1945) [bottle explosion].

Retailer's adoption of manufacturer's express warranty by resale of the goods, 25 *Minnesota Law Review* 246 (1941) [mascara].

Rule in Donoghue v. Stevenson, 56 *Law Quarterly Review* 20 (1940) [automobile].

Rule in Donoghue v. Stevenson, 56 *Law Quarterly Review* 436 (1940) [hair dye].

Sale of goods — by description — implied condition of merchantability, 7 *Canadian Bar Review* 197 (1929) [ginger-beer bottle].

Self-service merchandising and consumer protection before sale consummated, 47 *Columbia Law Review* 156 (1947) [bottle explosion].

Standard of care required of a retail dealer — duty to inspect, 22 *Minnesota Law Review* 743 (1938) [automobile].

Ultimate consumer may recover in tort from perfume manufacturer for injuries resulting from negligently compounded perfume purchased from retailer despite lack of privity, 34 *Georgetown Law Journal* 377 (1946).

Warranties — third persons, 12 *St. John's Law Review* 362 (1938) [shoe].

Warranty of particular fitness — effect of buyer's allergy on seller's liability, 24 *Iowa Law Review* 792 (1939) [face powder].

What constitutes adoption of manufacturer's warranty by a retailer, 29 *Illinois Bar Journal* 149 (1940) [mascara].

Table of Cases

Table of Cases

A

B

C

D

E

F

H

N

Y

Z

Index

Index

(References are to pages)

A

B

C

R

S

T

U

www.ingramcontent.com/pod-product-compliance
Ingram Content Group UK Ltd.
Pitfield, Milton Keynes, MK11 3LW, UK
UKHW020204290926
15470UKWH00001B/12

9 780837 157467